Themes and Issues in Judaism

WORLD RELIGIONS: THEMES AND ISSUES

Written for students of comparative religion and the general reader, and drawing on the chapters originally edited by Jean Holm and John Bowker in the *Themes in Religious Studies* series, the volumes in *World Religions: Themes and Issues* explore core themes from the perspective of the particular religious tradition under study.

Already published:

Themes and Issues in Christianity
Themes and Issues in Hinduism

In preparation:

Themes and Issues in Buddhism

Themes and Issues in Judaism

Edited by
Seth D. Kunin

CASSELL

London and New York

Cassell
Wellington House, 125 Strand, London WC2R 0BB
370 Lexington Avenue, New York, NY 10017–6550

First published 2000

British Library Cataloguing-in-Publication Data
A catalogue record for this book is available from the British Library.

ISBN 0–304–33757–9 (hardback)
  0–304–33758–7 (paperback)

Library of Congress Cataloging-in-Publication Data
Themes and issues in Judaism / edited by Seth D. Kunin.
    p. cm. — (World religions: themes and issues)
    Includes bibliographical references and index.
    ISBN 0–304–33757–9 (hardback). — ISBN 0–304–33758–7 (paperback)
    1. Judaism. I. Kunin, Seth Daniel. II. Series.
  BM561.T54 1999
  296 – dc21   99–10882
                                                                       CIP

Earlier versions of chapters appeared in the following books in the *Themes in
Religious Studies* series, edited by Jean Holm with John Bowker and published
1994 by Pinter Publishers: *Sacred Place*; *Rites of Passage*; *Myth and History*;
Sacred Writings; *Picturing God*; *Human Nature and Destiny*; *Women in Religion*;
Attitudes to Nature; *Worship*; *Making Moral Decisions*.

Typeset by York House Typographic Ltd
Printed and bound in Great Britain by Biddles Ltd, Guildford and King's Lynn

Contents

CONTENTS

The contributors

Dan Cohn-Sherbok was ordained a Reform rabbi at the Hebrew Union College and has served congregations in the United States, Australia, England and South Africa. Since 1975 he has taught Jewish theology at the University of Kent, and is a Visiting Professor at the University of Essex. He has been a Visiting Fellow at Wolfson College, Cambridge, and a Visiting Scholar at the Oxford Centre for Postgraduate Hebrew Studies. Rabbi Dr Cohn-Sherbok is a Fellow of the Hebrew Union College, and a Corresponding Fellow of the Academy of Jewish Philosophy. He is the author and editor of over thirty books, including *The Jewish Heritage*; *On Earth as It Is in Heaven: Jews, Christians and Liberation Theology*; *Jewish Petitionary Prayer: A Theological Exploration*; *Issues in Contemporary Judaism*; *The Crucified Jew: Twenty Centuries of Christian Anti-Semitism*; *Israel: The History of an Idea*; *Exodus: An Agenda for Jewish–Christian Dialogue*; *The Jewish Faith*; *Judaism and Other Faiths*; and *An Atlas of Jewish History*.

Seth Kunin is Senior Lecturer in the Department of Divinity and Religious Studies at the University of Aberdeen. He received rabbinic ordination from Leo Baeck College. He has studied at Columbia College, the Jewish Theological Seminary of America, and Cambridge University. His publications include *The Logic of Incest: A Structuralist Analysis of Hebrew Mythology* and *God's Place in the World: Sacred Space and Sacred Place in Judaism*.

Sybil Sheridan is the rabbi of the Thames Valley Progressive Jewish Community in Reading and a Lecturer in Bible, and Life Cycle and Festivals, at the Leo Baeck College, London. She is the author of *Stories from the Jewish World* (MacDonald, 1998) and contributed two chapters to *Creating the Old Testament*, edited by Stephen Bigger

(Basil Blackwell, 1989). Editor of *Hear Our Voice: Women Rabbis Tell Their Stories* (SCM, 1994), she is currently editing a second volume on women's ritual.

Norman Solomon is Fellow in Modern Jewish Thought, Oxford Centre for Hebrew and Jewish Studies, a member of Wolfson College, Oxford, and lecturer in Theology at the University of Oxford. He was previously Director of the Centre for the Study of Judaism and Jewish/Christian Relations at the Selly Oak Colleges, Birmingham. Dr Solomon was born in Cardiff, and educated there and at St John's College, Cambridge. He has been rabbi to Orthodox congregations in Manchester, Liverpool, London and Birmingham. He is a past President of the British Association for Jewish Studies, Vice President of the World Congress of Faiths and a Trustee of the International Interfaith Centre. His publications include *Judaism and World Religion* (Macmillan, 1991), *The Analytic Movement: Hayyim Soloveitchik and His School* (Scholars Press, Atlanta, 1993), *A Very Short Introduction to Judaism* (Oxford University Press, 1996) and *Historical Dictionary of Judaism* (Scarecrow Press, 1998), as well as numerous articles and reviews. From 1985 to 1991 he was editor of the quarterly *Christian–Jewish Relations*. Dr Solomon has participated in interfaith dialogue in twenty countries on four continents, and in 1993 he received the Sir Sigmund Sternberg CCJ Award in Christian–Jewish Relations.

Alan Unterman is Minister of the Yeshurun Synagogue, Gatley, Cheshire, and part-time Lecturer in Comparative Religion (Judaism and Hinduism) at the University of Manchester. He studied at the Universities of Birmingham, Oxford and Delhi and at *yeshivot* in London and Jerusalem. He has worked and taught in Israel and Australia. Among his publications are *The Wisdom of the Jewish Mystics*; *Jews: Their Religious Beliefs and Practices*; *Judaism and Art*; 'A Jewish perspective on the Rushdie affair' in *The Salman Rushdie Controversy in Interreligious Perspective*; and *A Dictionary of Jewish Lore and Legend*.

Alexandra Wright is rabbi of Radlett and Bushey Reform Synagogue in Hertfordshire, and Lecturer in Classical Hebrew at Leo Baeck College, London. She has written several articles on women and Judaism. Her area of research interest is the sixteenth-century Bohemian rabbi Judah Loew ben Bezalel.

Introduction

Seth D. Kunin

Judaism, like all of the world religions, is a diverse tapestry. It is composed of many different strands emerging from different cultural, theological and geographic points of origin. Although Judaism as a religion and the Jews as a people emerged from a single location in the ancient Near East, diaspora and history have enabled the community to flower in many ways in many places and times.

This book includes chapters which explore some of this cultural and theological diversity. It is written from the perspectives of insiders and thus allows us to explore Judaism as it is experienced and understood by individuals from different segments of the community. Because of the choice of authors, the focus of this book is on the Jewish community and traditions which emerged from Eastern Europe and which developed in Western Europe and the United States. Yet even within this specific geographic point of origin there is significant diversity, especially on the level of practice and theology. This aspect of diversity is one of the features of the chapters presented here. The authors, based on their own experiences and values, emphasize their own religious perspectives within the wider spectrum of Jewish tradition.

Although the book examines issues of relevance to the study of religion as its primary topics, many of the chapters take a phenomenological rather than analytical approach to the material.[1] In this sense they provide an essential resource for anyone interested in seriously studying Judaism. It is, however, necessary to provide an analytical framework which can unite many of the themes which are presented in the different chapters. Although culture – and Judaism is a culture (or cultures) as well as a religion – can be subdivided into different analytical categories, these elements should also be examined from a holistic perspective which seeks to indicate how the parts work

1

together to form an integrated whole.[2] This introduction seeks to provide a framework with which such a holistic perspective may be developed in respect of the material presented in the chapters.

The analytical framework presented here emerges from the field of social anthropology. It draws on several different strands of anthropological theory and methodology: symbol theory, structuralism and structural functionalism. Other aspects of anthropological theory related to particular topics, for example the work of van Gennep (1960) in respect of rites of passage, are also examined.

One of the key aspects of the anthropological approaches examined in this introduction is that of structuralism.[3] Structuralism suggests that culture can be examined on several levels and that one of the most significant levels is that of the recurrent patterning or structure that is found in all aspects of a particular culture. The analysis seeks to abstract the way in which symbolic elements are related to each other and categorized. It looks at both the groups or categories of elements and the way in which these groups are related to each other. It emphasizes that elements cannot be taken out of context, but must be analysed in terms of how they are related to each other. Thus a particular symbol does not stand on its own to be defined or explained in its own terms but must be examined in terms of its relations to other symbols. This contextual analysis also holds true for groups of symbols as depicted in, for example, myths or rituals. Structuralism also emphasizes the holistic aspect of the analysis of religion within culture. Religion does not stand alone in a separate compartment or separate from its cultural context. It is integrated into culture and both responds to and shapes its cultural context. Structuralism provides one key into the analysis of religion and is presented here as a model for integrating many aspects of Judaism.

Although structuralism is often presented as a static model, the variation of the theory presented here is transformative. The analysis emphasizes the transformations in Judaism and its underlying structural configurations over time. Religion and culture and their underlying structural configurations are constantly and subtly transforming in relation to changes in context. This process of transformation suggests that there is no authentic diachronic (through time) structural configuration. There are only synchronic examples of underlying structure at particular moments in time. Continuity of culture on the structural level is found in the patterns of transformation rather than in static and unchanging truths.

2

Some aspects of this transformative aspect of structure and the interrelationship between religion and culture are developed in Clifford Geertz's fascinating paper found in *Anthropological Approaches to the Study of Religion* (Banton, 1966). In that paper Geertz examines the key features of religion from an anthropological perspective. His analysis emphasizes the reciprocal aspect of validation between religion and culture and between the individual (within culture) and religion. It is this reciprocal process which allows religion both to function and to be dynamic. The paper also discusses what might be called the naturalizing process of culture/religion. The models created by religion and culture are constantly moving between models for (creative) and models of (descriptive). It is the perception of religion and culture as a model of reality that gives it much of its explanatory power and its validation as a uniquely true depiction and understanding of reality.

Geertz also emphasizes the affective aspects of religion, especially those associated with mood and motivation. These elements are developed in several of the chapters of the present book. The creation of pervasive moods is discussed in relation to worship, and more specifically in the discussion of *communitas* in Chapter 1. The motivational elements are developed in the chapters examining human nature and destiny (Chapter 6) and attitudes to nature (Chapter 8). These elements however, as suggested by Geertz, form the cornerstones of an all-embracing conception of reality which shapes the elements of religion and culture discussed in the other chapters as well.

One of the themes which emerges from the discussion presented in this introduction and throughout the chapters is the significant transformation in cultural forms between the Orthodox and non-Traditional movements within the Jewish community. Two additional points need to be emphasized in respect of these changes. First, modern anthropological thinking rejects any concept of cultural evolution or cultural progress. Thus the changes and developments which are highlighted below should not be understood as marking progress. It also implies that earlier forms should equally not be considered better because they are diachronically prior. All cultural and religious forms, from the perspective of the anthropologist, are of equal value. It is only for those within the religious system to make qualitative evaluations of the different elements of the system. Yet the evaluations themselves should be seen as data for study rather than as analysis. Second, many of the changes in all forms of Judaism are closely related to transformations in the wider cultural context.[4] Thus, a full understanding of the transformations can be gained only by placing them into this wider context.

Sacred place

Chapter 1, on sacred place, presents an extended example of the type of analysis suggested here. Several aspects of the analysis presented in that chapter are applicable to all of the areas examined. Based on a structuralist model, which seeks to examine the abstract categories of Jewish thought and to demonstrate how the relationship between categories is exemplified regarding space, it suggests that the basic formula underlying Jewish/Israelite thought is 'A not B'.[5] This equation indicates that different categories within the system are unique and mutually exclusive. Any element in one category will not be found in the other. In general the two categories in the formula are qualitatively distinguished; thus one category will be considered positive and the other negative. The chapter also demonstrates regarding space that the underlying structure of Jewish thought does not allow for intermediate or mediating categories, that is, categories which suggest that there can be elements which overlap the two primary categories or which can be found in both categories, A and B. It is argued that this structural model is also found in respect of the understanding of people and social structure. Structuralist theory suggests that it should also be found in other realms of Jewish culture.

Chapter 1 also indicates the importance of a historical perspective to the understanding of aspects of culture. It demonstrates the transformations in the Jewish understanding of sacred space and the relationship of these transformations to the internal and external historical context. Jewish culture and religion, like all other cultures and religions, is in a constant process of transformation and development. The changes, however, are not solely motivated by internal or by external forces. Both play a complementary role. The discussion indicates that depending on the cultural context, for example, whether there are strong external boundaries, different aspects of structure will be emphasized. It suggests that when external boundaries are strong, internal segmentation will be emphasized but where boundaries are diffuse, segmentation will be minimized.

One area, pilgrimage, touched on in the chapter demonstrates the limitations of general anthropological models and the need to test models in the crucible of particular ethnographic situations and contexts.[6] The discussion of pilgrimage suggests a need to modify the use of Victor Turner's model in consequence of a different valuation of liminality and transformation in Jewish culture. Turner emphasizes the liminal stage, the ambiguous period in which the individual moves between statuses, whether through pilgrimage or through rites of passage. The discussion of pilgrimage in the Jewish context suggests that this liminal stage is either insignificant or not present. This analysis challenges the general model and suggests that liminality is related to the structural model. While in cultures where it is possible to move between categories liminality will be emphasized, in those where such movement is not possible liminality will be de-emphasized or not present. This analysis has clear implication for the study of rites of passage in the Jewish context and is discussed below in relation to Chapter 2, on rites of passage.

Rites of passage

Although Chapter 2 suggests that the category of 'rites of passage' is not found within a Jewish framework, the rituals which are described can be related to the models proposed by both anthropologists and students of religion. The most influential work on rites of passage is that of Arnold van Gennep (1960). He observed that all societies possess rituals for marking transitions in life, whether biological, that is, birth and death, or social, for example, marriage or changes in status (moving from childhood to adulthood).

His cross-cultural analysis suggested that rites of passage had three characteristic phases which are referred to as pre-liminal, liminal and post-liminal. In the pre-liminal phase the individual is taken out of his/her original position or status. The liminal stage is one which mediates between the old status and the new. It tends to be a period of ambiguity, and is often perceived of as a period of danger. The final, post-liminal state is that through which the individuals are reincorporated into their community bearing their new status. The liminal stage has been emphasized in the work of Victor Turner in respect of both rites of passage and pilgrimage. Turner argued that one of the key features of the liminal period was the creation of *communitas*, a feeling of group identity and solidarity created through shared experience and crisis.

The chapter on rites of passage presents several rituals which can, at least in part, be conceptualized within this analytical model. Thus, for example, *bar mitzvah* is a rite of passage through which a boy moves from the status of child to that of an adult. There is, however, a significant difference in emphasis between the Jewish rites of passage and those described by van Gennep. While the pre-liminal and post-liminal stages of separation and re-incorporation are clearly present, we do not find a clearly articulated liminal phase. Similarly, as all of the traditional rites of passage are individual there is no significant element of *communitas*.

The difference between Jewish rites of passage and those described by both van Gennep and Turner can be related to the underlying structure of Jewish culture. The liminal phase is one in which the individual overlaps boundaries, suggesting that the categories are not mutually distinct. As suggested above, this type of mediation is not allowed within the Jewish structural model; thus the liminal phase is either not found or significantly de-emphasized. We also find a significant difference in the type of transformation which occurs. Within Jewish culture the transformation is automatic and occurs whether the ritual is performed or not.

The only significant exception to this is that of *berit milah*, the covenant of circumcision. In order for a boy to enter the covenant he must be circumcised. Yet even in this case the categories are clearly maintained (unless there is a medical reason for not performing the operation). Prior to circumcision the boy is in effect not yet considered viable; he has no name and does not require a proper funeral service. If he is never circumcised he is considered anomalous and is moved into the negative category. To some degree, prior to both *berit milah* and *bar mitzvah* the child is not in the outside category, that is, not Israel, but rather is not yet properly categorized. As indicated, prior to circumcision on the eighth day the boy is not considered viable and prior to *bar mitzvah* at 13 the boy is not considered responsible. His father is responsible for all of his actions.

The only significant exception to this structural pattern is found in the Progressive movement's use of Confirmation or *kabbalat Torah* (receiving the Torah). This ritual is usually conducted several years after the age of 13 (often at 15 or 16) and is always a group ceremony. To some extent, the period between 13 and Confirmation may be considered a liminal phase, with some communities not seeing the young people as full members of the community until after Confirmation. *Communitas* is also an important feature of the experience, with much of the preparation focusing on group dynamics and identity. It is not unlikely that these elements reflect the influence of the wider cultural environment in which both liminality and *communitas* are significant. This, however, is not meant to suggest that the ritual was consciously shaped to copy rituals from the Christian cultural context. Although the term 'confirmation' is clearly taken from the Christian ritual, the time, structure and content of the rituals are very different. The aspect of structural transformation is an unconscious phenomenon reflecting broader patterns of transformation, many of which are found in all segments of the Jewish community.

Myth and history

Chapter 3, on myth and history, brings together many significant elements found in all religions and cultures, that is, stories or models which allow people within the particular cultural community or religious tradition to make sense of their past, present and future.[7] It suggests that myth, history and time itself are interrelated categories. Depending on the particular cultural context, these categories will be differentially emphasized.

Although the term 'myth' has been understood in a wide variety of ways, including stories of acts of gods or humans doing fantastic things, it seems more useful to define it more broadly as narratives (stories or otherwise) which enable communities to define how they understand themselves, how they place themselves in the continuum of past, present and future. In respect of this definition history, in part, should be seen as a sub-category of myth. It is often defined in opposition to myth – perceived as presenting a factual view of events, while myth either is metaphorical or fictional. While this opposition is significant, it is the way that both 'myths' and 'histories' are used within culture that places them within a conceptual category. On a different level, both the narrow definition and the opposition between fact and metaphor are often built on an ethnocentric framework: 'we have history (fact) while other cultures or religions have myth (fiction)'.

The opposition between the two is, however, a significant feature of the analysis of myth and history presented in the chapter. It can be associated with the categorization of myths as living, broken, or dead. Living myths are those which are considered to be 'factual' and thus

7

include historical models of the past. Broken myths are those whose factual basis has been challenged but which retain metaphorical significance. Dead myths are those which are no longer significant within a particular cultural community. What is of particular interest to the analysis of any mythological tradition is how the myths are divided into these three categories. Within the Jewish framework different segments of the community will categorize the myths differently. These differences will depend to a large degree on their respective understanding of revelation and their acceptance or non-acceptance of modern models of history and biblical criticism.

The author of the chapter presents a continuum of transformation from myth to history based on her community's model of differentiation; thus Genesis 1 and 2 are considered mythological because they do not fit in with current scientific models of cosmogony, while stories about Abraham and Moses, for example, are increasingly historical. Within the framework of the approach all of the narratives still contain at least metaphorical meaning. The dead myths are those from Mesopotamia from which the biblical myths emerged. If the categorization of stories were done by a member of another segment of the community, for example, an Orthodox Jew, it is not unlikely that they would draw the line between living and broken myths at very different points.

The valuation of history is significant in the Jewish framework from an additional perspective: that is, validation of the present, in Geertz's terms giving the present cultural/religious values an aura of factuality. Within the Jewish tradition religious truth has not tended to be validated by direct experience of the divine. History and connection with the past and past experience, especially the covenant on Sinai, validate the present covenant and connection with God. Thus, the emphasis on the biblical text as history and our existence as the outcome and descendants of the events and actors are essential building blocks in the reciprocal validation which is the foundation of the tradition as a whole.

The chapter also introduces the Jewish understanding of time, especially in respect of the movement of history towards a messianic future. Time is analytically significant in several respects. Although we often consider time to be an integral part of the natural world, and thus separate from culture and cultural models, our experience and understanding of time and perhaps the concept itself are intrinsically culturally determined. Each culture develops its own way of expressing and experiencing time. In some cases it is considered (and experienced) in a circular pattern, in others in a linear pattern, and in others as a constant unchanging flow. Israelite and Jewish material suggest that their concept of time is structured in a similar way to that presented above in respect to sacred place. Time is divided into two categories: the present is category A and the past and future are category B. To a great extent the past and future represent time out of time, symbolized by the garden of Eden and the world to come or paradise. These two realms are conceptually elided in the metaphor of garden. The end is a return to the beginning. These two realms are opposed to the purely human realm in between. To some extent the B category almost does not exist, as indicated in the grammatical structure of Hebrew in which the past and future are interchangeable and the present tense does not exist.

The understanding of the messianic future is also significant. This is emphasized by the transformation of this concept in the nineteenth century by Reform thinkers: that is, from a messiah to a messianic age. The Messiah represents a complete break with history, in effect the end of history. Although human action may help the coming of the Messiah, his coming will intrinsically transform the nature of the world. It should be emphasized, however, that he remains a human figure. He is not divine or semi-divine, as such a figure would bridge the unbridgeable category of human and divine. The messianic age, however, reflects a transformation of structure. It is within history and is brought about by gradual transformation. Thus the messianic age, like Confirmation, is based on a structure which includes some degree of mediation. Conceptually, the Messiah model might be related to the Christian model of events leading up to the final thousand-year reign of the saints, while the messianic age model is similar to the model of that reign.

Sacred texts

Several important issues are raised in the chapter on sacred writings (Chapter 4). Those of analytical significance include the relationship between Torah (in a narrow sense) and the continuous tradition of commentary and discussion, and the relationship between revelation through prophecy and revelation through argument as sources of authority.

Jewish tradition has tended to use the term 'Torah' in two senses, narrow and broad. The narrow sense refers to the first five books of the Bible, that is, Genesis to Deuteronomy. These books have the greatest authority and are considered by many Orthodox Jews to be the literal words of God given to Moses on Mount Sinai. Other Jews, while continuing to consider them to be of central importance, may accept an inspirational view of their origins – often accepting aspects of the modern critical approaches; a minority consider the texts to be of purely human authorship. The broader sense of Torah refers to the continuous tradition of Jewish commentary and discussion which begins at Sinai and is unfolding into the present day. To some extent these two senses are encapsulated in the concepts of Written and Oral Torah.

In line with the analysis presented above these two categories can be seen as fitting into an 'A not B' structure. The Written Torah, that is, the first five books of the Bible, is a unique and unbridgeable category qualitatively distinct from the Oral Torah. This distinction is emphasized by the aspect of authority. Although the Oral Torah is authoritative, its authority is contingent and changeable. The authority of the Written Torah is absolute and unchangeable.

The transformation in Reform structure is also found in respect of these two categories. Reform thinkers have tended to play down the divine nature of the Written Torah. They have also emphasized its sociological and historical context and thus introduced the aspect of changeability. To a large extent they have merged the Written Torah into the broader context of Torah in the wide sense, ignoring the opposition between the Written and Oral Torah. Torah becomes a constantly unfolding revelation, with roughly equal weight given to all levels of discussion and commentary.

The opposition between the two types of revelation is also significant. Jewish tradition makes a clear distinction between prophecy and rabbinic debate. It argues that prophecy as a mode of divine communication ends with the last of the biblical prophets. In spite of this, God's revelation continues through a different mode, that is, rabbinic discussion and debate based on a struggle with the biblical text, primarily the Torah. This creates an opposition between two types of authority. Prophetic authority is creative and direct from God. Rabbinic authority, although the unfolding of God's will, emerges from a rational human process of discussion and debate based on a clear process of decision-making. As in the case of the distinction between the Written and Oral Torahs with which it is intrinsically related, the type of authority is qualitatively different. The authority of prophecy is essentially divine, unchangeable and unique while that of the rabbinic process is essentially human, contingent and to an extent changeable.[8]

Picturing God

Ways of viewing God or gods have been examined from a number of different perspectives in the development of sociological and anthropological thought. Some of the most influential groundwork was established by Emile Durkheim (1926) in his *Elementary Forms of Religious Life* in which he suggests that the idea of God is an image of or emerges from a culture's perception of itself. This theme is further developed in the work of Berger and Luckmann, who focus on the relationship of religion to the organization of culture.[9] A structuralist perspective adds to this approach an analysis of the way in which views of God or gods exemplify the relationship between categories: for example, whether there is an overlap between the categories of human and divine, natural and supernatural. It argues that the picture of God will reflect the underlying structural relation. Monotheism or polytheism and other models emerge from structure rather than being independent realities or spiritual or intellectual insights. This is to suggest not that the structure on the surface level cannot be elaborated or intellectualized through the development of theologies, but that its basis rests in a broader cultural equation which is equally reflected in other aspects of culture.

Some of the key issues raised in Chapter 5 are the problems of anthropomorphism and doctrinal formulations about God in the Jewish tradition from the biblical until the modern period. Both of these problems are exemplified in the work of Moses Maimonides, who in effect denies the possibility of God having any form or image which could be literally pictured, or even the possibility of the human mind intellectually understanding or encompassing God.

This thread of Jewish thought, which can be minimally traced back to the rabbinic period (second century CE) and maximally into the Biblical text, can be understood from a structuralist perspective as emerging from the 'A not B' pattern. If human and natural are in one category and divine and supernatural are in the second with no possible overlap, then it is logical (within the Jewish system of categorization) that the two categories must be absolutely distinct. If God were in any way anthropomorphic (or indeed similar to any other feature of the natural world), then the integrity of the system could be challenged.

Similarly, the emphasis on monotheism also logically emerges from Jewish underlying structure. The biblical variant on the structure was highly centralized (see the discussion in Chapter 1). It emphasized a strong opposition between Israel (the people), as a whole, against the nations, and Israel (the land, exemplified by the Temple) against the rest of the world. Such a structural emphasis would lead to a centralized or monotheistic view of God in opposition to the world (as a whole).

Chapter 5 also discusses the development of certain mystical ideas which move in a slightly different trajectory. Ultimately the mystical tradition in its Zoharic and Lurianic manifestations begins to develop an aspect of mediation between the infinite unknowable God and the finite and knowable world. This mediating aspect, the *sefirot*, becomes progressively less infinite and more knowable. It is possible that under the influence of neo-Platonic thought and other cultural influences this reflects a transformation in structure in which the categories are no longer absolutely impermeable. To some extent this is reflected in a pantheistic element in which the entire realm of creation can be seen as the unfolding of the divine and thus not absolutely separate from it. Similar trends might be found in modern Jewish communities in the feminization of aspects of God. (This aspect is discussed in the chapter in the section 'Feminism', pp. 157–60.) The discussion is emphasized by a complementary transformation in structure, with a move away from opposition to metamorphosis.

Human nature and destiny

Human nature, as suggested by the above discussion, is directly related at the level of structure to the understanding of the divine and the supernatural. This is true not only of the opposition between human and divine but also in relation to human destiny, that is, the fate of human beings after death.

Structuralist analysis suggests that human beings and indeed the world as a whole are set in structural opposition to the divine. This opposition is emphasized in Jewish texts by the concept of creation. Throughout most of the history of Jewish thought there is an emphasis on both creation *ex nihilo* and the direct creation of human beings by God. This establishes the opposition of God (uncreated) to world and human beings (created). The opposition between humans and God, however, seems to be challenged by the concept of creation in the 'image of God'. Eventually this aspect of apparent mediation is minimized through the concept of emulation of God's attributes rather than a literal image of them.

Chapter 6 also introduces the concepts of free will, evil and atonement. The role of evil in creation creates certain problems within the Jewish framework. Because of Judaism's emphasis on a strong version of monotheism, built on the underlying structure, dualism is not a possible solution to the existence of evil. To a great extent, it can be argued that within the traditional Jewish framework evil has no independent existence (and in some cases its actual existence is denied). Although the concept of the 'evil inclination' gives evil an aspect of existence, it does not, until late mystical texts, give it an independent existence in opposition to God. It is possible that although the world as a whole could have been evil in structural opposition to God's goodness, because of God's creative role the opposition was between absolute, determined goodness (that is, God) and non-absolute undetermined goodness/badness (that is, creation). The very undetermined nature of creation within the opposition implies free will and allows for reward and punishment or theodicy. If matter was evil, yet humans could transcend it, then they would be a mediating category between God and the world, which would conflict with the underlying structure.

The question of the fate of human beings after death is also related to the underlying structure. Within the Jewish tradition there are three possible models: no existence after death, resurrection of the body, and immortality of the soul separate from the body. Of these models only the first two are compatible with the underlying structure. Separation of the body and soul would suggest that the soul was a mediator between the world of matter, which is finite, and that of the divine, which is eternal. Most Jewish texts until the Middle Ages (and to some extent into the modern period) emphasize the resurrection of the body, and suggest that the body and soul are created together and exist together. Some of the philosophical texts which make a distinction between body and soul attempt to get around the structural problem

13

by arguing that the soul's immortality is in effect provisional (unlike God's, which is actual). The soul has a beginning in time and is kept in existence by God rather than intrinsically. In line with many trans-formations in structure found in the modern period, there is a comparable move to the third model, immortality of the soul. This is in part connected with modern rational models which see resurrection of the body as irrational, but it also fits in with many transformations which introduce aspects of mediation into the structural model.

Women in religion

Women as a subcategory within human nature are often a significant structural marker in respect of their structural relation to the other subcategory of men. From a structural perspective it would be expec-ted that the relationship between the subcategories will mirror that of the higher-level categories. Thus, the structural opposition between men and women should mirror that between humans and God. In biblical, rabbinic and Orthodox Judaism we find that the opposition between men and women is based on a clear 'A not B' pattern. To a large extent, as indicated by the prohibition on their access to the inner courts of the Temple, women are intrinsically distinct from men.

This opposition is played out in many aspects of surface-level structure. The clearest area is found in respect of participation in public ritual life. Public ritual is distinctly the arena of men, with clear prohibitions against the access or participation of women. The opposi-tion is often stated today in the terms that each category, men and women, has their proper place of action within Judaism: for men the synagogue and for women the home. The chapter also exemplifies this opposition in both mythological texts from the Bible and rituals connected with childbirth and purity.

In non-Orthodox streams of Judaism (and to a lesser degree in Orthodoxy itself[10]) there are moves to remove this opposition. Thus, in the Progressive Movements (Reform and Liberal) and in the American Conservative Movement the roles of men and women have to a great extent been equalized; all these movements allow women full partici-pation in services, do not separate men and women in the synagogue, and allow women to become rabbis.

Although this transformation is a result of external cultural influ-ences, unlike many of the transformations discussed above it does not involve the introduction of a mediating category. Women have not become mediators; they have been moved into the same category as the men.[11] This process reflects a significant mechanism of structural transformation. In consequence of changes at the surface level of culture, that is, the feminist movement, the opposition between men and women no longer serves a structural need and is indeed in conflict with cultural norms; thus the opposition is removed and men and women are placed into the same structural category. This process does not reflect a transformation in structural equation but rather a transformation in content.

Attitudes to nature

The chapter examining attitudes to nature (Chapter 8) focuses on how nature should be treated and the Jew's (or human's) relationship with it. One issue which is not explicitly examined is whether there is a conceptual distinction between humanity and nature, and between culture and nature. In respect of the structural categorization this issue can be examined on two different levels. Because structural relations recapitulate at different levels, the conceptual distinctions are paradoxically both significant and insignificant.

The significance of the opposition depends on the level of structure which is brought into play. On the macro-level, in structural opposition to God there is no significant distinction between humanity and nature. God stands in the same relationship to all of creation. This level of structure is perhaps suggested by Genesis, chapter 2, in which humans are commanded to be stewards of the world, that is, to be part of it and to take care of it.

One level down in structure, however, we do find an opposition between humans and nature. Although human beings are part of creation they are separately created and commanded to rule and subdue nature rather than be part of it. The two different levels of opposition and the differentiation in valuation of the symbols are particularly significant in understanding symbols in general. The meaning and value is not intrinsic to them but depends on the other symbols which they are over and against, and on the level of structural relation.

There are several other areas in which the Jewish understanding of nature is shaped by underlying structure. One of the most culturally significant areas is in respect of divisions within the animal world, as Professor Mary Douglas pointed out in a series of seminal papers (1966, 1971 and 1975). The animal world is divided into a number of categories which are shaped by the same underlying structural equations as found in other spheres of Jewish culture. Animals are divided in to a number of unique and unbridgeable oppositions. Thus, animals are clean or unclean (as indicated in Genesis 7:2), edible (*kosher*) or inedible (*treif*), domestic or wild, fit for sacrifice or unfit. In each of these oppositions animals are in one category or the other. The oppositions are developed in the context of both legal decisions and narrative mythological texts. Thus, example texts from Leviticus make a clear opposition between domestic and wild animals. Domestic animals can be sacrificed while wild animals cannot. This opposition is found explicitly on the narrative level in the opposition between Jacob and Esau in Genesis. Jacob is associated with the tents and domesticated animals, feeding his father kid (goat), while Esau is associated with nature. He is a hunter and plans to give his father venison. The text clearly rejects Esau and wild or nature in favour of Jacob and domestication or culture. This opposition is also found implicitly in many names given in the Bible. Israel often uses names derived from domesticated animals while the nations have names derived from wild animals.

This structural categorization of nature works on two related levels. First, as underlying structure is the basis of how a particular cultural group organizes its conceptual universe, it would be expected that the same patterns of categorization would be used in respect of all different levels of their thinking and experience. Second, culture undergoes a continuous process of naturalization, that is, attempting to justify itself by demonstrating that it is natural, that there is no opposition between the structure of nature and that of culture. Thus, if it can demonstrate that nature is structured through the same equations, then it validates itself and its boundaries.

Worship

Although the chapter on worship (Chapter 9) touches on some aspects of the liturgy, it focuses primarily on the structuring of time. It examines the cycle of the year, beginning with the weekly cycle moving from Shabbat to Shabbat, and then the cycle through the year moving from festival to festival and beginning again with each new year.

This structuring of time is closely related to the naturalization process discussed in respect of nature and the structuring of geography discussed in respect to sacred place. Like the natural world and sacred places, time is divided into categories of sacred and profane each of which is unique and unbridgeable. This is most clearly seen in the opposition between the Shabbat and the rest of the week. The texts of Genesis 1 and 2 clearly indicate a qualitative distinction between the two. This opposition is further emphasized in later traditions by associating the Shabbat with the world to come. Shabbat becomes a taste of paradise in this world. The mystics further emphasized the opposition by stating that we are given an additional soul on the Shabbat which we will have permanently in the world to come.

Other sociological aspects of religion which are worth mentioning are those associated with group identity. Within Judaism worship has both an individual and a communal aspect. Although individuals do engage in worship there are many aspects of the Jewish tradition, including the reading of the Torah and the recitation of the mourners, *kaddish* (recited in memory of the dead), which can only be done in a communal setting (minimally ten men in Orthodox communities and ten people in non-Orthodox communities). Thus, worship in bringing people together, especially in times of crisis, is a significant feature in supporting and creating communal identity. The communal reading of the Torah as symbolic revelation also emphasizes the communal aspect of the covenant with God. In Jewish tradition the covenant is essentially communal rather than individual.

The aspect of identity validation and creation is reflected in the diversity of synagogues and traditions – identity is created and supported by attending a service in which people share similar values and traditions. The very liturgy and form of service is shaped to both reflect and validate these values. In many cases the identity created is sufficiently strong that individuals are uncomfortable worshipping in different synagogues or traditions.

Making moral decisions

Chapter 10, on moral decisions, covers many aspects which have been touched upon already, for example, free will and emulation of God or *imitatio dei.* It introduces one further area which it is useful examining here: the possible opposition between law and morality or ritual and morality. This is also touched on under the heading of natural law. Within modern Judaism this opposition is often highlighted with an emphasis on the aspect of moral law as the heart of Judaism. This approach was initiated in the work of Moses Mendelssohn, who saw moral law as being the true essence of religion.

The trajectory of Jewish tradition, however, has not emphasized or developed this opposition. Rather, it views the two realms of morality and ritual as being equivalent. This equivalence can be explained in the light of the structures examined here. If there was a qualitative distinction between ethics and ritual then a pattern of mediation might develop. The two primary categories might be moral law, defined as good action, and sin, defined as bad action. Ritual law would fall somewhere in the middle, not being precisely equivalent to moral law. By creating the equivalence, however, the two are set in equal opposition to forbidden actions or sin and thus no problem of mediation is created.

It is suggestive that within Progressive Judaism there is a structural shift which recategorizes and requalifies the relationship between moral and ritual action. Progressive Judaism, especially in the nineteenth and early twentieth centuries, placed a strong emphasis on moral law and to a great extent moved ritual law into an anomalous position – being amoral and therefore standing between moral action and sin. This creates a mediating structure in which ritual action can fall into either major category, depending on the context. As suggested above, this transformation reflects a structural development which underlies many of the developments in Judaism in the modern period. It should be emphasized that these transformations, although different in degree, are found in all segments of the modern Jewish community.

Conclusions

This introduction has attempted to highlight some of the issues raised in the chapters. It presents an analytical framework through which the phenomenological material presented can be analysed from a holistic perspective. The structuralist perspective developed here is only one possible approach to the material; readers are encouraged to apply their own approaches and insights.

The structuralist approach is especially useful in respect of the type of material discussed here because it facilitates a holistic approach. The brief discussion in this introduction indicates that all of the aspects of Jewish culture are shaped by the same underlying structural equation. This pattern, 'A not B', is also found in other aspects of Jewish/Israelite culture which fall outside of the remit of this book. Thus, both the patterns of social organization and the emphasis on endogamy are also structured in the same way.

As suggested above, this book is also useful in highlighting some of the different strands of Jewish tradition and thought. It illustrates both current diversity and the ongoing processes of development and transformation. All living cultures and religious traditions are continually changing in response to both internal and external forces and contexts. Although some traditions might view themselves as being unchanging and static, perhaps preserving some ancient pattern of belief and practice, when these are examined from an anthropological perspective and a historical perspective, we find a continuous pattern of transformation. Even the attempt to remain the same involves a change in emphasis and consciousness. Because of this theme of change and development, no one thread or tradition within Judaism or any tradition should be taken as the authentic tradition by which all others should be measured and from which all others have emerged. Each tradition is an authentic response to the world and an attempt to find a meaningful way of living in it. Orthodox, Conservative, Reform, Liberal, Reconstructionist or Humanist are all responses to modernity and are all threads in the growing tapestry of Judaism and Jewish culture.

Notes

1   It must be emphasized that, in many cases, because of their internal perspectives the authors are not intending to present an up-to-date presentation of critical academic scholarship. Rather, they occasionally use different academic approaches to highlight their own ways of understanding the material.

2   For useful discussions of religion see Geertz (1966) and Spiro (1966).

3   See for example Lévi-Strauss (1963) (especially chs 2, 9, 10 and 11) and (1976) (especially chs 1, 9, 10 and 14); and Kunin (1995) (especially chs 1 and 11).

4   See for example the discussion of the move from ritual to belief in

Douglas (1973), pp. 19–39. Many of the transformations highlighted in this book are related to a move from an emphasis on the body as a means of religious expression to an emphasis on words and belief. In some respects Judaism has moved from a tradition with a high degree of 'group', emphasizing shared and obligatory forms of bodily expression and action with a low degree of 'grid', shared and obligatory world-view, to forms which increasingly focus on 'grid'. Within the non-Traditional community this is associated with a significant reduction in 'group', with bodily elements reduced to a minimum and ritual and religious action left to individual choice. Within the Orthodox community, while 'grid' is increasingly emphasized, with progressively less room for individual variation in respect of world view, the element of 'group' has also been maintained and in some cases strengthened even further. For a sophisticated discussion of the relationship between 'grid' and 'group' in respect of ritual and religious structures see Douglas (1973), pp. 77–92.

From a slightly different perspective the relationship between grid and group provides an interesting approach to the absence of dogma in Jewish tradition. Given the strong emphasis on group and the need to establish a clear and accepted, if provisional and contingent, set of practices, this provided a strong basis for communal identity and continuity. The foundation of group allowed the element of grid, belief and world-view to be much more flexible and open-ended. Thus Judaism, in effect, replaced dogma, common belief, with *halakhah*, common behaviour.

5   See Kunin (1996), which compares the basic structures of Hebrew thought with those of the New Testament and the Book of Mormon.

6   See Turner (1969) and (1978). See also Kunin (1998) for a detailed discussion of pilgrimage.

7   For a detailed discussion of different theories of myth see Kunin (1995), pp. 19–48.

8   See for example *Mishnah Eduyot* 5 and 6, which suggest that future courts of Jewish Law can overturn the legal decisions of past courts.

9   See Berger and Luckmann (1967).

10   One very recent development in Orthodoxy in the United States has been the appointment of women as interns, standing in a semi-rabbinic role. Although thus far this has only occurred in two Modern Orthodox congregations, it will be interesting to see if it expands to a wider constituency within the Orthodox community.

11   It is possible that some elements of Conservative practice may reflect an aspect of mediation. Women were subdivided into two categories: women who accept the obligations of men and are to a great degree seen as equivalent to men, and women who do not and remain in the status

traditionally given to women. Although this structure is implicit in many of the Conservative movement's decisions in respect of the role of women, in actual practice there are no clear distinctions and the categories of men and women are joined together.

References

Banton, M. (ed.) (1966) *Anthropological Approaches to the Study of Religion*. London: Tavistock Publications.

Berger, P. and Luckmann, T. (1967) *The Social Construction of Reality*, London: Penguin.

Douglas, M. (1966) *Purity and Danger*. London: Ark Paperbacks.

Douglas, M. (1973) *Natural Symbols*. Harmondsworth: Penguin Books.

Douglas, M. (1975) *Implicit Meanings: Essays in Anthropology*. London: Routledge.

Durkheim, E. (1926) *Elementary Forms of Religious Life*. New York: Free Press.

Geertz, C. (1966) 'Religion as a cultural system' in Banton (1966).

Gennep, A. van (1960) *The Rites of Passage* (1st edn 1908). London: Routledge and Kegan Paul.

Kunin, S. (1995) *The Logic of Incest: A Structuralist Analysis of Hebrew Mythology*. Sheffield: Sheffield Academic Press.

Kunin, S. (1996) 'The death/rebirth mytheme in the Book of Mormon' in D. Davies (ed.) (1996) *Mormon Identities in Transition*. London: Cassell, pp. 192–203.

Kunin, S. (1998) *God's Place in the World*. London: Cassell.

Lévi-Strauss, C. (1963) *Structural Anthropology*. New York: Basic Books.

Lévi-Strauss, C. (1976) *Structural Anthropology*, Volume 2. Chicago: University of Chicago Press.

Spiro, M. (1966) 'Religion: problems of definition and explanation' in Banton (1966).

Turner, V. (1969) *The Ritual Process*. London: Routledge.

Turner, V. (1978) *Image and Pilgrimage in Christian Experience*. Oxford: Blackwell.

1. Sacred place

Seth D. Kunin

This chapter discusses the biblical, rabbinic and modern understanding and use of sacred place in Judaism. The first half examines two interrelated aspects of sacred place, that is, the Temple in Jerusalem and the relationship of the land of Israel to the rest of the world. The Jewish understanding of pilgrimage and the modern understanding of the land of Israel are discussed in the context of these two elements. The second half discusses the two key elements of modern sacred place, that is, the synagogue and the home. A case study comparing the differing use of sacred place among the Orthodox and the Progressive Jewish communities highlights the key aspects of sacred place in Judaism.

In order to understand properly the use of sacred space and place in Jewish thought and culture, the concept must be examined on two interrelated levels: the ideological and the functional. The ideological level is based on an abstract understanding of the structure of reality as it is realized in the Israelite and rabbinic understanding of geography and in the structure of the Temple and *mishkan* described in biblical and rabbinic texts. (The *mishkan* was the portable structure used to house the Ark of the Covenant during the forty years in the desert.) Although this level has its basis in biblical and rabbinic thought, it is still relevant to the understanding of the modern Jewish attitude towards sacred space, though it functions entirely on the abstract level.

The functional level is found in the structure of the synagogue and in the place of the home as the replacement for the Temple.[1] The functional level which we find today developed as a response to the diaspora and the destruction of the Temple. It has been continually transformed over the last 2,000 years to remain in alignment with the needs of Jewish culture as it developed during each specific period.

This chapter shows that the conceptualization of diaspora and pilgrimage, as two aspects of sacred space, can be understood only through the interaction of the ideal and functional levels. It also presents a comparison of the use of sacred space in Progressive and Orthodox synagogue architecture and religious services as a case study for the practical application of the concept of sacred space in Judaism.[2] The comparison also indicates ways in which the concept of sacred space is transformed in respect to transformed cultural needs (or perceived needs).

Ideological sacred space

The clearest depiction of the rabbinic model of sacred geography is found in the following text taken from *Mishnah Kelim*.[3]

> There are ten degrees of holiness: the land of Israel is holier than other lands ... The walled cities of the land of Israel are still more holy ... within the walls of Jerusalem is still more holy ... The Temple mount still more holy ... the rampart is still more holy ... the courtyard of the women is still more holy ... the courtyard of the Israelites is still more holy ... the courtyard of the Priests is still more holy ... between the 'sea' and the altar is still more holy ... the sanctuary is still more holy ... the Holy of Holies is still more holy, for none may enter therein save only the High Priest on the Day of Atonement. (*Kelim* 1:6–1:9)[4]

This text presents a model for organizing space into a coherent pattern. The model works from the outside in. Israel is contrasted with the rest of the world, Jerusalem is contrasted with the other cities of the land, the Temple is contrasted with Jerusalem, and the Holy of Holies is contrasted with the Temple. The text combines two levels of geography. It presents the relationships within macro-space, that is, the world, Israel, Jerusalem and finally the Temple. It then presents micro-space which is a recapitulation of the structure of macro-space, that is, the various areas within the Temple. The micro-level focuses an association of space with humanity. All people can enter Temple Mount; yet as we move inward, the groups of people who are allowed to enter are progressively reduced.

The text presents space as consisting of progressively smaller opposing domains. One way of modelling these domains is as a set of concentric circles.[5] Each ring of the set of concentric circles is qualitatively compared (in terms of holiness) with its two adjoining rings. It is qualitatively positive with respect to the ring outside it, and qualitatively negative regarding the ring inside it. The negative and positive qualitative values are the degree of relative holiness.

It might be thought that this pattern of progressively wider domains of holiness extends beyond the circles listed here. This, however, is unlikely. The text itself compares Israel (i.e., the land of Israel) to the world (i.e., everything other than Israel). The structure of sacred geography is presented in Figure 1.1. Notice that while the inner rings are progressively more holy (indicated by + (plus) signs), the outer ring, the world, is profane (indicated by a − (minus) sign).[6]

This text from the Mishnah brings together several other significant elements. At each level the text offers examples from other cultural domains which distinguish that level from the previous level. With respect to the distinction between Israel and the world, the text states that offerings from agricultural produce, e.g., barley, are brought from Israel but not from the other parts of the world. Similarly, Jerusalem is

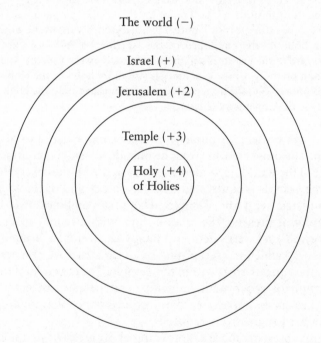

Figure 1.1 The structure of rabbinic ideological space

distinguished from the other cities by the fact that the lesser holy things and the tithe may be eaten in Jerusalem, whereas they may not be eaten in the other cities.

As observed above, the micro-levels of holiness, that is, the Temple and its courts, are distinguished by the people who may enter them. This is exemplified by the final ring, the Holy of Holies, which may be entered only by the High Priest. These distinctions emphasize the role of sacred space in organizing many levels of culture. They also reveal that sacred space is one of many related cultural hierarchies which organize experience into culturally manipulatable domains. We shall return to this aspect below (see pp. 26–9).

THE BIBLICAL MODEL OF IDEOLOGICAL SACRED SPACE

A similar model of sacred geography is also found in the biblical text, especially regarding the structure of the Israelite camp as described in Exodus and Leviticus. As in the rabbinic model, space is divided into a pattern of progressively smaller concentric circles. The camp is distinguished from the world. This distinction is found in the association of pure and impure with these two domains. Pure objects or people could remain within the camp and impure objects had to be removed from the camp. This separation of the camp from everything outside it supports the argument that the concentric circles of the rabbinic text also end with the borders of Israel, which are analogous to the boundaries of the camp. Israel and the camp are holy (albeit to a lesser degree than the inner circles) while the world and outside the camp are impure and profane. The enclosure was distinguished from the camp, the tent of meeting from the enclosure and the Ark from the tent of meeting. As in the division of pure and impure found between the camp and the outside world, the individuals permitted into each sacred space are progressively limited, culminating in the High Priest being the only person allowed into the presence of the Ark. The biblical model is depicted in Figure 1.2.

A second model, which allows a more precise depiction of the structure of ideological sacred space, both biblical and rabbinic, is that of segmentary opposition. The ideological structure of sacred space found in these texts is in many ways analogous to a segmentary opposition model. Each circle or space comes into play depending on what is being opposed to it. The land of Israel is used in opposition to

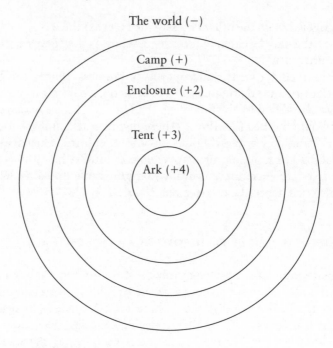

Figure 1.2 The structure of biblical ideological space

the world. At smaller levels of opposition, smaller spaces are compared. As in the segmentary opposition model, like must be opposed to like and the smaller units come into play (as relatively more sacred) only when working on a micro- rather than a macro-level. Ultimately the comparison is between Israel and the rest of the world.

Structure and sacred space

We have already observed that space, like other aspects of experiential reality, is culturally structured to fit into an overarching pattern. Both the biblical and the mishnaic texts implied divisions within humanity and the Israelite community which mirrored those in geography. The pattern allows individuals within the cultural community to give meaning or value to particular events, people or places. The structure of space, e.g., its division into sacred or profane, is closely related to more general structural patterns, and therefore must be examined in the context of general cultural structures. This synthetic approach is especially relevant as it explains the relationship between the various circles in Israelite sacred geography.

Structuralist analysis suggests that Israelite social structure can be depicted by two related models. On the one hand the Israelites, as indicated in the above discussion, could be subdivided in relation to holiness, e.g., who was allowed to enter various holy spaces or eat specific holy foods. Figure 1.3 illustrates this model of humanity. Notice that the outer circle of 'the nations' corresponds to the circle of 'the world' in the geographic models.

It is, however, with the second model for humanity that the relationships in the other models can be clarified. This structure is based on a segmentary opposition model in which each smaller level is qualitatively more positive than the previous level. The model relies on a strong association of a preferential rule of endogamy, with the family being the smallest unit. Although one was legally obligated to marry beyond the basic family unit, ideologically the preference was to marry as close as possible. Each level of kinship further away was less ideologically preferable. This system of increasingly large and negative

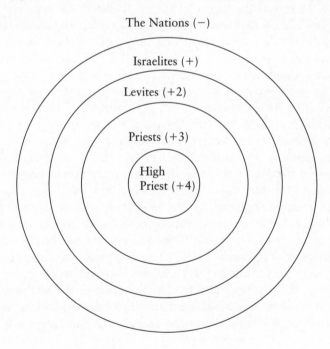

Figure 1.3 The structure of humanity

27

concentric circles is limited. The rule of endogamy ultimately defines a boundary of inside and outside – people considered inside are acceptable marriage partners and those considered outside are unacceptable partners. Thus, the ring of concentric circles logically ends with the culturally defined border of membership in the Israelite or Jewish people.

The model of sacred geography, as well as the other models already presented, is based on an identical structural pattern. Within a certain boundary, i.e., in respect of geography, the borders of the land of Israel, there is a pattern of graded holiness with the inner circles being progressively more holy. Yet in each case there is a clear boundary between sacred and profane. Regarding sacred geography in both biblical and rabbinic thought, sacred space ends at the borders of the divinely ordained space for Israelite occupation. In the rabbinic text sacred space is static; it is associated with a specific land and progressively more holy places within that land. In the biblical text discussed here, sacred space is mobile. It is the space in which the Israelites live, surrounded by the wilderness – a barren land associated with the rest of the world and non-Israelite humanity.

The biblical/rabbinic model of geography and the related sociological model of segmentary opposition ultimately grow from a simple structural expression: 'A not B'.[7] Thus the various models are based on non-overlapping circles in which categories/circles of equal size are set in opposition to each other, and joined in opposition to large circles or categories. This pattern can be best understood by using a standard genealogical table to exemplify the relationships. Figure 1.4 presents such a table. At the lowest level each 'brother' is a single circle set in opposition to the other brothers. At the next level, the brothers together form a complete circle set in opposition to cousins, etc.

Figure 1.5 illustrates this pattern in a more abstract form. The two largest circles are Israel and the world respectively. The smaller circles within the Israel circle are the next two smaller units which make up the category Israel. From the macro-perspective, the basic opposition is between Israel and not-Israel, which is progressively mirrored on the micro-level. It is due to this recurring pattern that the micro-structure mirrors the macro-structure. The first half of the mishnaic text presents a macro-view of sacred space. In the second half of the mishnaic text and in the biblical text the Temple and the Tabernacle represent one aspect of the micro-level.

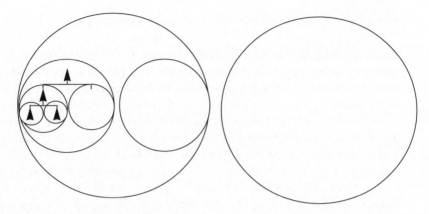

Figure 1.4 Genealogical model of sacred space

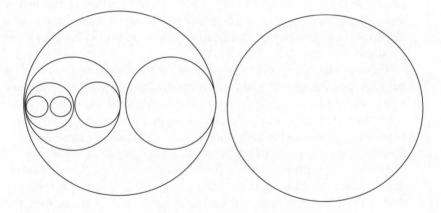

Figure 1.5 Abstract model of ideological sacred space

Alternative models of sacred space

This model of sacred space and place, however, is not the only one found in the biblical text. Several narrative texts suggest some related and some contradictory models for organizing space. The two related models presented above are associated with a qualitative understanding of directions on the horizontal (that is, north, south, east and west) and the vertical planes (that is, up and down). The models of sacred place which contrast with the two models presented above are associated with the identification of competing holy places.

29

THE STRUCTURAL SIGNIFICANCE OF EAST AND WEST

There appears to be an association between the directions of the compass (at least regarding east and west) and the ideological quality of the events which take place or move in those directions. In Genesis all events which move in an easterly direction are qualitatively negative. In the early chapters of the book, movement in an easterly direction represents the descent of humanity into degradation. When Adam and Eve are expelled from the garden by God for eating the forbidden fruit, they leave the Garden of Eden towards the east (Gen 3:24). After killing Abel, Cain moves to the east of Eden, where he founds the first city. This ties the origin of civilization to the descent into sin (Gen 4:16). The founding of civilization is logically opposed to the discovery of spiritual realities by the descendants of Seth, who remain in the west. In later chapters the men of Babel move east before building their doomed city. The move to the east is associated with a challenge to God's power and leads to the confusion of language and conflict between people (Gen 11:1–9).

There is also an association of 'east' with the nations other than Israel. When Abraham[8] and Lot divide the land, Lot chooses the east side of the Jordan, leaving the west bank to Abraham and the Israelites who came after him. Similarly, Abraham gives his descendants, other than Isaac, lands to the east (Gen 25:6). The text therefore makes a double association: west (or westward movement) is equivalent to holy and is the proper setting for Abraham and his chosen descendants, while the east (or eastward movement) is associated with evil and is the proper setting for the other nations. It is likely that this qualitative categorization of east and west is due to the geographic position of Israel. Its placement on the shore of the Mediterranean, the boundary of civilization, meant that it was, in a sense, as far west as possible, while most of the nations with which the Israelites fought were to the east of Israel.

This qualitative understanding of direction, however, has not survived the transformation of the Israelites into a diaspora people. With the movement into Europe, to the west of Israel, east lost its symbolic power. In fact, the qualitative characterization of east has been inverted; it now has a positive qualitative value.[9] The Ark, the most important part of the modern synagogue, is placed on the eastern wall, and services in a synagogue are conducted facing east, that is, towards Jerusalem and the Temple. It should be noted, however, that west has not been equally inverted. It has little or no qualitative value in the modern Jewish understanding of space. The west's primary occurrence in modern Jewish sacred geography is the Western Wall which is one of the retaining walls of the Temple Mount in Jerusalem. In this particular case, west does have positive symbolic value.

THE STRUCTURAL SIGNIFICANCE OF UP AND DOWN

The vertical directions, i.e., up and down, are also given qualitative value in the biblical text. Perhaps because they have no direct or necessary historical association, this value has been retained. 'Up' is consistently portrayed as a positive direction in opposition to 'down'. This opposition is best illustrated by comparing two narrative texts: Genesis 22 and Genesis 37. In Genesis 22 Abraham is commanded by God to sacrifice his son Isaac upon a certain mountain which God will show him (the text actually initially says 'place', which turns out to be a mountain). Abraham prepares to offer his son as a sacrifice, and when he is stopped God blesses him because his actions showed his faith in God.

The positive value of the upward direction is indicated in several aspects of this text. God commands Abraham to bring Isaac to the top of the mountain, and to set him upon a raised altar. The actual act of sacrifice is called in Hebrew *laha'alot*, that is, 'to raise up'. Sacrifice must be understood as a positive and purifying death, and thus supports the positive value of the upward direction. Thus, movement in the upward direction is qualitatively positive and ultimately brings a blessing and fruitfulness – God promises Abraham a multitude of descendants.

Similarly, mountains and the direction up are qualitatively positive in several other key biblical texts. Moses, for example, receives the Ten Commandments (and the entire Torah) upon Mount Sinai, and the Temple in Jerusalem is built upon a mountain. It is significant that the sacrifice of Isaac is said to have occurred on the site of the Temple.

In Genesis 37 we find the association of 'down' with evil. In this text Joseph's brothers, acting, in a sense, against God's command, attempt to murder their brother by placing him in a pit. Whereas in Genesis 22 the upward motion is associated with positive death, that is, sacrifice, in Genesis 37 the downward movement is associated with negative and polluting death, that is, murder.

31

The negative association of downward movement is illustrated in two other elements of the text. First, Jacob tells his sons that Joseph's death will cause him to 'go down to Sheol', that is, cause his own death. Secondly, Joseph's journey into slavery is called a descent, and later, when he is sent to prison by Potiphar, the text refers to it as a descent. Thus, 'up' and 'down' should be understood as standing in qualitative opposition, with 'up' being qualitatively positive and 'down' negative.

THE ROLE OF THE LIMINAL IN SACRED SPACE

Both of these vertical directions share a significant element in relation to the Israelite understanding and categorization of space. Both should be considered liminal spaces (that is, for example, movement in either direction, up a mountain or down into a pit, is movement into a liminal space). The direction 'up', especially in regard to mountains, joins the domains of earth and the firmament, or perhaps the divine space. It is in this intermediate area that most communication with God occurs. Sacrifice, therefore, is doubly positive in biblical thought. It involves an actual raising of the object sacrificed and, at least during the Second Temple period, was performed only in Jerusalem on the Temple Mount.

The direction 'down' also joins two domains, the surface of the earth which is the place of the living and the underworld which is portrayed in the idea of 'Sheol' as the place of the dead. Thus, downward movement is symbolically the opposite of upward movement. The negative aspect of the depths is found throughout the biblical text. Two examples of this negative value are Psalm 30 and Jonah 2.

In the anthropological literature, liminal spaces are usually regarded as ambiguous. They are the places where opposing domains meet and perhaps overlap. This ambiguity is especially relevant in the context of the material discussed here. As we have observed, a basic pattern of Israelite structure is 'A not B'. The structure relies on a clear and complete distinction between A and B. A cannot be B, B cannot be A, and similarly they cannot overlap. Such an overlap would diminish the distinction between the two.

Thus, liminal spaces are structurally problematic. Israelite mythology and ideology cloud or remove this structural crisis by transforming the liminal spaces into non-liminal spaces, i.e., they transform or remove the ambiguity. The two directions, up and down, are transformed, not surprisingly, in opposite directions. 'Up' is moved to positive, semi-divine space and 'down' becomes negative space, the domain of the dead or sinful.

The text exemplifies the nature of these two different types of space through associating them with different types of death. We have already noted the association of 'up' with sacrifice, positive, transformative death. On the most basic level, through sacrifice sin is removed and the giver or sacrificer transformed. On a mythological level – especially in respect of Genesis 22 – the sacrificed, or symbolically sacrificed, is transformed or divinely reborn as a result of the sacrifice. The direction 'up' is also associated with several other positive deaths. Both Moses and Aaron die on mountains after transferring their blessing or mantle on to the next generation. Both these deaths fit into the transformative aspect of sacrifice. The fact that the location of Moses's tomb remains secret or unknown also suggests a bodily transformation to spiritual space.

The aspect of sacrifice and transformation from human to semi-divine is most apparent in the case of Elijah. 2 Kings 2:11 states:

> And it came to pass, as they still went on, and talked, that, behold, there appeared a chariot of fire, and horses of fire, which parted them both asunder; and Elijah went up by a whirlwind into heaven.

This text and the verses before it contain all the aspects of the positive and divine aspects of the direction 'up'. As in a sacrifice, Elijah is transported to heaven by means of fire and wind. The element of fire is emphasized by being mentioned twice. Fire is tied to sacrifice directly in the texts about Elijah; see, for example, 1 Kings 18:20 and following. The transformative aspect of sacrifice is found on two levels. First, Elijah is transformed from an earthly being into a divine being. This element is emphasized in later Hebrew mythology, with Elijah becoming the precursor of the Messiah. Secondly, the transformation also occurs on the human level. Elisha is given Elijah's mantle and is transformed into a prophet and miracle worker.

The transformation of 'down' from ambiguous to negative is also exemplified by types of death in the biblical text. The symbolic murder of Joseph is only one such example. The clearest example of this usage of the direction 'down', an example repeated throughout later books

33

of the Torah, is the fate of Korah. He and all his followers are swallowed up by the earth. Thus, because of the needs of Israelite structure, liminal spaces are transformed into non-ambiguous spaces. Up is positive and transforming, while down is negative and polluting.

Conflicting models of sacred space

There are, however, examples of sacred space which are based on a different model from the dyadic segmentary model which organizes the majority of textual material. Throughout Genesis there are a number of texts which highlight sacred spaces other than Jerusalem. Two examples of this type of text are: Genesis 28:10–22 and Genesis 35:1–14. Both of these texts establish Beth El as a holy place. In the first, Jacob dreams of God's presence and declares that the place is the house of God. The second text gives an explanation for its sacredness. Both of these texts justify Israelite worship at Beth El, and possibly explain the establishment of a dream cult at that temple. There are many similar texts in the Bible which either justify the position of a place as sacred space or reveal the use of such places. One such text is 1 Kings 18:20–40. That text makes it clear that Elijah rebuilt the altar of God, implying that Mount Carmel was an established Israelite holy place. One attribute which many of these alternative sacred spaces share is their raised position, fitting in with the liminal and sacred aspects of raised places. Although this alternative version of sacred space can also be understood using the segmentary opposition model, yet there is a clear difference between the model used in this approach and that presented above. This model never culminates in a single space which is distinguished from the rest, it probably has no necessary outside boundary and is not based on the pattern 'A not B', and it is not essentially dyadic. These three elements are basic to the primary understanding of biblical/rabbinic sacred space.

As suggested below, the primary distinction between the two models emerges from a different attitude towards endogamy. The multiple holy place model emerges from a society which does not emphasize endogamy,[10] and the single sacred space model emerges from one which does. It is possible that the two models, that is, a single sacred space and multiple sacred spaces, are tied to a more general transformation in Israelite culture. With the return from the Babylonian exile in 538 BCE, the Temple, which was rebuilt in Jerusalem, became the political and religious centre of the re-established community in opposition to the centres which had been established during the exile by those who remained. It is likely that several of the boundaries within different cultural domains (including a strong opposition between Israel and the nations) based on an 'A not B' structure which became dominant in Judaism were established during this period. These new mechanisms included a strong emphasis upon endogamy. The new emphasis is an essential element of the basic structure discussed above. This transformation is equally reflected in an emphasis on the Temple in Jerusalem in opposition to any competing holy place. It is possible that the alternative model which allowed for multiple sacred spaces pre-existed the return from exile.

What makes space into sacred space?

Thus far we have concentrated on the organizing aspect of sacred space but have not addressed the question of what makes a space sacred. We find a pattern of evolution of this concept within the biblical text. In some texts, especially in regard to the Tabernacle and the Ark, God is viewed as actually dwelling in these objects or places. Similarly, there are texts which describe God in anthropomorphic terms, and thus almost physically present in a specific place at a specific time. Thus, in these texts the sacredness of the space is due to God's presence there as opposed to God's being anywhere else. In other texts, however, there is a gradual transformation and displacement. In Deuteronomy there appears to be a clear theological transformation in the understanding of the Ark and the Temple. The text emphasizes that it is God's glory which is present, rather than God's actual physical presence. Presence of God's glory in one space is not mutually exclusive; God's glory can be present elsewhere as well.

This type of transformation continues throughout the development of Jewish thought. Rabbinic texts emphasize that although God was present in the Temple in Jerusalem, this did not prevent him from also being present, perhaps in a slightly less concentrated form, everywhere else. This idea is developed in the following rabbinic metaphor:

> God's presence in the Temple was like the sea in a cave. The cave can be full

of the sea without reducing the amount of water in the sea as a whole. (Urbach, 1979, p. 46)

Thus, the rabbis preserved the pre-eminence of the Temple (while it still existed) as a sacred place, because of God's concentrated presence, while also allowing other places to be sacred by emphasizing that God's substance and presence were not diminished by its concentration in the Temple. Other rabbinic texts even further emphasize God's omnipresence, suggesting that sacred places were not such by particular divine presence. They stated, for example, God is the place of the world, the world (and therefore any specific space) is not God's place (*Genesis Rabbah* 1:18).

Other texts develop an even more fundamental understanding of God's relationship to space, and therefore the nature of sacred space. Many rabbinic *midrashim* suggest that God, as it were, went into exile with his people. Thus, God's presence is not tied to a specific place. Instead, it is tied to the presence of God's people, that is, Israel, who bring God's presence to wherever they are. This dynamic aspect of God's presence, and therefore dynamic understanding of sacred place, is also illustrated in the following text from the Mishnah: 'If two men sit together and occupy themselves with the words of the Torah, the *Shekhinah*, God's presence, is in their midst' (*Mishnah Avot* 3:2).[11] The rabbis took pains, however, to emphasize that this understanding of God's presence did not suggest that God could be divided or that there were many *Shekhinot*.[12] The metaphor of water (discussed above) was one such attempt. A second metaphor, that of the sun, was also used to similar purpose: 'It [the sun] shines on each individual and at the same time, upon the world as a whole' (Urbach, 1979, p. 48, adapted from BT *Sanhedrin* 39a).

The second aspect of the rabbinic understanding of the relationship to time and space is fundamental for the functional and modern Jewish use of sacred space and place. Both of the rabbinic concepts depend on a significant ideological innovation. The rabbis distinguished between two aspects of God. The essential essence of God is ultimately distinct from the world and transcendent. Yet one attribute of God, his presence or *Shekhinah* – coming from the Hebrew word meaning 'dwelling', or 'indwelling' – is immanent and present both with Israel and in the Temple in Jerusalem. As is seen, the *Shekhinah* itself is not necessarily tied to one place or location but can be found in any place. A second version of the text cited above (that is, 'If two men . . . ') gives the number as ten men. Ten men (a *minyan*) were seen by the rabbis as the minimum number of people needed to make a community. Thus the sacredness of a place depends on the presence of a community of people who allow God, or God's *Shekhinah*, to enter.

The implications of ideological sacred space

In the beginning of this discussion we made a distinction between ideological and functional sacred space. The former is abstract in two respects. On the one hand, ideological sacred space is an abstract hierarchical categorization of geography. On the other hand, the centralization of sacred space in Jerusalem and the Temple is also primarily ideological rather than functional. By the time that the rabbinic texts were written (or edited), the Temple in Jerusalem had been destroyed and Jews were forbidden to live in Jerusalem itself. A large proportion of the community was already living in other parts of the world, for example, Babylon and Rome.[13] Even in the biblical text describing the Tabernacle, it is likely that there is a similar ideological element. These elements come from texts which were probably written during the Babylonian exile and thus describe a situation which no longer existed or never existed.

It seems likely that ideological sacred space and place with its focus on Israel and Jerusalem also has messianic implications. This possibility is supported by the use of 'Jerusalem' in the Passover *seder*. At the conclusion of the *seder* the words 'next year in Jerusalem' are read. Jerusalem, in this context, is always understood to be the heavenly or messianic Jerusalem rather than the material city of Jerusalem as it exists today.

This messianic understanding of the ideological levels of sacred space is significant in the transition to functional sacred space. We have already observed one aspect of that transition, that is, the dynamic aspects of the *Shekhinah* – moving from a view of God tied to a single and specific object or place to one in which God can be present in many places or indeed all places simultaneously.

A second implication of this understanding is found with respect to pilgrimage. In the biblical text (and those rabbinic texts which describe cultic celebrations while the Temple still stood), in which ideological space at least ideally existed in practice, there is a clear obligation to make pilgrimages to Jerusalem three times a year; this emphasizes

Jerusalem's role in the ideological structural model. This obligation did not survive the destruction of the Temple and the move from ideological to functional sacred space. Although throughout the centuries Jews have made pilgrimages to Jerusalem and other holy places in the land of Israel, such pilgrimages are not obligatory in Jewish law. With the transformation of ideological space into messianic space, return to the Holy Land, as a religious expectation or obligation, is left to the time of the Messiah. There is no special merit, as there is in Islam, for pilgrimage. On several occasions in Jewish history mass movements to the Holy Land have been associated with messianic movements or expectations. Although secular Zionism called for a return to the land, this is not due to the land's sacredness, but for nationalist and cultural reasons. The relationship of secular Zionism to sacred space is discussed below (see p. 48).

There is also a further spiritual distinction between ideological, messianic space and functional space. The rabbis considered prophecy to be possible only in the Holy Land. Although they considered prophecy to have ended in the fifth century BCE, it is primarily associated with the transition between the Temple and the synagogue, or between an ideological space and a functional space. Although it is likely that the rabbinic view of prophecy was shaped as much by political authority as by theological considerations, it does, however, reflect a significant transformation in the rabbinic view of the nature of Israel (the people) and the spiritual role of the land. Whereas the Temple and prophetic period were based on a hereditary caste of priests and a group of individuals in direct personal, idiosyncratic communication with God through prophecy, the rabbinic model was non-hierarchical within Israel, and any properly trained person could be involved in the process of halakhic, 'legal', decision-making. In essence it was non-priestly. This transformation is especially significant with respect to the traditional understanding of the synagogue. This aspect is discussed below in the examination of the nature and role of the synagogue as a sacred space (see pp. 41–3). The spiritual distinction between the Holy Land and the lands of the diaspora is strengthened by medieval Jewish thought. Jehudah HaLevi, for example, states that prophecy and direct communication with God were limited both to the people of Israel and to the land of Israel (Altmann et al., 1981, pp. 64–70).

MACRO- AND MICRO-STRUCTURE

The transformation of sacred space from one to many, from the Temple to individual homes and synagogues, reflects a general change in Israelite/Jewish culture. During the biblical period (as reflected in biblical myth and law) we find two related structures: macro-structure and micro-structure. Macro-structure used the concept, 'A not B' to distinguish between Israel and the nations. This level is tied to the Israelite preference for endogamy. On the spatial level this structure is reflected in the distinction between the Land of Israel and other lands.

Micro-structure is also tied to structural opposition and is focused on the individual family and the preference to marry as close to the family structure as possible. It is associated with two different aspects of Israelite structure. On the one hand, the dyadic form reflected in the inner structure of the Temple recapitulates the basic equation exemplified in macro-structure. On the other hand, a non-dyadic variant of this level of structure may be reflected on the spatial level in the early Israelite pattern of multiple holy places.

Macro-structure and non-dyadic micro-structure are most clearly developed in Genesis 10, the 'Table of Nations'. The text includes two types of genealogy: segmentary and linear. The segmentary genealogies reflect micro-structure and the linear reflect macro-structures.

In the biblical text and the culture it reflects, there is a clear emphasis on macro-structure (and recapitulated dyadic micro-structure). This emphasis is found on the spatial level with the centralization of the cult and sacred space in the Temple in Jerusalem. The macro-level emphasizes the unity, the oneness of Israel, and therefore the cult as opposed to the unity of the nations. It is likely that macro-structure is highlighted to support the ever stronger preference for endogamy. This may have been threatened in the cultural and historical context which saw the redaction of the biblical text.

Later rabbinic texts and the community which emerged in the diaspora focus on non-dyadic micro-structure. No longer is there a single focus of sacred space or, on the human level, a single group or hierarchy with a monopoly in sacredness or cult. As in the segmentary opposition model, the system accentuates the smallest unit, that is, the family.

Functional sacred space

Functional sacred space brings together many of the elements of ideological sacred space which are discussed above. With the transformation of the community from one based in the Holy Land to a diaspora community, and with the destruction of the Temple in Jerusalem, functional sacred space became primarily dynamic, following the community rather than being a specific place or places.[14] Sacred space in the diaspora is focused on two separate domains, the home and the synagogue.

THE HOME AS A SACRED SPACE

In rabbinic thought the home replaces the Temple as the central locus of sacred space. The family table and the family meal are seen as replacing the altar in the Temple and the sacrificial cult. Similarly, the two loaves of bread, the *hallot*, are symbolically associated with the shewbread which was part of the Temple ritual. The rabbis called the house a *mikdash maat*, a 'small sanctuary', using the same word, *mikdash*, which is used in the biblical text to refer to the Temple and the Tabernacle. Thus, the rabbis make a direct association between the two. During the Passover *seder*, the leader of the service, in imitation of the High Priest, washes his hands, linking the *seder* with the paschal sacrifice in the Temple. An equivalence is also made between the *seder* table and the altar in the Temple. Many other aspects of home ritual make a similar analogy between the home and the Temple cult.

A second aspect of the spiritual importance of the home is its place in the *halakhah*, the Jewish legal system. With the probable exception of the synagogue, the home is the focus of more laws than any other location. Thus, the role of the home as a sacred space may also be tied to this legal concentration. The home is holy because through being in it, eating in it, one can fulfil God's laws.

The home as a sacred space fits in with the structural patterns discussed above. It is the logical extension of the pattern of structural opposition. Structural opposition is ultimately based on the smallest unit of the system. In this case the household is the smallest unit. Thus, by making the home a sacred space, the system brings together key elements of both the social and the spiritual systems. The unity of the two areas means that they mutually support each other: the sacredness of the home justifies the focus on the family, and likewise the focus on the family unit gives additional strength to the holiness of the home. The home is also significant as a sacred space because it also reflects a move to non-dyadic micro-structure – by definition homes are multiple.

THE SYNAGOGUE AS SACRED SPACE

The synagogue also fits within this model of micro-structure.[15] Each synagogue, symbolically based on ten men (or ten people in the Progressive community), is the smallest community unit and is the communal equivalent of the family in the structural pattern. It is likely that the cultural transformation reflected in the structural transformation is a change in internal and external relations. Prior to the diaspora, endogamy needed to be enforced internally, and therefore the structure reflected this need by emphasizing macro-structure. In the diaspora period the community was isolated, with endogamy being enforced externally. In this situation an emphasis on macro-structure was not needed and thus micro-structure could come to the fore.[16]

The home is not alone in being perceived as being contiguous with the Temple; the synagogue also has elements of such continuity. The clearest tie of this sort is in the concept of *avodat halev*, 'service of the heart'. One major rabbinic innovation with the destruction of the Temple was the transformation of the means of communication with God. Prior to the destruction, the primary means was through the sacrificial cult, the *avodah*. By the time of the Second Temple period all such sacrifices were conducted by the priests in the Temple in Jerusalem. With the destruction of the Temple came a spiritual crisis resulting from the closing of this channel. The rabbis resolved this crisis by declaring that service of the heart was equivalent to service in the Temple. Although service of the heart, or prayer, was also associated with the home, it was primarily associated with the synagogue. Thus, the synagogue in this respect was seen as being contiguous with, and replacing, the Temple as the space where one could communicate with the divine. This is reflected in the many rabbinic texts which associate God's presence with activities performed in the synagogue.

The internal structures of the synagogue retain many of the elements of sacred space which were developed on the ideological level. These elements are most apparent in the traditional form of the synagogue. Thus, the first part of this discussion will focus on the traditional synagogue, with reference, when appropriate, to the differences in non-traditional patterns.

The synagogue has a section in which men pray and a second section for women. The women's section is often a gallery or a section separated from the main part of the synagogue by a partition. The primary focus of the synagogue is the Ark, which is placed on the eastern wall. Most of the service, however, is conducted from the *bimah* (the raised reading desk), which is often in the centre of the synagogue. The men's seats are placed along the north, south and west walls facing the *bimah*.

Like the Temple in Jerusalem, the synagogue is divided into spaces in which only specific segments of the community are allowed. There is, however, a difference for this type of division between the Temple and the synagogue. In the Temple the division of spaces was based on relative purity, while in the synagogue women are excluded from the men's section through fear that their voices (or presence) may be seductive and draw men's minds away from prayer. This division in space is one of the primary differences between traditional and non-traditional synagogues. Non-traditional synagogues will usually have men and women sitting together.

The synagogue also has a hierarchy of sacred spaces. The building itself has an element of sacredness. This is reflected in many ways, e.g., laws concerning the disposal of a building which had been a synagogue, and the fact that a synagogue does not need a *mezuzah*.[17] Within the building, the sanctuary, the room where the services are conducted, is relatively more sacred. This is followed by the *bimah*, the reading desk, and culminates in the Ark, where the scrolls of the Law are kept.

This pattern of sacred spaces is, however, not as exclusive as that in the Temple. All the sacred spaces are open to all male members of the community (the position of women is discussed above).

The synagogue also includes several other reflections of ideological sacred space. The significance of 'up' has been maintained. This significance is found in several areas. The *bimah* is always on a raised platform. Thus the most important elements of the service are led from a symbolic mountain or positive liminal space. The positive and sacred aspect of 'up' is also found in the word used to describe the action of being called to the Torah: *aliyah*, that is, a 'going up'.[18] (Interestingly, this same word is used by modern Zionists to describe going to live in the state of Israel.) The Ark is also built in a raised position in, or on, the wall.

We have already alluded to the transformation of the significance of compass directions. In the biblical text, west was positive while east was negative. In most diaspora communities this relationship has, at least in part, been inverted.[19] In most synagogues the orientation of prayer and the Ark are towards the east. The eastward alignment is linked to the connection between the synagogue and the Temple, and the ideological priority given to the Temple as a locus for communion with God. Although the rabbis recognized that prayer was possible anywhere, they still recognized in the Temple a more concentrated presence of God. Synagogues face towards Jerusalem and the Temple.

Some non-traditional synagogues have intentionally moved away from this directional orientation. This transformation is linked to a significant ideological change. Non-traditional Jews, especially Liberal and American Reform Jews in the early part of the twentieth century, rejected two key elements: one was the importance of the Temple and a desire to return (in the messianic age) to the sacrificial cult practised there; the other was the notion that Jews were a nation with national aspirations, tied to a specific national homeland. Thus, the rejection of the eastward orientation reflected the rejection of both the Temple and the Zionist dream of a national homeland.[20]

Sacred time and sacred space

Before we examine the use of sacred space among Orthodox and Progressive Jews, one other aspect of sacred space needs to be mentioned. To a degree, sacred space in rabbinic Judaism has been transformed to sacred time. Thus Shabbat, a time rather than a place, has become the locus of much of what once was the essence of sacred space. Shabbat is understood as being a taste of the world to come, and it thus replaces the Temple as the focus of messianic hope. By celebrating and keeping Shabbat, one carries sacred space to wherever one is. This is reflected in a statement by A. J. Heschel (1951): 'The Shabbat is a palace in time.' This statement reflects the close connection between the concept of sacred space and sacred time in Jewish thought. Shabbat and other festivals are therefore the most extreme examples of dynamic sacred space.

A case study: comparison of Orthodox and Progressive use of sacred space

By a comparison of the use of sacred space between the Orthodox and the Progressive Jewish communities, many significant aspects of modern Jewish sacred space and place are clarified.[21] The key difference between the two approaches is the issue of the democratization of sacred space. While in the Orthodox community there is general access to sacred space for the male members of the community, in the Progressive community, which gives equality to men and women, there also appears to be an emphasis on the priestly function of its rabbis, thereby reducing general access to sacred space.[22]

In order to contextualize this comparison, a summary of the key aspects of a Shabbat morning service is necessary. The service begins with a preparatory section. This section is recited individually in an Orthodox synagogue. In a Progressive synagogue this section is shortened and recited by the leader and the community together. The second section, the 'Shema and its blessings', is introduced by a communal call to worship; it centres on a statement of belief and obligation. The third section of the service is then a prayer section called the Amidah. In an Orthodox community this is first recited silently by the congregation and then led aloud by the leader. In most Progressive synagogues it is only read aloud, and concluded by a short period of silent prayer. The fourth section of the service continues with the reading of the Torah, which is the central focus of the service. During this segment a section of the Torah is read. In an Orthodox service seven men will be called to recite blessings before and after the Torah reading. In a Progressive service, sometimes only one person is called. The final section of the Progressive service includes concluding prayers and a memorial prayer. The Orthodox (and American Conservative) service includes here an additional service called Musaf. This includes a repetition of the prayer section with some changes focusing on the sacrificial service in the Temple and concluding prayers.[23]

One of the primary distinctions between the two forms of service is the use of individual as opposed to communal reading of prayers. As we have mentioned, the Progressive service includes little or no individual reading. The congregants read as a group when indicated in the prayerbook and listen to the leader when it is indicated that he/she should read. In an Orthodox service much of the reading is done individually at one's own pace. This distinction is linked to the enhanced priestly function of the rabbi which is discussed below.

There is also a clear difference in atmosphere between an Orthodox service and a Progressive service. Orthodox services are much less decorous. People talk throughout the service and greet each other. In many ways the service feels more informal. This type of atmosphere is in keeping with the general pattern of non-dyadic micro-structure which is focused on individual access to sacred space. The Orthodox community is, in general, more comfortable with its sacred space than is the Progressive community. The Progressive service is much more decorous. Rubrics in the prayerbook are often taken seriously, and individuals are apparently more respectful. This pattern of behaviour is associated with a strengthened priestly function and a more exclusive use of sacred space.

The respective architectural plan of Progressive and Orthodox synagogues is the first area which reveals the different approaches to sacred space. The Orthodox community places the *bimah* in the centre of the sanctuary and therefore in the centre of the community. The community is thus made part of all that occurs on the *bimah*. The architectural plan of a Progressive synagogue usually contains a significant difference. The *bimah* is placed in front of the congregation, almost as a stage. The Ark is on the wall facing the congregation at the back of the *bimah*. There is no women's section, as men and women sit together. Unlike the Orthodox synagogue in which actions are performed in the centre of the community, the service and the actions take place on the *bimah* and are thus separated from the congregation. The Progressive synagogue plan is similar to that of Christian churches and thus supports the priestly aspect of the rabbinical role.

The use of the *bimah* is equally significant. In the Orthodox synagogue the leader of the service faces in the same direction as the congregation and thus is not distinguished from the congregation; in the Progressive synagogue the leader usually faces the congregation. Thus in some sense, he/she is leading rather than praying with the congregation.

The choice of person to lead the service (and to read the Torah) also reveals a similar trend to that revealed by the respective architectural plans. In Orthodox synagogues where there is a rabbi, the rabbi will not necessarily be expected to lead the service. Often, knowledgeable laypeople will lead significant parts of the service. Equally, many men other than the rabbi will read from the Torah scroll. In Progressive synagogues, however, the rabbi will be expected to lead the majority of the services and usually read from the Torah scroll. It is possible that this distinction, at least in part, stems from the fact that often the rabbi is the only person (or one of the few people) in a Progressive synagogue with the skills needed. Whatever the reason, this distinction in roles further enhances the separation of the Progressive rabbi from the congregation and thereby the priestly aspect of the Progressive rabbi's role.

Several other rituals associated with the Torah are relevant to this discussion. In a traditional service (on Shabbat) seven men are called up to the Torah (to do a blessing before and after the reading of the scroll). Several other men also participate in taking the scroll to and from the Ark. Thus, a large number of individuals participate in this part of the service. In a Progressive service the number of blessings is often limited to one, and occasionally only the rabbi recites the blessing. In some Progressive synagogues only two or three people participate in this part of the service.[24] The respective atmosphere of the synagogue during the reading of the Torah is also indicative of this general pattern. On the one hand, in an Orthodox synagogue there is an audible connection between the congregation and reader; everyone is reading with him. Should he make a mistake, members of the congregation will correct him. On the other hand, in a Progressive synagogue there is a profound silence. No one would dream of interrupting or correcting.

The procession of the scroll is also significant. In an Orthodox service the Torah scroll is processed around the synagogue twice during the service. As it passes, men touch it with their prayer shawls. This ritual emphasizes both that the Torah is part of – i.e., not separated from – the community and that each individual has a personal connection with it and therefore with sacred space. The Torah is treated with respect but also familiarity. Within many Progressive synagogues the Torah processions were removed as being undignified and perhaps even verging on idolatry. In these communities the Torah has a strong aspect of respect but very little familiarity in the community.

These few examples reveal a general pattern. In Progressive synagogues we find a strengthening of sacred space. The *bimah* and the Torah are increasingly becoming the preserve of an almost priestly caste – the rabbis – who are almost qualitatively distinguished from the congregation. In the Orthodox community, although sacred space is maintained, it is less exclusive. This trend in Progressive Judaism is probably tied to the cultural shift mentioned above. On the synagogue level, the Progressive community is using a macro-model which emphasizes the exclusive aspect of sacred space. Because of the Progressive community's higher level of assimilation and participation in the wider culture, there is a corresponding quicker movement to a structural model which emphasizes group identity. In the Orthodox community, because of its separation from the wider community, we find a slower movement towards the macro-model. Many aspects of Orthodox synagogue ritual still reflect the micro-model's emphasis on the individual within a pattern of segmentary opposition. Thus, at the level of sacred space, Orthodox communities appear to be more egalitarian than Progressive communities.[25]

The Hasidic community and the *Rebbe* as dynamic sacred space

A similar phenomenon is found in developments within the ultra-Orthodox Hasidic community. The Hasidic community emerged at the same time as the Jewish community was being allowed to enter into closer connection with the wider European society. Thus in many respects it is responding to the same pressures as the Progressive community. The Hasidic community moved in the opposite direction, emphasizing traditional practice rather than modernization. We do, however, find a similar cultural transformation moving towards macro-structure. Although the Hasidic community has emphasized the importance of the individual, it has simultaneously re-created the priestly function and a new form of sacred space. This priestly function is concentrated in the person of the *Tzaddik* or *Rebbe*. The *Tzaddik* is understood as being the direct conduit between the individual Hasid and God. Sacred space is concentrated in and around the person of the *Rebbe*.

This transformation and concentration of sacred space is exemplified among the Habad Hasidim. Their preferred place of residence, even above the state of Israel, is Crown Heights in New York City – the area in which the *Rebbe* lived. The focus on the *Rebbe* and Crown Heights is further emphasized by the fact that the Habad Hasidim built a house for the *Rebbe* in Israel which is identical to the home in which he lived in New York. The focus is reversed: Israel is tied to New York and the *Rebbe*, rather than New York being tied to Israel. The home in Israel was built in preparation for the coming of the Messiah, which was seen as being the only time when the *Rebbe* would go to Israel. The hope that the *Rebbe* was the Messiah also reflects the emphasis on ideological macro-structure, with tri-annual or annual pilgrimages to the *Rebbe*'s court replacing the ancient pilgrimages to Jerusalem. Thus, the Hasidim, like the Progressive community, in the face of a more open community which no longer externally supports the rule of endogamy, emphasize the distinction between the Jewish people and the nations by accentuating the priestly function and the macro-model of sacred space.

The state of Israel as secular sacred space

We find an interesting related phenomenon in the development of the state of Israel and secular Zionism. This phenomenon is also closely tied to the transition in emphasis from micro- to macro-structure. Whereas in the earlier form of macro-structure the land of Israel was spiritual sacred space, in modern Jewish thought (especially in Western communities influenced by Zionism) the land has become secular sacred space.

Although it retains many of the attributes of the spiritual form, it exhibits them in a secular way. This transformation is most apparent in the mission statement of the World Zionist Organization. This statement lists the following goals of Zionism and the state of Israel:

> The unity of the Jewish people and the centrality of Israel in Jewish life; The ingathering of the Jewish people in its historic homeland ... through aliya from all countries; The strengthening of the State of Israel which is based on the prophetic vision of justice and peace; The preservation of the identity of the Jewish people through the fostering of Jewish education and of Jewish spiritual and cultural values. (Hirsch, 1993, p. 14)

Notice that the spiritual aspect of the land is left to the end. The statement emphasizes the centrality of the land in relation to the national and therefore secular existence of the people. In effect the text is a secular form of macro-structure. (The land of) Israel is the embodiment of the unity of the Jewish people in structural opposition to other peoples and cultures.[26]

Commandments and sacred space

There is one element which joins all loci of sacred space, both ideological and functional. Each space, be it the Temple and the Holy Land on the ideological level, or the home and the synagogue on the functional level, is the focus of *mitzvot*, that is, commandments. Although there are commandments which have no spatial focus, each one of these locations has a large number of commandments which must be performed there. Thus, from this perspective, sacred space becomes such through the performance of God's word. The difference between the two levels, however, is maintained. The commandments associated with ideological space can be performed (for the most part) only with the existence of the Temple and thus will come into force only with the messianic age. The commandments associated with the home and the synagogue are in force both in the diaspora and in the Holy Land.

Conclusions

In this chapter we address several aspects of the Jewish understanding of sacred place. The first dichotomy addressed was the distinction between ideological and functional sacred space. Ideological space is primarily concerned with the nature of geography and an abstract understanding of space. It is seen that two interrelated models structured the understanding of space. The initial model is based on a pattern of concentric circles with the smaller circles being progressively more sacred. This model ultimately relied on the external distinction between Israel and the nations. The second model is based on the social structure of segmentary opposition. This aspect of the structure worked from the smallest level to ever larger levels, culminating with the borders of Israel. It is shown that the models applied to both geography and social structure. The two models work together to create a structural pattern which, although it is based on a recurring structure, is significantly also a closed structure. The pattern of decreasing holiness concludes with the borders of the Holy Land. Land and space outside these borders, on the ideological level, are, by definition, profane. It is suggested further that macro-structure can be viewed via the concentric model, or perhaps more precisely as a dyadic version of the segmentary model.

We examined two aspects of functional sacred space: the home and the synagogue. Both of these spaces are distinguished from ideological space through being essentially dynamic. They are not based on specific locations. Rather, they are based on the presence of a community or as loci of commandments. It was suggested, however, that the home and synagogue have key structures based on ideological space. Both of these spaces, for example, were understood as being analogous to the Temple in Jerusalem. The influence of the ideological level was also apparent in the structural plan of the synagogue, which is based on a hierarchical pattern similar to that found in the concentric model of structure. Other related elements included the use of raised areas and direction as symbols emphasizing the sanctity of certain areas within the synagogue. This sanctity arises from either the sacredness of the space (or objects kept in the space), e.g., the Ark, or the importance of the rituals conducted from that space, that is, the *bimah*. Direction was also used to make a symbolic association between the synagogue and the Temple in Jerusalem.

One of the underlying themes of the discussion is the relationship between macro- and micro-structure. Macro-structure is based on the distinction between Israel and the nations. It is tied to the need to maintain the preference for endogamy. On a geographical level the structure makes clear distinctions between sacred and profane spaces, echoing the distinction which it makes between people, i.e., Israel and the nations. Both dyadic and non-dyadic micro-structure are based on the logical extension of Israelite endogamy and social structure culminating in a pattern based on segmentary opposition, focusing on the smallest geographic spaces. It is suggested that, although both macro- and micro-structural patterns are always present, the relative weight given to either pattern will depend on broader cultural situations and contexts. Thus, macro-structure, which emphasizes and justifies the preference for endogamy, is itself emphasized when that preference is endangered.

In the chapter it is shown that one period of cultural transformation, which is reflected in a change in the respective weight of macro- and micro-structure, is the move from a centralized community based in the land of Israel to a diaspora community.[27] In the Holy Land, during the Persian period (fourth century BCE and beyond), the preference for endogamy needed to be maintained internally in the face of a culturally mixed society. Thus there appears to be a progressive centralization and unification of sacred space based on the macro-model. During the diaspora, in consequence of anti-Semitism and the ghettoization of the

Jewish community, endogamy was in effect enforced externally, and thus the micro-model became the dominant pattern. One of the key aspects of this initial realignment was the democratization of sacred space.

It is suggested that the Jewish community's becoming more connected with the modern Western multi-ethnic community, and more assimilated, will be associated with a realignment of structural weight. This realignment is seen in both the Progressive and Hasidic communities. Both have re-emphasized aspects of the priestly element of Jewish culture and the associated aspect of exclusive sacred space. It is suggested that the modern state of Israel also plays a part in this structural realignment. In a sense it has become secular sacred space, emphasizing the Jewish people's nationhood in structural opposition (within the macro-model) to other people's nationhood.

Notes

1 It is clear that during the biblical period, just as today, there must have been a functional level which worked in relationship with the ideological level. The biblical text preserves and is the basis of the ideological level. It also includes hints of the biblical functional level. The ideological level should not be understood as merely pertaining to the biblical period; it interrelates with the modern functional level as well as playing a significant role in its own right in modern Jewish thought.

2 The term 'Progressive' is used here to include all non-traditional forms of Judaism except for the American Conservative Movement. Thus it includes a wide range of practice and belief. The cases examined come from several different Progressive communities.

3 The Mishnah is a rabbinic text which was edited in the second century CE (see Chapter 4, pp. 117–19). It is significant that the text under discussion was edited (and probably written) at least 100 years after the destruction of the Temple in Jerusalem.

4 This text comes directly after a text listing the degrees of impurity. Thus it suggests that in this aspect of the ideological model impurity is the structural opposite of sacredness. The significance of this opposition is seen below in the discussion of the reasons given for women being refused access to sacred objects in some Progressive synagogues.

5 A more precise structural model based on a segmentary opposition model is presented on p. 29.

6 The key elements of the structure can be illustrated by the set of equations Israel:Jerusalem :: Jerusalem:Temple :: Temple:Holy of

Holies) :: World:Israel :: Profane:Sacred. : is used here to mean 'is to', which indicates that the two elements are in some type of relationship. In the equation here they are in opposition. :: is used here to mean 'as'; this indicates that the two elements in the second half of the equation are related in a similar way to the first two elements.

7 The simple equation essentially states that elements placed in one category will never be found in the other; thus no overlap between the categories is possible. In the biblical/rabbinic variation of the model, no movement is permitted between the two categories.

8 We use the name Abraham here in order not to cause confusion. The biblical text actually uses the name Abram.

9 It is possible that in recent years east has regained some of its negative connotations. During the Holocaust, going east was analogous to being sent to the concentration camps. Equally, going west during the last hundred years was associated with going to the New World and therefore qualitatively positive.

10 It must be noted that this difference is based on emphasis rather than practice. Although both variation of Israelite culture may have been ideologically endogamous, one variant needed to emphasize this practice while the other did not.

11 It should be noted, however, that the rabbis maintained both the static and the dynamic understanding of God's presence. *Sifre Zuta*, for example, states: 'The land of Canaan [i.e., Israel] is fit to contain the House of the *Shekhinah* [i.e., the Temple] but TransJordan is not fit for the House of the *Shekhinah*' (*Sifre Zuta*, Naso, vol. 2, p. 228). For a complete discussion of this aspect of sacred place see Urbach (1979), pp. 37–46.

12 *Shekhinot* is the plural form of *Shekhinah*.

13 It is likely that the dynamic nature of the *Shekhinah* developed in relation to the needs of the diaspora community. A similar development occurred in the prophetic texts which described God as going into exile with his people during the Babylonian exile.

14 It must be emphasized that it is not suggested here that the synagogue only came into existence with the destruction of the Temple, rather that it was the destruction which led to a cultural transformation moving the emphasis from ideological centralized space to functional decentralized space.

15 A comprehensive discussion of the synagogue as sacred space is found in Heilman (1976) *Synagogue Life*. There are, however, several significant problems in his exposition. Many of the problems are due to a fundamental misunderstanding of the nature of holiness in respect to Jewish ritual objects. Thus, he attributes holiness to the candle used in the ceremonies opening and closing the Shabbat. He bases this under-

standing on the fact that the light of these candles may be used only for the light of the celebration and not for any other purpose. The candles, however, are sacred only by virtue of their being used for the performance of a commandment, not for any particular virtue of their own. Almost any object can gain such contextual holiness through being associated with the performance of a commandment. This problem is also seen in his discussion of profane objects, e.g., a light switch or the *tefillin*, neither of which may be used on Shabbat. He states that touching them on Shabbat is taboo (Heilman, 1976, p. 49). Like the candles, the objects themselves are neutral; they gain contextual 'tabooness' because one is forbidden to use them on Shabbat. It is not because they are profane in and of themselves, but rather because their use is considered to be work (which is forbidden on Shabbat). Many aspects of functional holiness are contextually rather than essentially holy. The only objects which are essentially holy are those which have the name of God written in them, e.g., prayer-books and Torah scrolls. One distinguishing feature of intrinsically holy objects is that they must be buried, not thrown away.

16   In modern Judaism the situation has again changed. With the emergence of the Jewish community from the ghetto, the external community no longer enforces endogamy. It is likely that as structure develops there will be a gradual emphasis on macro-structure and centralized institutions.

17   A *mezuzah* is a box containing verses from the Torah which is placed on the door-post of all Jewish buildings with the exception of synagogues. A synagogue does not require a *mezuzah* because it (the building) serves as its own *mezuzah*.

18   In a traditional Shabbat (Saturday) morning service seven men are called up to recite a blessing before reading a section of the Torah portion. The Torah is divided into weekly portions which are read in the synagogue during the Shabbat morning service.

19   The symbolic power of the direction west is occasionally reflected in rabbinic texts. One such text, admittedly based on an attempt to distinguish between the orientation of Jewish prayer and that of Christian prayer (also towards Jerusalem), suggests that prayer should be towards the west because 'the *Shekhinah* is in the west' (Urbach, 1979, p. 62). Interestingly, many early synagogues were built with a westward rather than an eastward orientation (Urbach, 1979, pp. 62–3).

20   For the most part, all Jews have accepted the importance of a homeland. This is in part tied to the Holocaust and the insecurity which it created, but it is also tied to the movement back towards macro-structure. Nationalism emphasizes unity in opposition to other nations.

21   Although most of this discussion refers to ritual patterns among the

British Liberal and the American Reform community, many of the conclusions and observations are applicable to the Progressive community as a whole.

22 By priestly function we mean the interrelationship of several factors: a distinction between the rabbi and congregation in terms of participation in ritual; a view of the rabbi as being in some way spiritually distinct from the congregation (ranging from being a spirituality professional to being a conduit of communication with the divine); and giving the rabbi a monopoly of access to sacred space. This priestly function is in structural opposition to the more traditional role of rabbi as teacher and judge of Jewish law. It should be noted that in almost no Progressive community have rabbis taken on all elements of the priestly function. Rather, these elements must be understood as extreme forms at the ends of polar axes.

Two conscious examples of this emphasis on the priestly function are the use of the word 'temple' for the synagogue, and the inclusion of the 'Priestly Benediction'. In the American Reform movement synagogues are called 'temples'. Although this de-emphasizes the centrality of the Temple in Jerusalem, it also introduces a conscious association of the synagogue with the Temple and thereby with a specific kind of priestly sacred space. At the conclusion of the service in most Progressive synagogues the rabbi recites the 'Priestly Benediction'. Very often the rabbi will raise his hand in imitation of the priests in the Temple. This makes a direct association of the role of the rabbi with that of the priests as being a conduit of blessing for the congregation.

23 This section was removed from the Reform/Liberal service for several reasons. First, these movements chose to remove repetitive elements which were felt to lengthen the service unnecessarily. Second, this section was perceived as objectionable because of its emphasis on sacrifice and the Temple in Jerusalem.

24 There is one area in which the Orthodox include a priestly element not found among Progressive communities. The Orthodox reserve the first two Torah blessings: one is reserved for a Cohen, a descendant of the priests, and the second for a Levi, a descendant of the Temple functionaries. In a sense, these two groups open the sacred (the Torah) to make it available for the rest of the community. This, however, is not relevant to the priestly function of the rabbi or the general access to sacred space because both the Cohen and the Levi are now part of the general community.

25 It is possible that this trend is also reflected in respect to women. We have already mentioned that women are excluded from the men's section in the Orthodox community because of their sexual attraction. In some Progressive synagogues, which limit the role of women (and,

granted, most give full equality), we find a very different reason given. People will say that women are not allowed to read from the Torah because they might make it impure if they are menstruating. (In Jewish law, however, it clearly states that a Torah can never be made impure.) Thus the reason given is symbolically associated with macro-structure which used purity as the primary category for access into sacred space.

26   There is an interesting concomitant transformation in modern Jewish thought. Earlier in the twentieth century the model used for Jewish cultural creativity was bi-polar, with the diaspora (or America) and Israel as the two poles. This reflected a transition from the earlier micro-model, which was more multifaceted. In more recent years there has been a progressive shift to viewing Israel as the primary centre for the development of Jewish cultural creativity, thus moving to a stronger version of the macro-model. This transformation is reflected in a paper published by World Union for Progressive Judaism in which the authors suggest that acceptance of the bi-polar model is 'a depreciation of Zionism as the vital preservative and creative force of Jewish life' (Hirsch, 1993, p. 14).

27   It is possible that the Persian period reflects an earlier realignment. In some biblical texts we find a multiplicity of sacred spaces. Other texts emphasize the pre-eminence and exclusiveness of Jerusalem as a sacred space. If a strong form of the preference for endogamy was primarily an innovation of Ezra and his followers after the return from exile, then it is likely that the weight given to macro-structure in the biblical text reflects that specific cultural transformation. The texts emphasizing micro-structure may reflect earlier cultural patterns.

References and further reading

Altmann, A., Lewy, H. and Heinemann, I. (eds) (1981) *Three Jewish Philosophers*. New York: Atheneum.

Cohen, A. and Mendes-Flohr, P. (eds) (1987) *Contemporary Jewish Religious Thought*. New York: Free Press.

Douglas, M. (1966) *Purity and Danger*. London: Ark Paperbacks.

Heilman, S. (1976) *Synagogue Life*. Chicago: University of Chicago Press.

Heschel, A. J. (1951) *The Sabbath*. New York: Farrar Straus Giroux.

Hirsch, R. (1993) *The Israel–Diaspora Connection*. Geneva: World Union for Progressive Judaism.

Turner, H. W. (1979) *From Temple to Meeting House: The Phenomenology and Theology of Places of Worship*. The Hague: Mouton Publishers.

Urbach, E. E. (1979) *The Sages*. Cambridge, MA: Harvard University Press.

2. Rites of passage

Alan Unterman

The ritual framework of Judaism is determined by *halakhah* (law) and *minhag* (custom) which make up traditional Jewish praxis.[1] Neither in *halakhah* nor in *minhag*, however, do we find any terms equivalent to 'a rite of passage'. In other words Torah, the general term for the 'teaching' of both Scripture and the traditions of Rabbinic Judaism, does not distinguish between rituals associated with birth, puberty, marriage and death and other rituals. It is thus artificial to isolate rites of passage rituals from the ritual corpus of Jewish life. The idea of a ritual transition from stage to stage, or from status to status, is referred to in kabbalistic (i.e., mystical) texts which take a 'sacramental' and 'instrumental' view of ritual. From the point of view of *halakhah*, however, the notion of a rite of passage is an external idea, useful though it may be in analysing a religious tradition.

Birth

According to Jewish teaching, while a child is in its mother's womb a candle burns beside it and an angel teaches it the whole of the Torah. Just before birth the angel touches the child on its lips, and it forgets all it has learnt. This is why a child is born with a cleft upper lip, caused by the fiery angelic finger. Learning God's Torah in this world beyond the womb is, thus, really a process of remembering. The birth of an individual is foreshadowed in the biblical creation story. Adam and Eve are not only the father and mother of all humans, but are also paradigms of every particular man and woman. *Adam* means 'man' in Hebrew. He was shaped by God from the dust of the earth, and the spirit of the Lord was breathed into him. He is thus a being of the lower world, on a par with the animal kingdom, but he is also made in the image of God and is a partner with God in the work of creation. At death his dust-nature will be returned to the earth from which he was formed while his spirit will return to God. His female companion, Eve, the mother of all life, was formed out of Adam's rib. Although woman was not actually made from the dust, yet she shared the dust-nature of man from whom she was shaped.

In some midrashic and kabbalistic interpretations of the biblical text, Eve is not the first wife of Adam. This is based on the disparity between chapter 1 of Genesis ('male and female created he them') and chapter 2, where God creates Eve specially as a companion for Adam. The first wife was Lilith, who was created together with Adam, but who was unable to stay married to him and fled to the Red Sea. When Adam complained to God, three angels, Sanvi, Sansanvi and Samangelaf, were sent to bring her back but she refused to go with them. They did, however, manage to extract a promise from her that she will not harm humans when she sees the names of these three angels.

Lilith is jealous of the married state of the descendants of Adam and Eve, and she is particularly jealous of their children. She sleeps with men at night, conceiving demons through their nocturnal emissions, and she attacks women in childbirth and kills new-born babies. Jewish folk traditions prescribe a number of methods for protecting mothers and children against Lilith and her demons. During pregnancy and immediately after birth, holy objects, such as a *sefer torah* (a Torah scroll), or *tefillin* (phylacteries) may be brought into the confinement chamber. An amulet with the names of the angels on it might be hung around the neck of the mother, or placed on the wall. Sometimes a magic circle is drawn round the bed of a woman in labour and the names of the three angels written inside this circle, thus making it out of bounds to Lilith.

In pre-modern times these techniques were taken as seriously as ante-natal and post-natal care are taken today, and in more traditional families there is still considerable reliance on prophylactic measures. Most of these practices, however, are regarded as superstitions by modern Jews. What has remained for them is the recitation of prayers in the synagogue for the welfare of the mother. These prayers exist in two basic rites (and many minor variations). The Sephardi rite is that of Jews of Iberian origin, most of whom lived in Muslim countries after their expulsion from Spain in 1492, and today it is subscribed to by about half of the Jews in Israel. The Ashkenazi rite is that of Jews of

German origin who eventually settled all over central and eastern Europe until modern times; today Ashkenazim make up the bulk of Jews in Western countries (see Chapter 4, pp. 115–16).

The Ashkenazi version of this *mi sheberah* ('May he who blessed') prayer is said in Hebrew, and in it the Jewish name of the mother and of her mother are used:

> May he who blessed our ancestors, Abraham, Isaac and Jacob, Moses and Aaron, David and Solomon, may he bless and heal So-and-So, the daughter of So-and-So, because her husband commits himself to a donation of such and such to charity on her behalf. In the merit of this deed may the Holy One, blessed be he, be filled with mercy for her to cure and heal, to strengthen and revive her. And may he send her speedily a perfect healing from heaven in all her limbs and nerves, in the midst of the other sick ones of Israel. Now, speedily and soon; and let us say Amen.

NAMING THE FEMALE CHILD

The births of a female and of a male child are celebrated differently. A girl undergoes a ceremony of name-giving which takes place in the synagogue usually on the next Shabbat ('Sabbath day', i.e., Saturday) after her birth. The father is called up for an *aliyah* ('going up') to make a blessing over the reading of the Torah. After the *aliyah* in Ashkenazi communities the following *mi sheberah* prayer is said for the mother and daughter and the name of the infant is announced (this time it is the father's name that is used in 'the daughter of' clauses):

> May he who blessed our ancestors, Abraham, Isaac and Jacob, Sarah, Rebecca and Leah, may he bless the woman who has given birth to So-and-So, the daughter of So-and-So, and her infant daughter who was born to her with *mazel tov* 'good luck'). Her name shall be called in Israel So-and-So the daughter of So-and-So. Because her husband, and her father, commits himself to a donation of such and such to charity on her behalf, in reward for this deed may her parents merit to raise her to Torah, to the wedding canopy and to good deeds.

The Jewish name given in this ceremony is the one by which the girl will be known for all religious purposes: it will appear on her wedding certificate, it will be used when *mi sheberah* prayers are recited for her recovery from illness or when she gives birth, and it will appear on her tombstone. It is announced ritually so that it has a public role in the community.

Among diaspora Jews today the Jewish name for both boys and girls is often completely different from the secular name. Sometimes there is a similarity of sound or meaning between the two names; thus a girl might be given the Jewish name Faige from the Yiddish *feigel* meaning 'a bird') and the similar sounding, but totally different, secular name Phoebe (from a Greek word meaning 'to shine'). Sometimes the secular name is a translation of the Jewish name into the vernacular. Thus Shoshanah might be known as Rose, although a better translation of this Hebrew word would be 'lily'.

CIRCUMCISION (*BERIT MILAH*, LITERALLY 'COVENANT OF CIRCUMCISION')

A newly born boy should undergo circumcision on the eighth day after birth, even if that day is Shabbat or a festival. The operation cannot take place before the eighth day but it may be delayed if there are medical grounds. Jaundice is one of the most common reasons for delayed circumcision, because the *mohel* ('circumciser') will not operate unless the colour of the baby's skin is normal. If the ceremony is delayed, however, as soon as the child is fit the operation should take place on the next available weekday.

When two sibling children, or two first cousins, have died after circumcision, a third child would not be circumcised until he had grown up and become strong. Obviously haemophilia or some other medical condition might make circumcision impossible, in which case the child is considered as if already circumcised. If the child is born without a foreskin, then a drop of blood ('the blood of the Covenant') must be removed from the penis as an act of symbolic circumcision. The same is the case with adult male converts to Judaism who need to undergo circumcision as part of the process of conversion. Some of them may have been circumcised by a doctor as youngsters and thus need to undergo symbolic circumcision when they become 'children of the Covenant'.

On the first Friday night after the birth of a boy, and in some communities on the night before the circumcision, family and friends gather at the parents' house to eat chickpeas and drink beer. This

59

ceremony is known as a *shalom zachar* (literally 'peace of the male'). This party has been understood as a mourning meal for the Torah the child had learnt in the womb and now forgotten. Chickpeas and other round foods are typical of a mourners' meal, and this gathering at the parents' home is like the custom of gathering at the house of mourners to comfort them.

The night before the circumcision is a time for guarding the child against the predatory evil spirits which seek to harm him. It is known as a 'night of guarding' or *vach-nacht* ('watch night') in Yiddish. There are a number of customs, the purpose of which is to protect the child from demons and from danger on the morrow. Thus, for instance, people stay awake all night studying Torah in the house of circumcision, preferably in the presence of a *minyan* ('number', i.e. a quorum of ten men). The Polish custom, still practised among some Ashkenazi Jews, is to bring a class of youngsters from the *heder* ('room', i.e, religion school) to the house to recite prayers. The sound of innocent little children at prayer was powerful enough to undermine even the most persistent demons. The circumcision knife might be placed under the pillow in the mother's bed and the father may recite sections from the kabbalistic classic, the *Zohar*, which are thought to have prophylactic power. In Israel, hospitals usually have a special room for circumcisions, but in the diaspora the ceremony most often takes place in the home. It is customary to light candles in the room where the operation will take place and to gather together a *minyan* of ten adult males. It is not customary, however, to invite people to the circumcision ceremony because it is a religious ceremony. Once invited, people would have to attend since they would not be able to refuse participation in a *mitzvah* ('commandment', i.e. religious obligation). Instead, the parents merely inform people that the circumcision will take place at a certain time on a particular date. This is considered information and not an invitation.

Someone is chosen by the parents to hold the baby on his lap during the operation. He is known as a *sandak* (or more commonly *sandek*), a word of Greek origin meaning a patron or co-father. A grandfather, the rabbi of the community, or the father himself usually fills the role of *sandek*, but it can go to any adult male. It is not customary among Ashkenazim for a woman to hold the baby during circumcision, but this does happen in some Sephardi communities. The child is brought from its mother to the circumcision room by a married female, specially chosen for this role. She hands the baby to her husband at the door of the room. The man and the woman are known among Yiddish-speakers as *kavater* and *kavaterin* respectively. These terms are from the Germanic root *gevatter*, meaning 'godfather'. The *sandek*, too, is thought of as a godfather who, together with the *kevaters*, will be responsible for helping the child in later life. Acting as *kevaters* is supposed to have *segulah* ('magical potency') for a barren couple, helping them to have children of their own.

When the *kevater* brings the child in, the assembled family and friends greet it with the words *barukh haba* ('Blessed be he that comes'). The child's father declares that he has appointed the *mohel* to circumcise his child, though in ancient times it was the father who performed the operation himself. The *mohel*, or the father, takes the child from the *kevater* and places him briefly on an empty chair, set up beside the chair where the *sandek* is sitting. This empty chair is for the prophet Elijah, known as 'the angel of the Covenant' (Mal 3:1), who attends every circumcision because he complained to God that the people of Israel were neglecting the Covenant. He is thus forced to return to earth to witness every occasion when Jews re-affirm the Covenant, and to act as a heavenly guardian to the child. Some scholars understand the greeting *barukh haba* to be words of welcome to Elijah who enters the room with the child. By being placed on Elijah's chair, the baby is thus placed on Elijah's lap immediately prior to the operation. In some communities an elaborately carved chair of Elijah is brought to the place of the circumcision for the invisible angelic guest to sit on. All those assembled remain standing during the ritual, except for the *sandek* (and Elijah, of course).

As the child is placed on the empty chair the *mohel* declares: 'This is the throne of Elijah the prophet, may he be remembered for good.' He then recites several verses from the Bible, mostly from the Book of Psalms, and addresses Elijah thus: 'Elijah, angel of the Covenant, behold your place is before you, remain on my right side and support me.' While the *sandek* holds the child on his knees, keeping its legs open, the *mohel* cleans the penis with disinfectant, makes a blessing and cuts off the foreskin. He then tears back the membrane covering the penis and sucks out blood from the wound, either with his mouth (the practice of pre-modern times) or with a glass pipette (a modern innovation to avoid the transference of germs). The actual operation takes only a few seconds, so the father immediately makes his blessing: 'Blessed are You O Lord our God, King of the Universe, who has sanctified us with his commandments and commanded us to bring him

61

into the Covenant of our father Abraham.' Everyone in the room responds with the words: 'Just as he has entered the Covenant so may he enter into Torah, the wedding canopy and good deeds.'

The foreskin that has been cut off is placed in a container of earth or sand. A bandage is then placed on the penis, the baby is dressed, and he is handed to someone appointed by the family to hold him for the name-giving ceremony.

NAMING OF A MALE CHILD

During the naming ceremony a cup of wine is held by the *mohel* or the rabbi as he recites two blessings followed by the naming formula. During the recital of the latter some drops of wine are placed into the mouth of the baby. The naming formula is as follows:

> Our God and God of our fathers preserve this child to his father and to his mother, and let his name be called in Israel So-and-So, the son of So-and-So (his father's name). May the father (or, if deceased, 'the father in Paradise') rejoice in the one who has gone out from his loins and may the mother (or 'the mother in Paradise') be glad in the fruit of her womb. [various biblical verses follow, including] It is written: 'And I said unto you: In your blood you shall live.' [At this point wine is placed in the baby's mouth]. May this little child So-and-So, the son of So-and-So, become great. Just as he has entered the Covenant so may he enter into the study of Torah, into the wedding canopy and into good deeds. Amen.

The *mohel* recites prayers for the spiritual welfare of the baby, which depict the circumcision as a sacrificial offering before the throne of glory. He asks for the angels on high to give the child a holy and pure soul with which to comprehend and keep God's teachings. He then prays for the baby's full recovery from the operation using the standard *mi sheberah* formula. A meal or light repast follows the ceremony. If a child dies before being circumcised, his foreskin is removed just before burial and he is given a Hebrew name. If a baby girl dies before being given a name, she too is named prior to burial. The naming is to ensure that God will have mercy on the child, and at the messianic resurrection of the dead the child will have a Jewish identity.

The custom today among Ashkenazim is for the mother to have the right to choose the name for her first child, usually calling him or her after a deceased close relative, particularly a parent. Until modern times the custom used to be for the father to have the right to name the first-born and the mother to have the right to call the second child after one of her relatives. Even today, if the father dies before the circumcision of his child, a male child is given his father's name. Since it is customary to name children after relatives, the same first names tend to recur in families. Ashkenazi Jews do not call a child by the same name as a close living relative. This is based on the folk belief that if the angel of death comes looking for the older relative it might kill the younger relative with a similar name by mistake. Sephardi Jews do not subscribe to this folk prohibition and do indeed call their children by the same name as living parents, grandparents, uncles, aunts etc. There is ample evidence from Jewish literature that the Sephardi custom better represents ancient practice. In talmudic times children were called after living relatives and sons were called by the same name as their father while he was still alive.

It is believed that the Jewish name parents choose for their child is actually put into their mouths by God Himself. This name is already the heavenly name of the child, engraved on the Throne of Glory, and it is a holy name representing the inner personality of its bearer. This explains why, in Jewish literature, there are many attempts to associate the names of biblical characters with their personalities and biographies. At the end of the *Amidah*, the central prayer of the liturgy, some people have the custom of reciting a verse from the Bible which begins with the first letter of their name and ends with the last letter. Through this association of their name with God's teaching, they prevent the forces of evil from taking the name into exile, and their name (symbolizing the divine element in each Jew) therefore remains holy. It further ensures that the Torah will save them from *gehinnom* ('purgatory') after death and their name will be remembered at the resurrection of the dead. It is even recommended by one authority that the verse should be recited by the name-bearer before any important undertaking.

It is the sanctity of the name which also lies behind the custom of giving boys their name only after their foreskin has been removed, and they have thus entered the Covenant. It is even customary for the parents, before the circumcision, to refuse to tell people the name they have chosen for their son. This prevents anyone casting an evil eye on the child, which is still in a vulnerable spiritual condition until the

circumcision. A leading seventeenth-century kabbalist, Abraham Azu-
lai, explained the mystical significance of the naming ceremony as
follows:

> A man is not called by the name of man except through the commandment
> of circumcision. Without it he is called a demon and not a man. As long as
> the demonic forces have a hold on a man, through the foreskin and the
> uncleanliness of man, it is impossible for the higher soul (which distin-
> guishes him as a Jew) to alight upon him and it is impossible for him to be
> called by the name of an Israelite. Thus it is customary not to give him a
> name until after the circumcision, when the foreskin and uncleanliness
> have already gone. Then the secret of the higher soul rests on him and he
> may be called an Israelite man through the commandment of circumcision.
> (*Chesed Le-Avraham* 2:52)

This kabbalistic view, that circumcision is a rite of passage which
inaugurates an individual into the community of Israel, is not, in fact,
in accord with the *halakhah*, which takes a less mystical view of the
matter. According to the *halakhah*, a child born to a Jewish mother is
already an Israelite by the biological fact of birth. Of course he needs
circumcision, but if his parents do not circumcise him he is still a Jew.
Indeed, there is a reference in one medieval text (*Sefer Chasidim*) to a
custom of calling a child by his Hebrew name as soon as he is placed in
his cradle, i.e. before his circumcision, and placing a copy of the Book
of Leviticus under his head to indicate his spiritual identity as a Jew.

The name of a sick person may be changed so that the heavenly
decree against the person with the previous name will not apply to the
new name. The additional name is usually one which means 'life' or
'healing'. If the sick person recovers, from then on the person and his
children, who are known as son or daughter of So-and-So, would use
the new name first, followed by the old name. If, however, the change
of name did not improve the person's health, then after the death, his
or her children would use the old name first, followed by the new
name. The reason why a new name is added to the old name, rather
than changing the name entirely, is because a number of mystics
insisted that the name given to a person at birth is the name which is
used in heaven and thus represents the very essence of a person. To
change it entirely might harm the person's life-force, except in the case
of a great saint whose life is itself focused on God, or if the name is
changed by a God-fearing sage who is able to call down a completely
new soul on the person. Sin can cause people's names to diminish so

that when they die and the angel of death asks them their name they are unable to answer because some letters of their name have simply slipped away.[2]

Bar mitzvah and bat mitzvah

In Jewish law adulthood is achieved by boys and girls when puberty begins; the sign of this is the growth of two pubic hairs. The examination of individuals to ascertain whether they have pubic hairs or not is obviously problematic, not least because pubic hairs may have grown and fallen out. The ages of 12 years for girls and 13 years for boys were therefore fixed upon as the average ages of puberty and adulthood. At these ages girls and boys become *bat mitzvah* and *bar mitzvah* respectively, and boys may now be counted as one of the ten men to make up a *minyan* for prayer.[3]

These ages have remained the accepted approximation for adulthood, but where the *halakhah* insists that only a true adult is needed they are not sufficient. Thus a *bar mitzvah* boy would not be allowed to read from the Torah on some special occasions, or be responsible for baking the unleavened bread for Pesach, unless he had pubic hair, or his beard hair had grown. Since the Middle Ages it has been customary for the community to celebrate the coming of age of a male child in a *bar mitzvah* ceremony. The term *bar mitzvah* ('son of the commandment'), and its female equivalent *bat mitzvah* ('daughter of the commandment'), indicate that the young adult is now subject to the commandments. According to the *Zohar*, the main mystical text of Judaism, from the age of 13 the boy inherits a new soul from God, and two angels begin to accompany him. They will be his constant companions for the rest of his life, signifying his good and evil inclinations.

The form which a *bar mitzvah* ceremony takes is for the boy to be called up for an *aliyah* to recite a blessing over a section of the *sidra*, or weekly Torah reading. The main Torah reading takes place on Shabbat morning, with smaller readings on Shabbat afternoons, and Mondays and Thursdays. In pre-modern times it was quite usual for the *bar mitzvah* boy to be called up on a Monday or Thursday, as it was impossible for everyone to have an *aliyah* on a Saturday morning. The practice today is to have the main *bar mitzvah* ceremony on Shabbat. The minimum that is expected of a *bar mitzvah* boy is the singing of the blessings before and after the Torah portion: 'Bless the blessed Lord.' The congregation respond: 'Blessed be the Lord who is blessed for ever and ever.' The boy continues: 'Blessed are you, Lord our God, King of the Universe, who has chosen us from all the peoples and give us his Torah. Blessed are you, Lord, who gives the Torah.' After the portion the boy continues: 'Blessed are you, Lord our God, King of the Universe, who has given us a Torah of truth, and planted eternal life in our midst. Blessed are you, Lord, who gives the Torah.' The section from the Torah may be read for the boy by the regular Torah reader. The *bar mitzvah*, however, can also read a section of the Torah, or the concluding section (*maftir*) of the Torah and the *haftarah* portion from the prophets which follows it. In the maximal case he may even read the whole *sidra* plus the *haftarah*. It can take around a year of special tuition for the boy to learn how to read the text and sing it to the liturgical tune.

The day of a boy's *bar mitzvah* is a testing time for him, when he will stand in front of the whole congregation. Apart from the Torah reading, the boy will usually also be expected to make a speech at the *bar mitzvah* party. In many Orthodox families it is taken for granted that the boy will do all the Torah reading. The real ordeal for him is to learn a subtle discourse on some obscure subject, written for him by his rabbi, which shows his attainments in the study of the Talmud.

What is common to all forms of *bar mitzvah* is the element of trial by ordeal, proving the worthiness of the boy to be an adult and to become a full member of the community. To the boy it conveys a sense of achievement and indeed matures him. The pain of preparation and of performance, however, is ameliorated by the presents which family and guests bring him. As the Jewish home has become more sec-ularized in modern times, so the ritual of *bar mitzvah* has become more important. In the past the *bar mitzvah* was the beginning of the serious ritual involvement of the child in Jewish life. Today it is often the last element of serious ritual involvement before the estrangement from religion which will characterize the boy's teenage years.

For the parents and the wider family the *bar mitzvah* represents a milestone, since the boy's last religious celebration was his circumci-sion. The family will host relatives and friends to a party to commemorate the boy's coming of age, and the *Zohar* actually com-pares such a party to a wedding feast. Indeed, it is a very emotional time, with grandparents often still alive who may not survive to see the wedding ceremony. The mother sees her son move from spiritual dependency to independence, and the father customarily makes a benediction after his son has been called up: 'Blessed be he who has freed me from responsibility for this child.' The rabbi's sermon on the Shabbat morning of a *bar mitzvah* will usually contain a special message for the boy and perhaps also some mention of the contribution of his parents and grandparents to the life of the community. At the end of the sermon in many communities the rabbi blesses the boy with the words of the biblical priestly blessing: 'May the Lord bless you and keep you. May he shine his face on you and be gracious to you. May he lift his countenance to you and grant you peace. Amen.'

Just prior to his thirteenth Hebrew birthday the boy will begin to put on *tefillin* (phylacteries) every weekday morning for prayers. These consist of two blackened leather boxes, bound to the left arm and head with black leather straps. Inside the boxes are biblical paragraphs handwritten on parchment. In many Ashkenazi communities the boy begins to put on *tefillin* up to a month before his birthday. In Sephardi communities, however, he does not put them on until his actual thirteenth birthday, and this day is celebrated by the family and guests. Those in synagogue are invited to a party after morning prayers.

A boy's thirteenth Hebrew birthday does not fall on the date of his thirteenth secular birthday because the Jewish ritual year is a lunar year of twelve months, considerably shorter than the solar year. Seven times every nineteen years an extra month is intercalated into the Jewish year to bring the two back together. This extra month, known as the Second Adar, leads to an anomaly concerning *bar mitzvah* boys. Suppose two boys are born in a leap year, the older one say on 25 First Adar and the younger one on 3 Second Adar. If their thirteenth year is not a leap year then the younger boy will be *bar mitzvah* first (on 3 Adar) and the older boy will be *bar mitzvah* three weeks later (on 25 Adar). One reason which is proffered in explanation is that spiritual maturity always follows the Hebrew calendar.

BAT MITZVAH

Although the coming of age of a girl, at 12 years, is as well established in *halakhah* as the boy's *bar mitzvah*, it receives far less attention in traditional communities. The main reason for this is that a woman's religious role is less public than that of a man. She does not lead the

67

prayers, is not counted as a member of a *minyan* quorum, is not called up for an *aliyah* to recite blessings over the Torah, and does not have to put on *tefillin*. Her coming of age, which sees the onset of menstruation and the ability to bear children, is therefore a more private matter. Among Reform Jews a much greater public role is assigned to a woman and there is no religious activity from which she is excluded, including acting as rabbi or cantor. In the nineteenth century a Confirmation ceremony was introduced by German Reform congregations for boys and girls around the age of 16, when they could understand more about their religion. This was meant to replace the *bar mitzvah* for boys and to provide an equivalent ceremony for girls. Confirmation is still practised in some USA Reform communities, but as it was borrowed from the Christian church, it never caught on sufficiently to displace the *bar mitzvah*. A *bat mitzvah* ceremony was therefore introduced for girls to parallel the *bar mitzvah* ceremony for boys. This was eventually adopted even by modern Orthodox synagogues.

The main difference between Orthodox and non-Orthodox *bat mitzvah* ceremonies lies in how closely the activities of the *bat mitzvah* girl imitate those of the boy in the *bar mitzvah*. In Reform and Conservative ceremonies girls prepare a Torah reading or *haftarah* reading, and are called up just like a boy. In Orthodox ceremonies the girl is never called up in a normal congregational service. Some Orthodox feminist groups, however, have started experimental *bat mitzvah* ceremonies attended only by women, where the *bat mitzvah* girl reads a portion from the Torah. It is more usual for a group of girls to be *bat mitzvah* together in an Orthodox synagogue on a Sunday, some time after their twelfth Hebrew birthday. They will prepare readings on a theme in Hebrew and English which they will present, accompanied by special prayers and a sermon. The parents host a reception or party afterwards to celebrate the coming of age of their daughters and their responsibility to keep the *mitzvot*. The earliest Orthodox support for *bat mitzvah* ceremonies was found among German rabbis who sought to combat the attractiveness of Reform. Even modified forms of the ceremony, however, have been condemned by ultra-Orthodox rabbis, who see in it a concession to Reform, or an imitation of Christian practices. They claim that such celebration involves too much of a change in the traditional status of women and that it has no precedent in the past. They even regard the festive meal, to which family and friends are invited, as without religious significance. Several halakhic authorities have prohibited the use of synagogues for *bat mitzvah* ceremonies on the grounds that holy places should not be used for purely secular purposes. In Israel, Orthodox *bat mitzvah* ceremonies do not take place in synagogues. Instead, the father of the girl is usually called up for an *aliyah* on the Shabbat after her twelfth birthday. She may then have a party at her home for her girlfriends.

Marriage

Adam was created alone, without a companion, unlike all the other animals which were created in pairs. God realized that being alone was not good for Adam; so he brought all the animals to him to see if he could find a partner, but they were unsuitable as companions. Adam managed to give each one a name, i.e. he comprehended its nature, but he found neither sexual fulfilment nor real relationship with them. So God put Adam into a deep sleep and took out one of his ribs which he then shaped into another human being, Eve, who became Adam's companion. According to a view found in rabbinic and mystical literature, it was not a rib that was removed from the first man: God actually split Adam down the middle. Till then he had been an hermaphrodite, half-male and half-female, with the two halves joined back to back. That is why, at the beginning of Genesis, it states 'And God created Adam in his own image, in the image of God created he him, male and female created he them' (Gen 1:27). In the operation God thus separated the man and woman and presented Adam with the other half of himself, to whom he could now relate. On seeing Eve he said 'Bone of my bone and flesh of my flesh' (Gen 2:23). The Torah concludes this story with the words: 'Therefore a man shall leave his father and his mother and cleave to his wife, and they shall become as one flesh.'

This context helps to explain the oft-reiterated idea that unmarried people are not really complete; until they have found, and married, a member of the opposite sex they have not found the other half of themselves. Thus it is said that the reason there is a reference to the creation of man in the seven wedding benedictions is precisely to teach this lesson that the birth of a person is always an incomplete thing. Until a man and a woman stand under the wedding canopy they are not properly born. Indeed, the canopy (*huppah*) in a sense symbolizes

69

the womb, for when the couples step out of it they are said to be born anew and all their sins are forgiven them. The day before their wedding is thus a fast day for bride and groom, modelled on the fast of the Day of Atonement, which is meant to call up God's forgiveness of sins.

The Jewish ideal is for a young man and a young woman to marry early, to 'build a faithful house in Israel' and to have as many children as God blesses them with. In traditional communities the sexes do not mix freely before marriage; so there is little opportunity of a girl and boy meeting and falling in love. It is a duty of parents to enable their children to marry; in the case of orphans or of paupers, the community has to take responsibility for this. Most traditional marriages are arranged by either a relative, a family friend or a professional marriage broker (*shadchan*); an arranged marriage is known as a *shidduh*. Once children are in their late teens their parents will expect them to meet members of the opposite sex on a *shidduh* with a view to finding a marriage partner. As the potential partner has been pre-selected by the amateur or professional matchmaker, there is no need for long court-ships before the couple make up their mind. After the initial introduction, three or four meetings are usually sufficient for them to decide in principle whether they wish to marry or whether they are not suitable for each other. There is no secular engagement party among traditionalists. Instead, they may have a *tenaim* ('conditions') cere-mony, which takes place in a private home. There, a document of commitment to proceed is signed on behalf of both families. Since this document is considered by many communities as absolutely binding, and not to be broken, they prefer not to put the engagement in writing. They still have a ceremony in a private house but it is accompanied with only a verbal agreement to marry, known in Yiddish as a *vort*.

THE WEDDING CEREMONY

A day or two before the wedding ceremony, the bride goes to the *mikveh* (ritual bath) for the first time.[4] She will usually be accom-panied by women relatives, and among Sephardi communities her visit is turned into a celebration for the community womenfolk. The *mikveh* is a pool of 'living water' made up from rain-water, or other natural water source, and kept in a tank. Ordinary tap water fills a large adjacent bath which is in contact with the contents of the *mikveh*. This contact transforms the tap-water into 'living water'. Women totally immerse themselves in the transformed tap-water a week after their menstrual period has ceased, before resuming sexual relations with their husbands, or, as in the case of the bride, before their first sexual encounter.

In strictly Orthodox families the wedding date will be arranged so as to fall shortly after the end of the seven clean days following the bride's menstrual period. During these days a woman has to examine herself with a cloth placed in the vagina to see if there are any bloodstains, indicating that the menstrual period has not quite finished. If it is feared that the bride will still be ritually unclean at the time of the wedding ceremony she may take a pill that delays the onset of her period. Among Ashkenazim there is a custom for a bride and groom not to see each other the week before the wedding, but the Sephardim impose no such restriction on the couple.

On the Shabbat before the wedding the groom is called up for an *aliyah*, known in Yiddish as an *aufruff*, in his home synagogue. He is greeted with traditional songs, and, among Oriental Jews, women shriek with joy and throw sweets at him. After the service the groom's family usually host a *kiddush* in honour of the forthcoming wedding.

On the wedding day the bride and groom will not be left alone, because demons are likely to harm them if they are on their own. It is customary for them to fast from dawn till after the wedding ceremony and to recite the confession of sins in their prayers. This day is a kind of private Day of Atonement for them. When they leave the *huppah* ('wedding canopy') all their sins are forgiven them and they are like newborn children. The wedding canopy consist of an embroidered piece of cloth supported by four posts, symbolizing the house of the groom. It can also be a simple prayer shawl (*tallit*) held up by four men.

It is customary for the wedding to take place in the bride's community, often inside the synagogue, as practised by modern Orthodox Ashkenazim, by most Sephardim, and by Conservative and Reform Jews. More traditional Ashkenazim prefer to set up the *huppah* under the open sky, as the stars are a symbol of fertility. A number of rabbis have objected to synagogue weddings, particularly with organ accompaniment, as imitation of Christian customs.

The wedding document (*ketubah*) is in Aramaic, a sister-language to Hebrew and the lingua franca of the Middle East during the early

71

centuries of the Common Era. The rabbi writes the Jewish date, the Hebrew names and patronymic of bride and groom, and the location of the marriage, all in Hebrew characters, on the printed *ketubah* text. The *ketubah* is duly signed by two witnesses who must be adult male Jews who are not close kin of either bride or groom. The *ketubah* guarantees the wife financial support should the husband divorce her, or predecease her. It also establishes the *bona fides* of the marriage, and if the marriage takes place under Orthodox auspices the *ketubah* will serve as sufficient proof of the Jewish status of both parties for Orthodoxy.

Among Ashkenazim the groom goes to the bride's room to cover the face of the bride with a veil, a ceremony known in Yiddish as *bedeken*. The biblical patriarch Jacob married the wrong girl because his father-in-law tricked him and he did not view the face of his bride beforehand (Gen 29:21–25). Even today, in certain Orthodox communities, the bride wears a thick veil under the *huppah* which completely masks her face.

The groom returns to the *huppah* accompanied by his best man, whose duty it is to guard him, and by members of his family. He stands facing towards Jerusalem, the holiest place for Jews. If the wedding is in the synagogue, then he will have his back to the congregation. The bride walks to the canopy either on her father's arm, between her parents or between the two mothers. The mothers may hold plaited candles alight in their hands as they accompany her. Either she goes directly to stand at the groom's right side or she circumambulates him three or seven times, depending on the custom, before taking up her place beside him. As she does so, the cantor sings the *mi adir* prayer:

> He who is mighty [*mi adir*] above all things, he who is blessed above all things, he who is great above all things, may he bless the groom and the bride.

The rabbi in charge of the ceremony then addresses the couple. He usually exhorts them to keep the traditions of Jewish married life (e.g. the kosher food laws, hospitality, the use of *mikveh*, or the rituals of Shabbat and festivals) and to follow the example of their parents and grandparents. After the sermon he takes a silver cup full to the brim with sweet red wine and recites two blessings over it. The first is the blessing over wine and the second is the betrothal blessing:

> Blessed are you, Lord our God King of the Universe, who has sanctified us

with his commandments and commanded us concerning forbidden sexual relationships. Who has prohibited to us those who are merely betrothed and has permitted to us those who have been married to us, through the ritual of *huppah* and sanctification. Blessed are you, Lord, who sanctifies his people Israel through *huppah* and sanctification.

The rabbi passes the goblet of wine to the parents, who stand beside the groom and bride under the *huppah*, to give their children some wine to drink. The groom then takes the wedding ring. This must be a plain band of precious metal, for if it contained any jewels the bride might be misled as to its real value. The rabbi asks the groom if it indeed belongs to him, and then he shows it to the two witnesses who satisfy themselves that it is of the requisite minimum value.

Holding the ring above the bride's right forefinger, the groom makes a Hebrew declaration, usually repeating the words after the rabbi and cantor:

Behold you are sanctified to me [*li*] with this ring according to the law of Moses and Israel.

He then places the ring on her finger and if she accepts it then she accepts him as her spouse.[5] The reason why the rabbi and cantor both prompt the groom, with the cantor saying the word *li*, is so that the congregation should not think that the rabbi himself was betrothing the bride.

The *ketubah* is then read aloud in Aramaic, and sometimes a précis of it is also read in the vernacular, to serve as a break between the two parts of the wedding ceremony: the *erusin* or betrothal, and the *nissuin*, or marriage proper. In ancient times the two parts were completely separate, with as much as a year elapsing between the giving of the ring and the recital of the seven benedictions under the *huppah*. Once the two parts were united into one ceremony it became customary to make a break between them with the *ketubah* reading, to show that they are indeed different rituals.

The *ketubah* is the property of the bride and it is handed to her after it is read. The cantor then takes the second cup of wine and sings the seven *nissuin* blessings over it. These blessings deal with the creation of man in God's image and the creation of woman from him, how Zion rejoices in her children, and God gives joy to the bride and groom. It ends with the longest of the seven blessings:

73

Blessed are you, Lord our God King of the Universe, who has created happiness and joy, groom and bride, rejoicing and song, gladness and merriment, love and brotherhood, peace and companionship. Speedily, O Lord our God, may there be heard in the cities of Judah and in the public places of Jerusalem the sound of happiness and joy, the voice of the groom and the voice of the bride, the jubilant sound of grooms from their canopies and youths from their feasts of song. Blessed are you, Lord, who rejoices the groom with the bride.

One parent from each side gives the groom and bride wine to drink from the wedding cup. A glass wrapped in cloth or paper is then placed before the groom, who smashes it by stamping on it with his right foot. This element of destruction in the midst of joy is to remember the destruction of Jerusalem, in line with the words of Psalm 137: 'If I forget thee, O Jerusalem . . . if I put not Jerusalem above my chief joy.' Reference to this psalm is also given as the reason behind the custom of smearing ash on the groom's forehead immediately prior to the wedding, ash being a sign of mourning for Jerusalem.

Jewish folklore has interpreted the breaking of the glass by the groom in a number of different ways. It is thought of as symbolic of the breaking of the hymen of a virgin bride. According to the kabbalists, it is an offering to the powers of evil, either to placate them so that they do no harm, or to prevent the evil eye emanating from one of the guests from harming the couple. It is said that if the groom is unable to break the glass at the first attempt, this means the bride will be the dominant character in the home.

At the end of the ceremony the rabbi blesses the couple with the words of the biblical priestly blessing. Among Ashkenazim the wedding ceremony ends with the couple being taken to an empty room, to spend some time alone together and to break their fast. This is know as *yihud*, and is witnessed by two witnesses. The bride and groom have to spend a few minutes together, sufficient time in theory actually to consummate the marriage. Since an unrelated boy and girl cannot be left alone without a chaperone, this *yihud* is a recognition by the community that they are now married. Most Sephardi communities do not have a specific act of *yihud* immediately after the wedding ceremony.

It is customary to have a party after the wedding ceremony, at the end of which the seven marriage blessings are recited immediately after the grace after meals. For the next week a smaller party is held every evening, hosted by family or friends, to entertain the couple with food, music and song. At these the seven blessings are recited if a *minyan* is present and there is a 'new face' who was not at the wedding or at any of the previous parties for this couple. The only day on which a 'new face' is not needed to recite the seven blessings is Shabbat, since the Sabbath day itself is considered a 'new face' guest.

Divorce

Jewish marriage is a religious bond which can only be dissolved by either the death of one partner or a religious divorce. In the latter case the husband has a document (*get*) written for him and his wife in a religious law court (*bet din*) by a scribe. The *get* is witnessed by two witnesses. He must then deliver the *get* to his wife of his own free will, either directly or via a third party, again in the presence of two witnesses. Among Ashkenazim the woman must accept the *get* of her own free will, and thus if either party refuses to participate in the divorce it has no validity.

Originally Jews practised polygamy, but this was prohibited to Ashkenazim in the Middle Ages. In theory, at least, polygamy is still possible for non-Ashkenazi Jews, although it is prohibited in the modern state of Israel. Since it was the rabbis who prohibited polygamy, if an Ashkenazi husband can gain the agreement of 100 rabbis then he can marry a second time, even if his first wife refuses to accept a *get*. A wife remains a 'chained woman' (*agunah*) if she cannot obtain a divorce. The most difficult case of an *agunah* is where the husband has disappeared and it is not known whether he is alive or dead.

Although the husband must divorce his wife freely, a *bet din* may put pressure on him to do so if they find that by law he ought to divorce her, e.g. if he has mistreated her, or he is impotent. In ancient times he was even beaten until he said 'I am willing [to give a *get*]'. The great medieval halakhist Maimonides explained this contradiction as follows. Every believing Jew really wishes to follow the dictates of God's law, and it is only the evil inclination in the husband that prevents him agreeing to give the *get*. The beating thus does not affect his free will: he simply overcomes his evil inclination. So when he declares 'I am willing', that is a genuine reflection of his inner will. In Israel there are a number of husbands who have spent years in prison but still refuse to divorce their wives and win their release.

75

Conversion

The most fundamental rite of passage takes place when a Gentile changes his or her religious status and converts to Judaism. Converts are literally considered as if they were newly born, having no biological family members. Their new father and mother are the biblical figures Abraham and Sarah, who first began to convert people to monotheism some 4,000 years ago. Kabbalists view converts as people who have been given a new soul, or who have been born with a Jewish soul in a Gentile body, which led them to undertake the spiritual journey to Judaism in the first place.

Conversion has to take place in front of a *bet din* of three judges (sing. *dayan*, pl. *dayanim*) who will open a file on a would-be convert.[6] The Talmud recommends that one should discourage converts while at the same time bringing them near, and so the *bet din* will initially try to discourage the would-be convert. If the *dayan* who interviews candidates is convinced that they are serious and determined, he will assign them a teacher. While studying, converts will be assigned a family to spend Shabbat and festivals with, and to learn about the dietary laws in a practical way.

A course of study for conversion may last for several years in the diaspora, although it tends to be shorter in Israel. It will usually involve both converts and their future Jewish spouses, and at the end of it converts must be willing to accept the whole Torah, without reservations. When the teacher concludes that a convert is ready, the *bet din* will be informed. They will consider the teacher's reports, interview the candidate, and if satisfied they will arrange for the conversion to take place. Many people drop out of the conversion procedure in the initial stages when they realize how much there is to learn about Judaism and how long it takes.

The actual process of conversion involves circumcision for the male, and immersion in the *mikveh* for both male and female converts in front of three *dayanim*. Once converted, the convert has to keep all the laws of the *halakhah*, and must be loved by his new co-religionists, never to be reminded of what he was in the past. Just as it is prohibited to oppress the orphan, so it is considered a terrible wrong to oppress a convert.

Death, burial and mourning

The world is described in rabbinic literature as a corridor leading to the world to come. Humans have to prepare themselves in the corridor before entering the hall which is their destination. Despite this, the message of Judaism does not concentrate on death and the hereafter, but on life. Indeed, the most common greeting exchanged between Jews when drinking together is *le-haim* ('to life').

Death has its own associated rituals. Before dying, persons should confess their sins, and if possible end their life with the declaration of the first line of the *shema* on their lips: 'Hear [*shema*], O Israel, the Lord is our God, the Lord is One.' It is particularly meritorious to die affirming the oneness of God. In the presence of a dying person it is prohibited to do anything which will hasten death, active euthanasia being abhorrent to traditional Judaism.

Death is defined as the cessation of breathing, which may be tested with a feather or a mirror. Recently some leading American Orthodox rabbis have accepted brain death, where breathing may continue on a respirator but there are no vital brain functions, as a sufficient criterion of death. This is an important innovation (though it has not won wide acceptance among halakhists) because it opens up possibilities of organ donation by Jews for transplant surgery.

A dead person should be buried as soon as possible after death, preferably on the same day. Leaving the body without burial is considered a desecration of the dead, as is cutting up the corpse in a post-mortem examination unless this is absolutely necessary. Jewish communities usually have their own *chevra kaddisha* ('holy fellowship'), societies of men and women volunteers to wash the body and dress it in a shroud before placing it in a coffin. Some earth from the land of Israel is put in the coffin with the corpse so that, symbolically at least, the dead are interred in the Holy Land.

Burial takes place in consecrated ground. Orthodoxy does not permit cremation because this negates the belief in bodily resurrection in the messianic age, though many Reform rabbis will officiate at cremations. Before the funeral service begins, a garment of each mourner is cut and the mourner makes the blessing 'Blessed are you, Lord our God King of the Universe, the true Judge.' A shortened form of this blessing, *barukh day ha-emet*, is used by everyone whenever the death of someone is announced. Close relatives are the first to cast earth into the grave and some recite a special version of the *kaddish* prayer at the graveside. After the funeral the family return home for a traditional mourners' feast, consisting of round foods such as hard-boiled eggs and chickpeas.

All members of the immediate family are in mourning for the first week after the funeral, known as *shiva* ('seven'). They stay indoors, sit on low chairs, wear a torn garment and non-leather shoes, do not shave or have a bath, and cover over all the mirrors in the house. Memorial candles are kept burning in the house of mourning for seven days and prayer services are held there. Memorial prayers for the dead are recited and members of the community come to comfort the mourners.

From the end of the *shiva* until 30 days after the death, known as *sheloshim* ('30'), the family are in a lesser mode of mourning. They return to normal life but avoid celebrations, particularly occasions where music is played. While spouses, parents and siblings end their mourning with the end of the *sheloshim*, children continue their semi-mourning for twelve months. Sons say the mourner's *kaddish*, a prayer praising God despite the pain of bereavement, for the first eleven months after death. The recital of *kaddish* is meant to help the soul of the deceased rise from the purgatory of *gehinnom* to heaven. If the *kaddish* were said for the full twelve months this would indicate that the deceased was a genuinely wicked person needing *kaddish* to be said for the full period.

The death anniversary, known in Yiddish as a *yahrzeit* ('year's time'), falls each year on the Hebrew date of death, and memorial prayers will be recited in synagogue on the previous Shabbat. The *yahrzeit* is marked by the kindling of a memorial candle, recitation of the mourners' *kaddish*, and, in some communities, by children fasting on their parents' *yahrzeits*.

Notes

1   Non-Orthodox practice is usually a variation on the practices described here. Some notes have been added where there is a significant divergence in practice. (Ed.)

2   Although there is no traditional covenantal service for the birth of a daughter equivalent to *berit milah*, some Reform, Liberal and Conservative Jews have developed covenant ceremonies to welcome the birth of a daughter. (Ed.)

3   Most non-Orthodox movements consider both a boy and a girl to be

ritually an adult at 13. Thus both the *bar* and *bat mitzvah* ceremonies tend to be held at 13. (Ed.)

4 Non-Orthodox Jews do not usually follow this practice of going to the *mikveh* either for weddings or for purity in general. *Mikveh* tends to be used only as part of the conversion process. (Ed.)

5 In many non-Orthodox communities the bride also make a similar declaration and gives a ring to the groom. (Ed.)

6 Among the non-Orthodox Jews in Britain it is usual for the proselyte to meet initially with a local congregational rabbi. The proselyte will be asked to spend at least a year attending services, learning about Judaism and living a Jewish life (as much as possible). At the end of this period the proselyte will meet with either the Reform Bet Din or the Liberal Rabbinic Board (both composed of three rabbis) who after interviewing the proselyte will determine if he/she is accepted into Judaism. (Ed.)

Further reading

Barth, L. (ed.) *Berit Milah in the Reform Context*. New York: Berit Milah Board of Reform Judaism.

Gennep, A. van (1960) *The Rites of Passage* (1st edn 1908). London: Routledge and Kegan Paul.

Goldin, H. E. (trans.) (1963) *Code of Jewish Law*. New York: Hebrew Publishing Company.

Golding, W. (1980) *Rites of Passage*. London: Faber.

Kaplan, A. (1983) *Made in Heaven: A Jewish Wedding Guide*. New York: Moznaim Publishing Corporation.

Kling, S. (1987) *Embracing Judaism*. New York: The Rabbinical Assembly.

Lamm, M. (1969) *The Jewish Way in Death and Mourning*. New York: Jonathan David Publishers.

Lamm, M. (1980) *The Jewish Way in Love and Marriage*. San Francisco: Harper & Row.

Siegel, R., Strassfeld, M. and Strassfeld, S. (1973) *The Jewish Catalog*. Philadelphia: The Jewish Publication Society of America.

Strassfeld, S. and Strassfeld, M. (1976) *The Second Jewish Catalog*. Philadelphia: The Jewish Publication Society of America.

Turner, V. (1969) *The Ritual Process*. London: Routledge.

Unterman, A. (1981) *Jews, Their Religious Beliefs and Practices*. London: Routledge and Kegan Paul.

Unterman, A. (1991) *Dictionary of Jewish Lore and Legend*. London: Thames and Hudson.

Zborowski, M. and Herzog, E. (1962) *Life Is with People: The Culture of the Shtetl*. New York: Schocken Books.

SIDDURIM (PRAYER-BOOKS)

American Reform: (1975) *Gates of Prayer*. New York.
Conservative: (1985) *Siddur Sim Shalom*. New York.
Liberal: (1995) *Siddur Lev Chadash*. London.
Orthodox: (1990) *Authorised Daily Prayer Book of the United Hebrew Congregations of the Commonwealth* (Centenary edn). London.
Reform: (1984) *Forms of Prayer*. London.

3. Myth and history

Sybil Sheridan

History is central to Jewish belief. The religion revolves around the worship of a god that is intimately connected with the history of the world and in particular the history of one people. God is the God of History, continually involved, intervening in events, supporting human beings and ensuring the divine purpose is carried out. The Jewish God is identified as the God of Abraham, Isaac and Jacob, as the Lord who brought the children of Israel out of Egypt – specific points in history in the drama of one nation. The uniqueness described in the Bible is that God is not only creator of the universe, but also creator of time.

> It was the glory of Greece to have discovered the idea of cosmos, the world of space; it was the achievement of Israel to have experienced history, the world of time. Judaism claims that time is exceedingly relevant. Elusive it may be, it is pregnant with the seeds of eternity. Significant to God and decisive for the destiny of man are the things that happen in time, in history. Biblical history is the triumph of time over space. Israel did not grow into being through a series of accidents. Nature itself did not evolve out of a process, by necessity; it was called into being by an event, an act of God. History is the supreme witness for God.[1]

As God is involved in time, so are the people who follow him. Jewish destiny is seen as a gradual unfolding of God's purpose in the world from the first act of creation to the end of time with the coming of the Messiah. The destiny is marked by the celebration of specific historical events: the Exodus, the destruction of the two Temples, etc., and looks forward to specific future events: the coming of the Messiah, the ingathering of the exiles.

Those celebrations that are clearly of agricultural origin have historical events superimposed upon them. The harvest festival, Shavuot, becomes the time when the Torah was given; Sukkot marks the wanderings in the wilderness.

In this process, much that is mythological becomes part of history. The agricultural origins of many celebrations predate Israel's settlement in the land of Canaan, and they contain elements of the cults that the Hebrew religion replaced. Other aspects have been demythologized to suit the theological needs of the Israelites. Some of the alterations are so great that the original myth becomes barely recognizable. On the other hand, important historical events appear to have been turned into myth. History, in Judaism, does not mean an enumeration of facts – accuracy is most certainly not its strongest point – rather, it is a theological interpretation of events designed to involve the believer and effect a specific response.

Contemporary Jews are to regard themselves not only as the inheritors of such historical traditions, but also as participants. Thus all Jews at the *seder* table are to think of the Exodus as if they too were in Egypt at the time, and all are understood to have stood at the foot of Mount Sinai and been witness to the theophany that took place there. In this way, history becomes myth. It is not so much the event itself but its meaning that is central to the belief, and the reinforcement of that meaning through a large variety of symbols and celebrations. This is particularly clear in Orthodox Judaism which, though holding history at the core of its beliefs, does not approach it historically, but thematically. Exile and return, sin and repentance, are ideas demonstrated again and again in the narratives of the Bible. From creation to the end of time, the same pattern of events unfolds. The patriarchs, Moses and other heroes have their place in this history, but they also act as pious examples that ordinary people can follow, and most of Jewish literature addresses these figures in such a vein. In this they belong in every age, offering a timeless quality and an immediate appeal.

Other movements within Judaism take a radically different line. Reform Judaism originated in Germany in the early decades of the nineteenth century and was greatly influenced by Christian biblical scholarship of the time. It therefore takes the Bible less literally as the Truth, and views it rather as expressions of truth as conceived in particular ages under particular circumstances. Non-Orthodox Judaism relies very heavily therefore on a historical approach to the religion, careful to separate the different strands of belief as they developed. Only through this approach can one make a distinction between myth and history in Judaism, for to Orthodoxy, myth is history and history myth.

The beginnings of time

THE FIRST CREATION STORY: GENESIS I – 2:4A

> When God began to create heaven and earth – the earth being unformed and void, with darkness over the surface of the deep and a wind from God sweeping over the water. (Gen 1:1–2)

The first creation story recounted in the Bible appears to have used elements found in the Babylonian creation epics. *Enuma Elish*[2] recounts how the primordial Apsu, Mummu and Tiamat are defeated by the gods they engendered. The heavens and earth are formed from the split body of Tiamat, and the triumphant god Marduk then holds a celebration and builds a city for his supporters.

There are clear similarities to be found in the primordial origins of the universe as a watery waste, and in the order of creation described, but unlike *Enuma Elish* Genesis records no indication of the battle for supremacy. God alone is. He creates out of emptiness. There are no other gods – even the use of the plural, thought to indicate the presence of a heavenly court, is in no way specific, and such lesser beings have no part to play in the creative process. While, for Genesis, creation is the central theme of the narrative, in *Enuma Elish* creation seems almost incidental to the main story, that of the great battle.

Other creation narratives in the Bible record more of the primeval battle. For example, in Psalm 74:13–14:

> It was You who drove back the sea with your might,
> who smashed the heads of the monsters in the waters;
> it was You who crushed the heads of Leviathan, who left him as
> food for the denizens of the desert;

Here the enemy is not Tiamat but Leviathan, which recalls the battle in Ugaritic mythology between the god Baal and Yam (the sea) in which the serpent Lotan figures. Yam is also mentioned in Job 26:1–13, alongside Leviathan and another protagonist, Rahab.

83

In these passages, the mythological elements are understood as poetic imagery. The prophet Isaiah places them more in a historic context by connecting them to the subsequent story of humankind and the future hope of redemption (Isa 51:9–11). The myth also becomes representative of eschatological expectation. God did not defeat the monsters at the beginning of time; rather, it is an expressed hope of the future messianic age.

> In that day the Lord will punish,
> With His great, cruel, mighty sword
> Leviathan the Elusive Serpent –
> Leviathan the Twisting Serpent
> He will slay the Dragon of the Sea. (Isa 27:1)

Rabbinic Judaism took over this use of the myth and enlarged upon it; the righteous will witness a contest between God and the two monsters: Leviathan and the great ox Behemoth. Having defeated them, God will serve them up as food in a great feast to celebrate the end of days.[3] This is the theme for a medieval poem, *Akdamut*, recited in Ashkenazi[4] synagogues, on the festival of Shavuot. The rather florid Aramaic has been translated thus:

> Then shall Leviathan's enthralling sight
> Divert them, with Behemoth's might
> On mountains bred, fast twined in mortal fight.
> As Taurus' lofty horn to gore begins.
> See, leaping Draco parries with his fins:
> Till his Creator wields His wondrous sword –
> And so prepared the righteous' festive board.[5]

In the first creation story of Genesis, however, none of these creatures appears. The battle, be it primal or eschatological, is irrelevant to creation and God's ultimate purpose. Creation provides instead the framework for a new and totally original idea – that of God resting. This becomes the reason for the observance of *Shabbat* by the children of Israel.

> Remember the sabbath day and keep it holy. Six days you shall labour and do all your work, but the seventh day is a sabbath of the Lord your God ... For in six days the Lord made heaven and earth and sea, and all that is in them, and He rested on the seventh day; therefore the Lord blessed the sabbath day and hallowed it. (Exod 20:8–11)

Creation itself is introduced within the framework of time. The seven days mark the beginning of time and, as such, are the first event in history. The Jewish year is calculated from the first day of creation – believed to have been the first of the month of Tishri (Rosh Ha-Shanah) 5,759 years ago.

THE SECOND CREATION ACCOUNT: GENESIS 2:4B – 3:24

While the mythological elements in the first chapter of Genesis seem to have been pared away, those in the second creation account and the story of Adam and Eve in the garden of Eden have kept much more of their original colour. This has been explained as the result of differing editing processes at quite different periods of Jewish history, but it may also have something to do with the subjects they cover. Genesis 1 is about God – and the Israelite perception of God appears to have been unique in the Near East – while Genesis 2 and 3 are about humanity and the human predicament – an issue shared by all peoples. The barren plain watered by a mist, God forming humanity out of the earth, the miraculous garden, the source of the four rivers, all have their counterparts in Sumerian, Akkadian and Ugaritic mythology.

In the *Epic of Gilgamesh*, Enkidu is formed by the goddess Aruru out of clay, and lives among the animals until, initiated into love by a priestess of the god Gilgamesh, he is rejected by them. As he is now like a god, the priestess clothes him, and brings him to Gilgamesh in the city of Uruk. Gilgamesh sets out to find the herb of immortality. He enters a paradise of jewel-hung trees, owned by the goddess of wisdom, but continues until he finds the herb at the bottom of the sea. He returns with it but it is subsequently stolen by a serpent at a freshwater stream.

The *Myth of Adapa* describes how the son of the god of wisdom is advised by his father to refuse the food of the gods, as they are seeking to kill him. Anu, the king of heaven, hears of this conversation and offers Adapa the bread of immortality instead. However, Adapa, heeding his father's words, refuses the bread and so condemns himself to die like mortals.

But while echoes of these stories remain in the Genesis account, there are significant differences. The yearning for immortality is replaced by the quest for knowledge. It has been suggested that the two trees in the garden of Eden were originally the trees of life and death.[6]

A warning by God against eating the tree of death makes for a simpler and less theologically challenging story – more in keeping with that of Adapa. But the myth as represented in the Bible introduces a moral element that becomes the foundation for its subsequent history.

Gardens of delight in mythology appear to have originally been ruled over by goddesses, and a serpent was invariably present.[7] At a later stage, according to Raphael Patai, male gods usurped them and reduced their status and power. In Eden, God is the only god, who walks alone in the garden he created. However, his creature, Adam, remains almost incidental to the story. The core event takes place between the serpent and Eve, and the subject of the discussion – the tree – can then be interpreted to be the acquisition of wisdom. The wise woman played a prominent part in Israelite society, her wisdom being related either to practical skills and diplomacy (2 Sam 13:39 – 14:7, 20:16–22) or to a magic, esoteric knowledge (1 Sam 28). However, in its later interpretations, it is humanity as represented by a man that becomes the subject of the piece. It is Adam who is told not to eat from the tree. It is his disobedience, not Eve's, that is noted by God, and it is not wisdom that he gains, but a sense of morality – of good and evil.

The reworking of the myth has one main object in mind: to provide a background for the history of the world in general and for the people of Israel in particular. By making the loss of innocence a moral issue – the result of disobedience – it explains the evils of the world not as the consequence of a mistake, or a trick as in its Near Eastern counterparts, but as the beginnings of a degeneration that is entirely humanity's own doing. Redemption is open to humanity through the same process: through moral action – from Noah, considered righteous in his generation, through Abraham, through his faith, and through subsequent history where kings are described as doing good or evil in the sight of God. Along with the gods, the principle of evil as an external force is eradicated from the story, and the myth, focusing on the notion of moral choice, becomes a 'historical drama of human rebellion and sin'.[8]

THE PRE-HISTORY: GENESIS 4–11:9

The stories that follow – of Cain and Abel, of the sons of God, of Noah and the Tower of Babel – can be identified with myths and folk tales of the region in which they were composed. But they have been brought together and altered by the editors to present meanings that may not necessarily have been part of the original telling. In particular, after the perfection of the original creation, the story describes the descent of humanity into moral depravity in a series of retellings of the second creation myth. In each tale, it is again humankind's decision to do wrong that brings changes with it, not only in relation to the environment, but also in relation to God. Each cycle of creation and fall takes humanity further from God till, in Babel, God does not speak to the people at all.

But the myths do not remain disjointed. The whole process is historicized with the introduction of genealogies. These occur from the beginning, linking the independent narratives, making unrelated characters part of the same family, and connecting unconnected events in terms of the changing but continuing relationship with God. Creation itself is seen as a historical process. The juxtaposition of heavens and earth in Genesis 2:4 serves to link the two creations and also to emphasize their difference – the first creation is of the universe, the second of the world. Two genealogies precede the flood and two follow it. Each pair has a longer and shorter form. There are ten generations before Noah and ten after him, giving him a special place, as it were, at the halfway point in pre-history. This clearly is not factual history but theological history. That the genealogies are not historically accurate is not important. They are history in that they reflect the forward motion of time, of change and development, and it is these genealogies that link the mythology of the first chapters of Genesis with the family history that follows.

The patriarchs

As we enter the lives of the patriarchs, we encounter a very different mode. The biblical text no longer deals with universal elements, but focuses on the domestic lives of specific people. While Adam, Cain and Noah were also named individuals, they represented 'Everyman', and their experience was that of all human experience. Abraham, Isaac and Jacob, however, are significant for the opposite reason. They stand out as individuals distinct from the rest of humanity, they are called by God to follow an individual path.

While in the first chapters the events are interpreted theologically, the patriarchal narratives are interpreted historically. The former's interest in humanity's relationship with God is replaced in the main by the human concerns of progeny and land. With the story of Abraham we are at the beginning of the history of the Jews.

ABRAHAM

It cannot be proved whether Abraham actually existed as an individual. Archaeological evidence of names and places, legal and social situations described in Mesopotamian, Egyptian and Syrian documents seems to confirm the situations described in the stories relating to him. Vast migrations took place through the Fertile Crescent in the Middle Bronze Age. To move from Ur, to Canaan, to Egypt and back was not uncommon – nor to marry one's half-sister (Gen 12:19), adopt a servant as one's heir (15:2) or use a concubine as a surrogate mother (16). Moreover, there is evidence of power alliances of several kings combining forces against other kings during the period from 2000 to 1750 BCE (Gen 14). This places Abraham very firmly within a known context at a known period in time and certainly suggests the veracity of much of the narrative.

However, other elements are clearly mythological: the angels visiting Abraham at his tent (18), the fate of Sodom (19), the saving of Ishmael (21). Both the historical and the mythological, however, are transformed by the editor to present one overriding theme – that of exile and return. This theme dominates subsequent Jewish history and, it can be argued, the events related about Abraham's life are read back from the standpoint of the Exodus from Egypt.

The first chapter of the Abraham saga encapsulates all of Jewish history. Abraham is called to leave all he knows, to go to a new, strange and unspecified land, one that God will show him (12:1). Once in the land of Canaan, his movement, from the north of the country to Shechem to the Negev, marks the boundaries of what will be the home of the future nation. At Shechem, God promises that the land will be given to Abraham's descendants, a promise reiterated again and again to Abraham and to his descendants. Then famine drives him to Egypt (12:10), just as famine will force Jacob to Egypt. Abraham returns, apparently with great riches, after Pharaoh is afflicted with plague. In just the same circumstances, the children of Israel leave Egypt, and they ultimately settle in the land that once was settled by Abraham.

The rest of the saga expands this theme. The covenants (15:7-21 and

17:1-15) promise the land and progeny. The stories relating to Lot emphasize the land, its division (13) and its conquest by Abraham (14). Subsequent chapters concern the search for an heir: Eliezer (15), Ishmael (16), the promise of the birth of Isaac (18), the jeopardizing of that promise in Gerar (20), Isaac's birth (21), and near-sacrifice in the *akedah* or binding of Isaac (22). Finally, in the death of Sarah and the purchase of a burial plot (23), the subject returns to that of the land. All point to a very heavy editing of the original material to concentrate on this theme.

One of the most apparent changes occurs in the chapters concerning the visitation of the angels to Abraham and to Lot (18 and 19). It contains the familiar tale of hospitality rewarded: the childless couple get their child, the 'wicked' man loses all he has. However, Lot appears as hospitable as Abraham – it is the people of Sodom who flout the convention. Indeed, hospitality is not mentioned at all. The sin of Sodom is a moral outrage, and it seems that Lot's punishment is because he chose to live in such evil surroundings. Moreover, dominating the whole sequence is the conversation of Abraham with God on the nature of justice. The tale has been altered as we have seen myths altered before – to emphasize a moral dilemma.

In Jewish tradition, Abraham has become important as the man of faith, the first Jew. Though the Bible gives no such indication, tradition has it that humanity descended into idolatry and the one true God was forgotten. Terah is pictured as a maker of idols; so the question arises, how did Abraham come to know God? Genesis 12:1 suggests a prehistory, and this the *midrash* provides.[9] Abraham, observing his father making the idols, feels they cannot be gods. He then watches the moon, stars and sun, and worships them in turn as each appears to supplant the other. Finally, he feels that there must be some prime mover of all the heavenly bodies. Another *midrash* describes how Abraham smashed all his father's idols except the largest one and then told his father that the large idol got angry and destroyed the others. When Terah remonstrates, Abraham retorts 'If you do not believe the idol can do this, how can you worship him as a god?'

Abraham, the first Jew, becomes the 'father' of all converts to Judaism, who, to this day, adopt his name as their patronym. He is described as having spent his life converting others until a great many 'souls' follow him to Canaan (Gen 12:5). There, many more are converted wherever he builds an altar and 'calls upon the name of the Lord'. Yet Abraham's faith is constantly being tested. Each incident related of him in the Bible is regarded as such a test, with the binding of Isaac as the greatest and last of them.

> With ten temptations was Abraham our father tempted, and he stood steadfast in them all, to show how great was the love of Abraham our father. (Mishnah, *Avot* 5:7)

ISAAC

In comparison to the Abraham saga, what we are told about Isaac is brief and inconsequential. There is only one chapter (26) that narrates actions independent of either Isaac's father or his sons. The relative insignificance of Isaac is neatly summarized in 25:19: 'These are the descendants of Isaac, Abraham's son: Abraham was the father of Isaac ...' Moreover, most of what is recorded parallels the life of Abraham. His wife is barren for many years (25) before giving birth, and he too is faced with rival heirs. Like Abraham, he goes to Gerar at a time of famine (26), and passes his wife off as his sister, with the usual results. He has trouble with the Philistines over wells he digs, paralleling 21:25, and, like his father, makes a covenant with Abimelech, though the wording in Isaac's case is more reminiscent of Abraham's dealings with Melchizedek (14:18). Twice he receives God's blessing with the promise of land and progeny (26:3–5; 24), and, like his father, he builds an altar at Beer Sheva and 'calls upon the name of the Lord'.

It is his father's story in miniature. Isaac's wanderings never go beyond the Negev region in the south. Most of the parallels with Abraham occur in the one independent chapter, which opens with a prohibition against going to Egypt (26:2) – even Abraham's status as a precursor of the Exodus is denied him.

Yet Jewish tradition ranks him as equal to both his father and his son. Adonai is 'God of our fathers Abraham, Isaac, and Jacob'. God is *pahad Yitzhak* (31:42), translated as 'the fear of Isaac'. The prophet Amos uses 'the house of Isaac' rather than the more common 'house of Jacob' as a synonym for Israel (Amos 7:16). Midrash points out that because God named him, he is the only one of the patriarchs not to experience a name change. This reflects on his character, which is blameless. He is the perfect dutiful son; witness the *akedah*.

JACOB

His son Jacob, however, has all the vibrancy and full characterization of Abraham. As in the case of his grandfather, the narrative surrounding Jacob appears made up of separate incidents, real or imaginary, that were related of the patriarch. The editor has linked them into a continuous narrative, again with the purpose of showing the pattern of exile and return, and of setting the scene for the descent into Egypt. Central again are two blessings, promising progeny and the land. Jacob's movements again confirm the extent of the land. He leaves his father in the south, and moves northward via Bethel to Padan Aram, where he later establishes a border with Laban (31:51). He settles in Shechem and ends his days in Egypt, thus travelling almost to the extent of his grandfather's journeys. But the emphasis in the text is more on the progeny than on the land, for here, for the first time, it appears the promise may come true. His thirteen children's births and namings are all mentioned, and significant events in their lives are described. These stories may well also have been independent traditions, recording the leaders of clans or tribal groups, but they have been brought into the Jacob saga to provide the narrative of one large family – the early history of the people Israel.

This approach seems to vary from that of the narratives described earlier. The two very dramatic theophanies that are described, of the ladder at Bethel (28:10–17) and of the wrestling bout at the Jabbok ford (32:22–32), probably owe their origin to earlier mythic religious experiences. Unlike other such incidents we have encountered, they are not moralized or placed into a theological context. Each takes place at a moment of crisis in Jacob's life, and clearly they have a great impact on his own development, but what this is, is not spelt out.

The rivalry between Jacob and Esau harks back to that of Cain and Abel, and may well have the same mythological root. Yet it becomes in the Bible a recurring theme that appears again in the life of his son Judah (38:27–30), which, in turn, becomes a blueprint for the events of the book of Ruth. A new element is introduced then, linking the concerns of progeny and land to the establishment of the future kingdom under the rule of the ideal king – David.

In the stories of the patriarchs we see ancient history and myth combined to form a new history. S. H. Hooke[10] sees, underlying these stories, the earliest movements of ancient peoples. Abraham, the 'Hebrew' (possibly part of the 'Hapiru' mentioned in literature of the period), demonstrates the movement from Ur to the land around Hebron. Jacob, the 'wandering Aramean' also known as Israel, settled in Shechem. Isaac may represent a third people who lived an independent, settled, agricultural life around Gerar. Each patriarch is associated with a different epithet for God: the Shield of Abraham, the Fear of Isaac, the Champion of Jacob. Each patriarch is seen as choosing God for himself; each is blessed independently by God. It is possible, therefore, that each group had its own tribal god which, when later the nation of Israel emerged, combined to form the God of Abraham, Isaac and Jacob.[11]

In order to maintain the unity of the nation once formed (the books of Judges and Kings suggest it was at times a very precarious unity), the individual ancestors were also combined into a family – a family with clear limits of exclusion and inclusion, so that only one child of each generation becomes part of the chosen destiny. In this way the patriarchs can be seen to have historical origins, though somewhat different ones from those described in the narrative. Yet, to the Jewish tradition, such speculation is irrelevant. Without the patriarchs, there would be no Jewish people. The history of Israel begins here in the lives of three individuals and their actions echo on down the generations.

It is noteworthy that, despite the length given over in Genesis to the Joseph story, Joseph is not considered a patriarch. Though he becomes the ancestor of two tribes, he is only one of the sons of Israel, all of whom have an equal share in the promise.

Moses

In all of the history of Israel, the Jews and Judaism, the figure that dominates is that of Moses. Prince and prophet; shepherd and showman; leader and lawgiver: Moses alone was responsible for the formation of the nation Israel, and the foundation of the Jewish faith. Yet there is no evidence that he ever existed.

Archaeology has confirmed that there were Semitic groups in Egypt, some of which moved northwest towards Canaan. Under the Hyksos rulers of Egypt, foreigners (like Joseph) attained high office; when the Hyksos were thrown out, such foreigners were not likely to be kindly treated by the new dynasty. Furthermore, there are accounts of runaway slaves seeking asylum in other countries. The cities of Pithom and Ramses have been identified: built in the time of Ramses II in the thirteenth century. The Merneptah Stele (*c.* 1220 BCE), describes the nation Israel as being defeated in Canaan. The name 'Moses' seems clearly Egyptian, despite the etymology given in Exodus 2:10. All this gives great credibility to the story, and historians tend to date the events described in Exodus to the thirteenth century, with Ramses II as the Pharaoh of the oppression and Merneptah as the Pharaoh of the Exodus. But of Moses the man, or of a mass exodus of Hebrew slaves, there is no evidence at all. To the Jewish believer, such doubts are unthinkable. The Exodus and the Theophany at Sinai are absolutely central to belief. This is history that really happened – perhaps not entirely in the form given in the Bible, but it happened nevertheless.

While many of the stories in Moses' life can be seen as coming from the general pool of folklore and myth, the Exodus and the revelation of law on Mount Sinai are absolutely unique. Moreover Moses, despite the birth stories, his miraculous abilities and the success of his mission, never develops into a full-blooded hero type. He does not end up as king or conqueror but remains a shy stutterer, reluctant to fulfil his required role, and dependent throughout his life on the help of his brother Aaron, his father-in-law and the elders of Israel. Moreover, he dies before the people enter the promised land and so never sees the fulfilment of his mission. Such a person, the argument runs, would not have been invented – nor would such humble origins for the nation. Moreover, the Exodus event is so strongly imprinted upon the psyche of the Jew that the question of proof becomes irrelevant. It is in relation to this one event that the Jewish people are defined; all previous and subsequent history is interpreted in its light.

MOSES' EARLY LIFE

Moses was born to Israelite slaves in Egypt at a time of intense oppression (Exod 1:8–22), and experiences a rescue from death and an upbringing incognito, common to many a mythological hero. After killing an Egyptian, Moses is forced to flee to Midian (2:11), where he first encounters God, and his mission to rescue his people from the cruelty of Egypt is made clear. Moses returns to Egypt and approaches Pharaoh, who, after falling victim to ten plagues sent by God, agrees to let the people go (5 – 12). The Israelites leave, but Pharaoh changes his mind and chases after them (13:17). They finally escape when a sea of reeds (*yam suf*) miraculously divides and lets

93

them pass to the other side, while the pursuing Egyptians are drowned in pursuit (14:15–50).

The genealogy at the beginning of the book of Exodus (1:1–7), as in Genesis, links the narrative into the continuing historical line. With the description of the population explosion in Egypt, God's original promise to Abraham is seen to be half fulfilled. When Moses is called on Mount Horeb and God identifies himself as the 'God of your fathers, God of Abraham, God of Isaac and God of Jacob' (3:6), the indication is that he is now about to fulfil the second half of that promise. Yet it takes another four biblical books and another generation before this actually comes to pass. While the biblical editor is using the Exodus in the general context of exile and return, the event as described here and in subsequent history quite clearly had an independent life of its own.

Many of the events recorded of Moses' early life are the stuff of legend. The rescue from the water is reminiscent of several other birth stories, while Moses' magic staff, the plagues and the miracles have parallels the world over. However, the leaving of Egypt and the emergence into freedom of a nation of slaves is particular to Israel, and records the precise moment in history when the nation was born.

THE EXODUS

Form critics suggest that the narratives of the book of Exodus fall into two parts, relating to specific cultic celebrations at two different sanctuaries.[12] The first section covers Exodus 1 – 15 and includes stories regarding the birth, growth and call of Moses as well as the events surrounding the leaving of Egypt itself, while the second concerns the events leading up to the revelation on Mount Sinai and a celebration of the covenant of law. These originally localized festivities now find their universal application in the festivals of Pesach and Shavuot.

The Exodus itself begins with the preparations before the last plague (12), preparations that could well reflect the cultic observance of some event. God commands that the children of Israel select a lamb whose blood will be used to smear the doorposts of their houses and which will then be eaten just before they leave. This later becomes the Pesach, the paschal sacrifice offered in the Temple. But there is also evidence of another observance in this chapter, that relating to the feast of unleavened bread or Hag Hamatzot. Scholars suggest that two originally independent festivals are recorded here, one agricultural and one nomadic – both spring festivals but neither necessarily of Israelite origin. The nomadic Pesach later became specifically Israelite by linking it to the historical event of the Exodus; while Hag Hamatzot – possibly adopted once Israel had settled in Canaan – continued roughly in its original form. It is hard to say when the feasts were connected; biblical evidence suggests that the observance of Pesach was spasmodic at least until the time of Josiah (2 Kgs 23:21–23), but it is likely that the popular harvest festivals would have been regularly celebrated in their appropriate seasons.

The Exodus as a supremely significant event emerged in Babylon at the time of another exile, where the dreams of a return to the promised land shaped much of the history related in Torah. The return and restoration of the Temple saw a new observance: a lamb eaten at home to the accompaniment of psalms and the telling of the Exodus story.

As Israel suffered further defeats and humiliations at the hands of foreign enemies, the Exodus experience intensified as the symbol of nationalistic hopes until, under Roman occupation, the passage from slavery to freedom took on an intense metaphysical as well as political form. It is then that the Exodus became mythologized in the *seder* and its accompanying service book, the Haggadah. Though the form of the meal follows that of a Roman symposium, the intention is to recreate the last meal eaten in Egypt.

> In every generation each person is obliged to consider themselves as if they had personally come out of Egypt. As it is said: 'and you shall tell your children on that day, saying, "This is because of what the Lord did for me when I went out of Egypt."' (Ex 13:8) Not only our ancestors alone did the Holy One, blessed be He, redeem, but he redeemed us also with them, as it is written: 'And he took us out from there in order to bring us here to give us the land which he swore to our ancestors.' (Deut 6:23)[13]

Much of the Haggadah is concerned with telling of the events that took place in Egypt leading up to the Exodus, but with distinctive differences from the biblical account. Moses is not mentioned at all. Instead, all the credit and glory go to God, and the narration is punctuated with elaborate songs of praise and thanks to God:

> The Lord freed us from Egypt by a mighty hand, by an outstretched arm and awesome power, and by signs and portents. (Deut 26:8)

Yet the events take on a wider spiritual significance. The four cups of wine drunk are symbolic of the fourfold promise of God to Moses (Exod 6:6–7):

> I am the Lord. I will free you from the labours of the Egyptians and deliver you from their bondage. I will redeem you with an outstretched arm and through extraordinary chastisements. And I will take you to be My people ...

But there is another promise symbolized in the fifth cup of wine:

> and I will be your God.

This cup is not drunk, but saved for Elijah, who will return heralding the Messiah and the End of Days. The introduction of the messianic theme adds another level to the story. The biblical subject of slavery and freedom, which becomes interpreted in the Babylonian exile as exile and return and under the Roman yoke as occupation and liberation, is turned into the idea of the spiritual redemption that will come with the reparation of the world.

THE PARTING OF THE SEA

The crossing of the *yam suf* marks the final escape of Israel from the Egyptians. The story is told relatively simply in chapter 14, how God 'hardened Pharaoh's heart', who then set off in pursuit of his former slaves. The Israelites complain when they find themselves caught literally between the 'devil' and the deep blue sea, asking 'Were there not enough graves in Egypt that you had to take us into the wilderness to die?' (14:11). The way the story is written, its purpose appears to be to demonstrate God's saving power so that the Israelites will believe in him. Thus the last verse explains,

> And when Israel saw the wondrous power which the Lord had wielded against the Egyptians, the people feared the Lord; they had faith in the Lord and His servant Moses. (Ex 14:31)

But the sheer drama of the event has meant its use in many other contexts, most notably in the Psalms.

The waters saw You, O God,
   the waters saw You and were convulsed;
   the very deep quaked as well.
Clouds streamed water;
   the heavens rumbled;
   Your thunder rumbled like wheels
   lightning lit up the world;
   the earth quaked and trembled.
Your way was through the sea,
   Your path, through the mighty waters;
   Your tracks could not be seen.
You led Your people like a flock
   in the care of Moses and Aaron.

(Ps 77:17–21)

The personification of the sea as an adversary, and God's use of lightning and thunder, make this passage an echo of the Ugaritic myths.[14] It is God once more facing chaos and subduing it.

In the famous song of the sea which follows the actual event (Exod 15), similar themes are used. Though the enemy remains Egypt, and the sea God's agent rather than adversary, God is still described as a warrior, and the reward for victory is that he shall reign for ever in the abode he has built (15:17–18).[15] The song has clear references back to the Genesis account of creation. God's intentions are activated by his *ruah* – his breath – and again it appears that he is dividing the waters.

At the blast of your nostrils the waters piled up, the floods stood straight like a wall, the deeps froze in the heart of the sea. (Exod 15:8)

Today, the central feature of the service on the seventh day of Pesach is the singing of the song at the sea. Some Hasidic sects re-enact the event also in a special dance, where water is poured on the ground and crossed; others will go down to the sea shore and recite specific psalms. But in the main, Judaism today does not make as much of the event as it could.

There is every likelihood that in the past, the crossing of the *yam suf* was the most important feature of the Exodus story. After all, it concludes the event. It is the climax, the most impressive of all the miracles, and only at the very end of the story are the Israelites safely away from Egypt. Moreover, the crossing of the sea is deeply symbolic, reflecting a new creation, re-birth or baptism. It is here that the slaves become a nation. Yet in today's ritual, the first night of Pesach eclipses the last. The emphasis lies in Egypt with the oppression of the slaves and the retribution of the plagues. This reflects the reality of Jewish suffering under persecution down the ages. Jews are all, as it were, still in Egypt: occasionally sharing the triumph of a temporary respite as after a plague, but not yet having achieved the complete liberation experienced by crossing the sea.

REVELATION AT SINAI

The second cultic cycle takes the Israelites through the desert to the mountain of God, where Moses and all the people of Israel are bound in a covenant relating to God's law. As with the Exodus narrative, the miraculous elements abound. There is God's providence along the way (Exod 16), there is the battle with the new adversary Amalek (17:8-13), and the great thunder when God descends upon the mountain (19:16-19). As with the Exodus narrative, there are what appear to be cultic preparations before the great event. In 19:10-25 bounds are set around the mountain, the people wash and get ready for Moses' ascent.

Yet the actual event is of far shorter duration. God descends upon the mountain top amidst thunder and lightning, smoke and blasts of the *shofar*. He then proclaims the Ten Commandments in the hearing of all the people. There are further laws (20:22ff.), the incident with the golden calf and its repercussions (32 – 34), and the erection of the Tabernacle, but it is that first theophany at Sinai that has become the significant event. And again, despite the miraculous overlay, the event seems to record an actual historical happening of such magnitude as to be everlastingly imprinted upon the nation's mind. This is the event that gave the people its identity. It became the nation of God, forged into a special covenant of which perhaps only later generations could properly see the significance. Something happened at Sinai – exactly what, cannot be said – but some religious experience so powerful and involving so many of the people that all subsequent religious experiences seem somehow to have emerged there and all subsequent generations shared in that experience. This feature is central to Orthodox Jewish theology.

'And God spoke all these words saying' (Ex 20:1). R. Isaac said: The prophets received from Sinai the messages they were to prophesy to subsequent generations; for Moses told Israel, 'Nor is it with you only that I make this sworn covenant, but with him who is not here with us this day' etc. (Deut 29:14) ... Although they did not yet exist, still each one received his share. (*Shemot Rabbah* 28:6)

And similarly with rabbinic revelation.

When God revealed himself at Sinai to give the Torah to Israel, he communicated it to Moses in order: Bible, Mishnah, Talmud and *aggadah*, as it says, 'And God spoke all these words' (Ex 20:1). Even the question a pupil asks his teacher God told Moses at this time. (*Shemot Rabbah*, 47:1)

In a sense, then, history stopped at Sinai. All that followed is the fulfilment of prophecy. Yet in another sense, it is the beginning of history. The nation defining itself in terms of a relationship with God is a nation centred on the observance of his law. How many of the laws recorded in the rest of the Pentateuch are actually of Mosaic origin is hard to tell, but again in religious terms this is not relevant. What is important is that the Torah became the blueprint for all action – religious, civil, and personal. The Mishnah, written about 200 CE, expands and interprets the laws of Torah in the light of Palestinian life at the time of the second Temple. The Gemara (which, with the Mishnah, makes up the Talmud) comments on the Mishnah laws for the benefit of Jews living in Babylonia four centuries later. The process continues to this day. *Halakhah* is the term given to this constant interpretation of Torah into practical application, a word derived from the verb 'to walk', signalling a persistent movement, or change, or progression; yet Torah remains at the source and is never distanced by the process.

The revelation at Sinai is also the point where Reform, or Progressive, Judaism differs from Orthodox Judaism. For the various non-Orthodox movements, Sinai was the first revelation of God and so the most important, but nevertheless limited by its time and place. The prophets had their own individual revelations of God relevant to the people and circumstances of their time, as did the later rabbis in theirs. This is termed 'progressive revelation' and demands a rather different understanding of the historical process within Judaism. For the Orthodox, the rabbinic saying 'there is no before or after in Torah' holds sway. Chronology is irrelevant, the law all-important. For the Progressive Jew, chronology and an appreciation of history in general become more important than the laws.

The book of Joshua (8:30) describes a re-enactment of the events on Mount Sinai when, after the initial victories, Joshua assembles the entire nation to Mount Ebal where he records Moses' words on tablets of stone and initiates a series of blessings and curses in response to Deuteronomy 27:11. Today the celebration that takes place at Shavuot is less dramatic. In synagogue, the events of Exodus 19 and 20 are read from the Torah scroll but this is not seen as a reconstruction of the revelation in the way that the *seder* commemorates the Exodus. Shavuot, like Pesach, probably started out as a non-Israelite agricultural festival upon which the people overlaid a historical event. The same happened to Sukkot, an autumn feast which now commemorates the wilderness wanderings of the children of Israel. This is emulated by the 'dwelling in booths' – not skin tents as were used in the wilderness, but huts decorated with leaves and fruit which clearly did not grow in the desert but which celebrate the richness of a successful harvest.

Towards the end of time

The books that follow Torah in the Hebrew Bible – namely, the Prophets (see Chapter 4) – are largely historical in their approach. They trace the ongoing adventures of the Israelites from their first step across into the promised land, through their conquest of Canaan, the tribal rivalries and allegiances, their unification under the monarchy, the capture of Jerusalem and consolidation of territory, to the division of the kingdom into two and their ultimate defeats and destruction causing the disappearance of tribes and exile of leaders. As we move forward in history, it becomes easier to demonstrate the actual existence of the main characters and to validate their actions through external documentation and archaeological finds. But the history as written in the Bible is theological history. The events as they occur are less important than the interpretation put upon them. David's sons squabble because of his 'sin' with Bathsheba (2 Sam 12:11–12). The kingdom is divided because of Solomon's idolatry (1 Kgs 11:9–13), and so on. This becomes most clear in the treatment given in the Bible and in later literature to the figure of Amalek.

AMALEK

Amalek is first encountered in the wilderness by the Israelites just after their escape from Egypt (Exod 17:8–15). The battle that ensues is decisively won by Joshua, with miraculous help from Moses. There then follows this passage, surprising in its vehemence:

> Then the Lord said to Moses, 'Inscribe this in a document as a reminder, and read it aloud to Joshua: I will utterly blot out the memory of Amalek from under heaven!' And Moses built an altar and named it Adonai-nissi. He said 'It means "Hand upon the throne of the Lord!" The Lord will be at war with Amalek through the ages.' (Exod 17:14–16)

The decisive battle with the Amalekites came in the reign of Saul (1 Sam 15). God remembers what Amalek had done to Israel in the desert and instructs Saul to finish off the nation:

> 'proscribe all that belongs to him; spare no one but kill alike men and women, infants and sucklings, oxen and sheep, camels and asses!' (I Sam 15:3)

But Saul disobeys. He takes the livestock as booty, and though killing every other Amalekite, makes King Agag his prisoner. The prophet Samuel, when he hears of Saul's actions, is furious and personally kills Agag. Historically, we know that the Amalekites were not totally destroyed. They are mentioned again in Saul's reign (1 Sam 30:13) and presumably remained as a nation for some time after this. But tradition has another story: Agag, while imprisoned by Saul, sired a child and so his line was saved; in subsequent generations, wherever an enemy arose dedicated to the destruction of Israel, that enemy was sure to be a descendant of Agag.

The best-known example is that cited in the book of Esther, where the evil adviser Haman is described as an 'Agagite' (Esther 11). The story, possibly based upon actual historical events that took place in the Persian empire, has a more universal significance in Judaism as portraying the primal battle between good and evil.

Haman represents Amalek, upon whom 'the Lord will have war'; Esther – a form of the Hebrew *Hester*, meaning 'hidden' – represents God. There is no direct mention of God in the story and this is interpreted to mean that God has 'hidden his face' (cf. Ps 89:46; Ezek 39:29). At times when Israel sins, rabbinic interpretation explains,

101

God hides, or withdraws from the world. This allows for all manner of evil to emerge and punish the nation before God once again takes control.

In the story of Esther, a Jewish woman risks her life to save her people and her courage is rewarded, while the enemy Haman and all his sons are killed. This is celebrated today in the feast of Purim, where the story is read out, and at each mention of Haman's name, as much noise as possible is made with rattles and the stamping of feet, in order to 'blot out the name' and the 'remembrance of Amalek from under heaven'. The hanging of Haman's sons means, according to the story, that the centuries-old enmity is finally at an end. But tradition has it that the line did continue. Thus rabbinic literature describes Rome as Amalek, and late medieval commentaries attributed the lineage to Torquemada, the leader of the Spanish Inquisition. In our own time Hitler was the 'Agagite'; under the Third Reich it really did seem as if God had withdrawn completely from the world.

While the battle between Israel and Amalek is seen as ongoing throughout history, history itself does move forward towards an end-point: the last days when all the world will be judged, the world will return to its former perfection – as in Eden – and all peoples will enjoy the delights of the messianic age. The harbingers of this age, however, are regarded as historical figures whose appearance in the past assures their presence in the future.

ELIJAH

The Elijah of the Bible is a prophet of great and uncompromising zeal. Prophet during the reign of Ahab (ninth century BCE), he wages war on the idolatrous gods Baal and Asherah, killing 450 of their prophets (1 Kgs 18:40). His stance led him into direct conflict with the ruling house, which depended for its survival on good diplomatic relations – and marriages – with the neighbouring pagan kingdoms.

This made Elijah one of the great heroes of the Maccabean period (168 BCE) (1 Macc 2:58), where his example is set alongside that of Phinehas (Num 25:6–15), and both seem to have been emulated by Mattathias in his slaughter of those worshipping the statue of Antiochus (1 Macc 2:23–25). Yet, after the destruction of the Temple in 70 CE, the leader of the Jewish people was a completely contrasting character. Rabbi Johanan ben Zakkai was a pacifist who, according to legend, was smuggled out of besieged Jerusalem in a coffin. He then approached the general (soon to be emperor) Vespasian and made his peace with him. As a result of this new leadership image, the perception of Elijah underwent a transformation. His battles with Ahab and Jezebel are so interpreted as to make him the champion of the ordinary people against the might and wealth of the ruling class (1 Kgs 20). Much of Jewish folklore has Elijah wandering the earth in the disguise of a beggar who rewards those who are kind and charitable and brings punishment on those who cheat the poor. Above all, the prophet who killed 450 prophets of Baal is portrayed as a man of peace.

One of the most dramatic biblical stories is the account of how Elijah was translated to heaven in a fiery chariot (2 Kgs 2:1–11). This gives way to the notion that he never died, and returns to earth from time to time, to help rabbinic students get out of their difficulties when studying the Talmud, or to relieve oppression and right wrongs. But the most enduring belief is that of his return at the end of days. This has its basis in the Bible itself.

> Lo, I will send the prophet Elijah to you before the coming of the awesome, fearful day of the Lord. He shall reconcile parents with children and children with their parents, so that, when I come, I do not strike the whole land with utter destruction. (Mal 3:23–24)

Elijah becomes the forerunner of the Messiah, the announcer of the end of days, the proclaimer of the reign of peace and perfection. Thus it is that his company is sought in a great variety of Jewish rituals. It is in 'Elijah's chair' that a boy is circumcised. Elijah is one of the guests who enter the *sukkah*, and he is expected at every *seder* meal. His return is requested in the grace said after meals, and every Shabbat, at the close of the day, the ceremony of *Havdalah* concludes with a song enjoining him to come quickly.

> Elijah the prophet, Elijah the Tishbite, Elijah the Gileadite.
> Speedily in our days, let him come to us
> With the Messiah, the son of David.

DAVID

Of all the characters described in the Bible, more is written of David than anyone else. He is undoubtedly a historical figure, though much

103

of his life is embellished with legend, inevitable for a character whose youth and attractiveness, and brave deeds, would make him an obvious national hero. But the biblical account stays away from the miraculous. David is deeply religious, and his actions are motivated by a desire to serve God, but God does not 'act' in his story in quite the same way as he did for Moses.

David was a shrewd politician and diplomat, as well as a military leader of unquestioned ability, and his conquests brought Israel vast tracts of land way beyond the boundaries promised to Abraham, bringing many of the surrounding nations under Israelite suzerainty. But David's most significant achievement was to unite the different tribes more or less successfully under his leadership. He did this by capturing Jerusalem – a Jebusite city that was not part of the original division of the land, and so excited no tribal claim (2 Sam, 5:6–10). This he made his capital, and centralized all administration so that tribal leaders and officials would be obliged to reside there. He then divided the land into twelve districts, but districts that did not correspond with the original apportioning of the land to the twelve tribes. He made Jerusalem the home of the Tabernacle (2 Sam 6:1–15), and prepared to build a temple there, thus centralizing the cult. Finally, he made the High Priest subject to him, and the Levitical priests, who operated throughout the land, his agents.

To aid this policy, the 'myth' of Jerusalem as the city of God was actively encouraged. We see it reflected where David decides to build a temple: 'See now, I dwell in a house of cedar, but the ark of God dwells in a tent (2 Sam 7:2). In a dream, God tells David that he will not build the temple but that his son will.

> When your days are done and you lie with your fathers, I will raise up your offspring after you, one of your own issue, and I will establish his kingship. He shall build a house for My name, and I will establish his royal throne forever. I will be a father to him, and he shall be a son to Me. (2 Sam 7:12–14)

A link is made here between Jerusalem, as God's house, and the Davidic line, established 'forever'. This is made even more explicit in Psalm 132, which describes the bringing of the ark to Jerusalem (cf. 2 Sam 6).

> For the Lord has chosen Zion;
> He has desired it for His seat.

'This is my resting-place for all time;
    here I will dwell, for I desure it.
I will amply bless its store of food,
    give its needy their fill of bread.
I will cloth its priests in victory,
    its loyal ones shall sing for joy.
There I will make a horn sprout for David;
    I have prepared a lamp for My anointed one.
I will clothe his enemies in disgrace,
    while on him his crown shall sparkle.'
(Ps 132:13–18)

It receives its classic formulation on the completion of the Temple building.

... 'I have heard the prayer and the supplication which you have offered to Me. I consecrate this House which you have built and I set My name there forever. My eyes and My heart shall ever be there. As for you, if you walk before Me as your father David walked before Me, wholeheartedly and with uprightness, doing all that I have commanded you [and] Keeping my laws and My rules, then I will establish your throne of kingship over Israel as I promised your father David, saying, 'Your line on the throne of Israel shall never end.' (I Kgs 9:5)

But despite the assurances of eternity intended to boost David's position, the tribal rivalries soon overcame the central monarchy. After Solomon's death, the vast Davidic empire, stretching from the Euphrates to Egypt, was divided and eroded till the Northern Kingdom was no more, and eventually the Southern Kingdom followed it.

The descriptions of David's eternal greatness were reinterpreted into the hope that one day, in the future, his descendants would once more rule over a united Israel:

In that day,
I will set up again the fallen booth of David;
I will mend its breaches and set up its ruins anew.
I will build it firm as in the days of old,
So that they shall possess the rest of Edom
And all the nations once attached to My name
– declares the Lord who will bring this to pass.
(Amos 9:11–12)

At the same time, a shift in emphasis is perceived, from the emphasis on the eternity of the dynasty to the character of the future king.

In token of abundant authority
And of peace without limit
Upon David's throne and kingdom,
That it may be firmly established
In justice and in equity
Now and evermore. (Isa 9:6)

On the return from Babylonian exile, the Temple was rebuilt, but the Davidic dynasty was never restored to the throne.

When the Hasmonean leader Aristobulus took upon himself the kingship (104 BCE), and when the Romans dispensed with the monarchy and destroyed the Temple (70 CE), the motif of kingship and Jerusalem, exile and return, had developed an eschatological as well as political side. As one of the pseudepigraphical Psalms of Solomon says:

> Behold, O Lord and raise up unto them their king, the son of David, At the time in which Thou seest, O God, that he may reign over Israel Thy servant.
> And that he may purge Jerusalem from nations that trample her down to destruction ...
> And he shall gather together a holy people, whom he shall lead in righteousness. And he shall judge the tribes of the people that has been sanctified by the Lord his God. And he shall not suffer unrighteousness to lodge any more in their midst, Nor shall there dwell with them any man that knoweth wickedness. For he shall know them, that they are all sons of their God. (17:23–25)

The king of David's line has become the Messiah, the Anointed of God. His role in rabbinic literature is various. He will do battle against Israel's enemies and win. He will gather the exiled of Israel back to the land and restore each tribe to its original inheritance (the very inheritance that the original David tried to downplay). The Messiah will also, it seems, act as judge alongside God, and he will establish the rule of justice and peace, and reign over a perfected world till the end of time.

The belief in a Messiah who would come and restore Israel and the world in this manner has kept Jews alive in hope at times of the deepest persecution. During the Holocaust, the words of Moses Maimonides' twelfth article of faith became a watchword for those in concentration camps:

> 'I believe with perfect faith in the coming of the Messiah; and though he tarry, yet will I wait daily for his coming.' (*Authorised Daily Prayer Book*, p. 255)

With the establishment of the state of Israel in 1948, Jews once more were in possession of the land of Israel, and the ingathering of the exiles from the camps of Europe, from North Africa and the Yemen began. The messianic age seemed to some to have arrived. Yet many religious leaders were against the establishment of the state on the grounds that the Messiah had not yet come and that to settle in Israel before then would be a blasphemy. Such a view is now a minority one, and most people distinguish between the Jewish state and the messianic kingdom which is to be established from on high.

Some of the Lubavitch Hasidim are convinced that the Messiah was here in the person of their late leader, Rabbi Shneerson. Their posters announce his imminent return as 'King Messiah', but this depends upon the penitence of all Jews living today. Thus messianic belief is today as strong as it has ever been.

Jerusalem is once again in Jewish hands, but the reign of peace and love is not yet at hand. So Jews today express their longing at Pesach, no longer in the traditional wish 'Next year in Jerusalem', but in the extended 'Next year in Jerusalem rebuilt', demonstrating their hope for a new David to dance once more with the Ark to Zion.

THE END OF TIME

The ingathering of the exiles is not necessarily the end. Judaism looks beyond to a point where time itself ends. Beliefs abound that when the Messiah comes there will be cosmic turmoil, a general resurrection, a judgement, and ultimately a time when all live in perfect peace and harmony.

Much of Judaism's eschatology is hazy and contradictory. Its ideas stem from Babylonian influences, but these have never been made their own in the way that so much of earlier mythology had been. Perhaps it is that Jews are better at looking back than looking forward, and of seeing life in the context of time rather than beyond it.

Jewish history and hope are ultimately summed up in Zechariah, who looks back to creation as well as forward to the end of time when all humanity is once again unified in its obedience to God:

> And there shall be continuous day ... of neither day nor night, and there shall be light at eventide.
> In that day, fresh water shall flow from Jerusalem, part of it to the Eastern Sea and part of the Western Sea, throughout the summer and winter.

107

And the Lord shall be king over all the earth; in that day there shall be one Lord with one name. (Zech 14:7–9)

Notes

The Biblical translations are taken from *Tanakh: The Holy Scriptures*. Philadelphia: Jewish Publication Society, 1985.

1　Abraham Joshua Heschel (1955) *God in Search of Man*. New York: Scribners, p. 206.
2　An epic recounting the triumph and kingship of the god Marduk over the first gods of the primordial waters, recited at the Babylonian New Year Festival.
3　BT *Bava Bathra* 75a, *Leviticus Rabba* 13:3, 22:10.
4　Jewish communities that originate in Germany or eastern Europe.
5　Translated by Raphael Loewe, in (1954) *Service of the Synagogue*. London: Routledge and Kegan Paul.
6　Gaster (1969), p. 32.
7　Graves and Patai (1964), p. 80.
8　Yehezkiel Kaufman (1972) *The Religion of Israel*. New York: Schocken, p. 295.
9　*Bereshit Rabba* 38:13.
10　Hooke (1963).
11　W. F. Albright (1957) *From Stone Age to Christianity*. New York: Anchor.
12　G. von Rad (1965) *Old Testament Theology*. Edinburgh: Oliver & Boyd.
13　The Passover Haggadah. For a good translation and commentary see Chaim Raphael (1972) *A Feast of History*. London: Weidenfeld and Nicolson.
14　See also Isaiah 51:9–11.
15　Compare Marduk and Baal, p. 83 above.

References and further reading

Childs, B. S. (1959) *Myth and Reality in the Old Testament*. London: SCM.
Freedman, H. and Simon, M. (eds) (1939) *The Midrash Rabbah*. London: Soncino.
Gaster, Theodore H. (1969) *Myth, Legend and Custom in the Old Testament*. New York: Harper & Row.
Ginzberg, Louis (1909) *The Legends of the Jews*. Philadelphia: Jewish Publication Society.

Graves, Robert and Patai, Raphael (1964) *Hebrew Myths*. London: Cassell.

Hooke, S. H. (1963) *Middle Eastern Mythology*. London: Penguin.

Nicholson, E. W. (1973) *Exodus and Sinai in History and Tradition*. Oxford: Basil Blackwell.

Roth, Cecil (ed.) (1972) *Encyclopaedia Judaica*. Jerusalem: Keter.

Scholem, G. (1971) *The Messianic Idea in Judaism*. New York: Schocken.

Seters, J. van (1983) *Abraham in History and Tradition*. New Haven, CT: Yale University Press.

4. Sacred writings

Alan Unterman

The sacred literature of Judaism consists of a vast collection of texts, some dating back thousands of years and others composed in the recent past. In general, the older the text the more sacred it is considered to be, since it is closer to the textual revelation to Moses and the Israelites at Mount Sinai after their exodus from slavery in Egypt. Later writings are regarded as essentially interpretations and applications of the holy teachings of the past. The most up-to-date writings, though they lack the sanctity of early texts, carry great authority for the Jews because they draw on the views of all the sages of the past in formulating their conclusions.

Jewish sacred literature is traditionally divided into two categories: the Written Teaching, *torah she-bikhtav*, and the Oral Teaching, *torah she-baal peh*. As we shall see, the Hebrew term *torah*, translated here as 'teaching', is used both narrowly and broadly, and may refer not only to the Pentateuch or to the Hebrew Bible, but also to the whole of the Jewish tradition.

The Written Teaching

The Written Teaching consists of 24 books of the Hebrew Bible divided into three sections: *torah* (henceforth Torah), *nevi'im* ('Prophets') and *ketuvim* ('Writings'), known by the acronym *TeNaKh*. The Torah, or Pentateuch, contains Genesis, Exodus, Leviticus, Numbers and Deuteronomy (in Hebrew: *bereshit, shemot, vayikra, bemidbar, devarim*).

The 'Prophets' contain the books of Joshua, Judges, 1 and 2 Samuel and 1 and 2 Kings – known collectively as the 'Early Prophets', plus

Isaiah, Jeremiah, Ezekiel and the Twelve Minor Prophets (Hosea, Joel, Amos, Obadiah, Jonah, Micah, Nahum, Habakkuk, Zephaniah, Haggai, Zechariah and Malachi), known collectively as the 'Later Prophets'. The 'Writings' contain Psalms, Proverbs, Job, Song of Songs, Ruth, Lamentations, Ecclesiastes, Esther, Daniel, Ezra–Nehemiah and 1 and 2 Chronicles.

THE TORAH

The Torah is the central text of the Hebrew Bible. It is believed to contain the primary revelation from God to the greatest of the prophets, Moses, known in the Jewish tradition as 'Moses our Rabbi', who received the divine teaching face to face in the most direct way. These Five Books of Moses are also known as the *humash* (i.e. 'fifth', a popular abbreviation of *hamishah humshei torah*, 'the five fifths of the Torah').

The Torah tells of the story of humanity from the beginning of the world to the death of Moses. The main religious motifs are the creation of the first human couple, Adam and Eve, who ate the forbidden fruit in the Garden of Eden and were expelled from Paradise; the story of Noah's ark and the flood; the call of Abraham, the first 'Jew'; the life of the patriarchs; the slavery of the Israelites in Egypt; their redemption by God through the agency of Moses; the crossing of the Red Sea; the theophany at Mount Sinai and the giving of the Ten Commandments; the worship of the golden calf; and the desire of the Israelites to return to Egypt after the report of the ten spies about the land of Canaan.

The forty years' wandering in the wilderness which followed was a punishment for their lack of faith. During these years the remaining divine laws were revealed to the Israelites about subjects such as the Sacred Year, ritual purity, the Tabernacle and the sacrifices, correct behaviour between humans summarized in the command 'You shall love your neighbour as yourself, I am the Lord' (Lev 19:18), social mores and dietary requirements. The Pentateuch ends with the death of Moses after he had led the people of Israel to the borders of the promised land.

111

PROPHETS

It is believed that the books of the *nevi'im* were written by the prophets through the gift of prophecy, and they tell the story of the Israelites after they entered the promised land. The people were first ruled by judges until the prophet Samuel anointed Saul as the first king of Israel. He was succeeded by King David, who conquered Jerusalem and made it his capital. The first Temple was built in Jerusalem by David's son, Solomon, since David was not considered suitable to build the 'House of the Lord' because his hands were stained by the blood he had shed as a warrior king.

After the death of Solomon, who had taxed the people heavily to support both his building projects and his opulent lifestyle, the Holy Land was divided between the ten tribes in the Northern Kingdom of Israel and the two tribes who supported the Davidic dynasty in the Southern Kingdom of Judah. The Books of Kings tell of the corruption of kingly rule in Israel and Judah, where many of the kings 'did evil in the sight of the Lord'.

This culminated in the conquest of the Northern Kingdom by the Assyrians in 721 BCE and the exile of its inhabitants, who came to be known as 'the ten lost tribes'. The Southern Kingdom continued in precarious existence till 586 BCE when Jerusalem and the First Temple were destroyed by the Babylonians and the Judeans were taken into exile in Babylonia. The religious heroes of this second section of the *TeNaKh* are characters like Ruth, Deborah and Samson from the period of the judges, prophets like Samuel, Elijah, Elisha, Isaiah, Jeremiah and Ezekiel as well as minor prophets whose sayings and prophecies are recorded in the books named after them, and those kings of Israel and Judah who sought to eradicate idolatry and to live according to the teachings of Moses and the prophets.

WRITINGS

The *ketuvim* are books believed to be written under the influence of the Holy Spirit, a lesser degree of inspiration than prophecy. They contain works of Wisdom literature, like Proverbs and Ecclesiastes; devotional works like the Book of Psalms, which is much used in the later liturgy of Judaism; works in historical form, like Chronicles, Esther and Ezra–Nehemiah, which take the history of Israel up to the return from captivity and the rebuilding of the Second Temple.

According to the rabbinic tradition, Moses wrote the five books of the Pentateuch like a scribe copying from an ancient text. Indeed, the Pentateuch, in its heavenly form, pre-existed the world and was used by God as a blueprint of the creation. Rabbinic tradition said that Moses also wrote the book of Job, Joshua wrote the book of Joshua and also, according to one view, the last eight verses of the Pentateuch which tell of the death of Moses.

The prophet Samuel wrote the books of Samuel, the book of Judges and the book of Ruth. King David wrote the book of Psalms. Jeremiah wrote the book of Jeremiah, the books of Kings and the book of Lamentations. King Hezekiah and his associates wrote down the book of Isaiah, and the books of Proverbs, Song of Songs and Ecclesiastes (the last three originally composed by King Solomon). The Men of the Great Assembly wrote down the book of Ezekiel, the Twelve Minor Prophets, the books of Daniel and of Esther. Ezra wrote the book of Ezra and the major part of the books of Chronicles.

The Oral Teaching

The Oral Torah consists, in its widest sense, of the whole interpretative tradition which bases itself on scripture. It is important to note that the term 'Torah' is used here to refer to all of Jewish religious literature as well as the Pentateuch. Since *torah* means 'teaching', the term implies that God is the divine teacher who gives his teaching to the people of Israel, and through them to the world. When Moses ascended Mount Sinai he received not only the whole of scripture but also all future development of the Judaic tradition:

> At Mount Sinai Moses received the Ten Commandments, the Pentateuch, the Mishnah, the Prophets and Hagiographa, the Talmud, and even what the Scribes would innovate in the future. (Babylonian Talmud (BT), *Berachot* 5a and *Megillah* 19b)

Though of divine origin, Torah is always open-ended, and each statement, whether in the Bible, the Talmud, the codes, or theological texts, has to be interpreted and argued about by scholars. It is viewed from different perspectives rather than taken literally. By its very nature Torah has to be studied before it can be effectively implemented in the life of the community and in the life of the individual.

113

MIDRASH

The division between the Written Teaching and the Oral Teaching does not simply represent two parallel types of sacred literature, one written, one oral. The Written Torah does not exist as an independent literary genre, even though it is concretely expressed in the canonical text. The Hebrew Bible never stands on its own, it exists as scripture only within the context of the Oral Torah. The meaning of the written word is not given, even though there is a level of quasi-literal meaning (*peshat*) which recurs throughout the interpretative matrix.

This dependence of the Written Torah on the Oral Torah is illustrated by a rabbinic story told of the first-century sage Hillel. Once, a would-be convert came to Hillel and asked to be converted to Judaism, but the heathen wanted to accept only the Written Scripture, not the Oral Teachings. Hillel, surprisingly, agreed to accept him as a convert and began to teach him the Hebrew alphabet so he could study the written text. Next day Hillel continued with this lesson but this time he taught him the alphabet in the reverse order. The heathen objected, and Hillel replied that he wanted to show him that even to read the written text he needed to rely on oral teachings. How much more would this be true if he wanted to *understand* the written teaching (BT, *Shabbat* 31a).

The point of this story is that the Bible can be approached only through tradition, albeit a somewhat open-ended tradition. Since texts are opaque or, what amounts to the same thing, highly ambiguous, their meaning and message have to be searched out. The process of this exegetical searching out (*derash*) is characteristic of Jewish thought, and it is this method which shaped a vast body of hermeneutical literature known as *midrash*.

The Pentateuch contains brief references to the main body of Jewish law (*halakhah*) which presupposes a much wider unwritten background. Around these seminal references a variety of different interpretations grew up in the rabbinic schools of Palestine, and these were collected in halakhic *midrashim*, which in the main date back to the first few centuries CE. A little later in origin are those *midrashim* which deal with the non-halakhic parts of Jewish teaching (*aggadah*). Most of the aggadic *midrashim* involve the expansion of biblical stories, bringing in a host of folkloristic and theological themes. *Midrash* in general is thought to be the earliest type of Oral Torah literature, although those works of *midrash* which have survived were finally edited in the post-Talmudic period.

BIBLICAL COMMENTARY AND INTERPRETATION

Since the Hebrew Bible exists within a tradition of interpretation, the text is always in need of explication and from the early Talmudic period, side by side with the composition of the early midrashic collections, biblical commentaries serving specific interests began to be composed. The commentaries are the key to understanding the relevance and message of the Bible, and are the main repository of new ideas, new philosophies, and new approaches to Judaism. The earliest of these commentaries are the Aramaic *targumim*, which were composed in the early centuries of the common era for Jews who spoke Aramaic, the lingua franca of the whole Middle East. Since Hebrew had become a literary language and the preserve of scholars, the *targumim* are in essence translations (the word *targum* actually means 'translation'), but they vary greatly from each other. *Targum Onkelos*, the most famous *targum*, sticks closely to the text, alluding to midrashic interpretation and paraphrasing the anthropomorphisms of biblical Hebrew, while others introduce much midrashic material set among the translation of the text.

It was considered mandatory for every person to read the weekly portion of the Pentateuch twice to themselves, together with one reading of a translation. Throughout the early Middle Ages *Onkelos* was read regularly as the translation of the weekly Torah portion, and was indeed considered to be an inspired work. Aramaic ceased to be a spoken language, even among Babylonian Jews, after the spread of Islam brought Arabic in its wake. Many people therefore preferred to use the biblical commentary of Rashi (R. Shelomoh Yitzchaki, 1040–1105), which presents a somewhat literal interpretation of the text, and was written in a simple Hebrew style, using many Aramaic words, and translating difficult expressions into medieval French.

Rashi belonged to the Franco-German tradition, which subsequently gave rise to the Ashkenazi sub-culture. Ashkenazim were Jews who lived mainly in Christian Europe and whose lingua franca was Yiddish (a Jewish dialect of medieval German). When these Jews settled in the Slavic countries of central and eastern Europe, they took Yiddish with them and also the literature, customs and foods of

Germany and Austria. A distinctive Jewish life-style, known as *yid-dishkeit*, characterized the Ashkenazi world which, in the nineteenth and early twentieth centuries, was centred on Poland, Russia, Lithuania and the Austro-Hungarian Empire.

The other main grouping of Jews in the late Middle Ages were the Sephardim, or Jews of Spanish origin. After their expulsion from the Iberian peninsula, in the 1490s, Sephardim took their highly sophisticated Spanish-Jewish culture to the Netherlands, North Africa, the Levant and into the Islamic world of the Middle East and Asia. Some of them preserved Judeo-Spanish (sometimes called Ladino) (a Jewish dialect of Spanish) as their lingua franca, and maintained their Sephardi identity where they settled by preserving their own customs, by marrying only into other Sephardi families and even by putting the two Hebrew letters 'S' and 'T', standing for *sefardi tahor* ('pure Sephardi') after their name.

The Ashkenazim, who became the dominant Jewish sub-group in the late Middle Ages, revered Rashi. In the course of time, some of the sanctity associated with *Onkelos* attached to Rashi, and his interpretation of a verse became *the* interpretation in the popular consciousness. His writings were also popular among Sephardim.

The standard Hebrew Bibles print the biblical text together with *Onkelos* and sometimes one or two other Aramaic *targumim*. They also include Rashi's commentary and that of his grandson Rashbam (R. Samuel ben Meir, 1080–1174). The latter is more literal than his grandfather in his commentary and he does not include any midrashic stories. This, together with the fact that he sometimes criticizes Rashi's interpretations and that some of his comments run counter to traditional rabbinic exegesis, meant he never achieved a high level of popular acceptance. Many commentaries were actually written on Rashi's commentary, defending it from the criticism of other commentators.

A number of Sephardi commentaries are also usually included in standard Bible editions. The best known are those of Abraham ibn Ezra (1089–1164), a Spanish grammarian and philosophical exegete who has harsh things to say about interpretations he disagrees with, even when they are of talmudic origin, and of Ramban (R. Moses ben Nachman, 1194–1270), a Spanish mystic. Ramban had to flee Spain after defending Judaism too vigorously against Christianity when he was forced to participate in the Disputation of Barcelona in 1263. A number of super-commentaries exist both on ibn Ezra and on Ramban.

THE MISHNAH

At the beginning of the third century CE collections of halakhic material, extracted from their original location in *midrash*, were gathered together and eventually formed into the Mishnah, the first published work of the Oral Torah. It was composed in Hebrew, although it was not originally written down (since there was opposition to the writing down of oral material) but was memorized. It contains 60 tractates divided into six sections:

1 'Seeds', covering agricultural laws and benedictions.

2 'Festivals', covering the Sabbath, the festivals and the fasts of the sacred year.

3 'Women', covering marriage, divorce and vows.

4 'Damages', covering duties and responsibilities in interpersonal and business relations, the function of law courts and the punishments meted out for crimes. This section also includes five chapters on ethical matters known as the 'Chapters of the Fathers' (*Pirkei Avot*).

5 'Holy Things', covering the Temple, the sacrificial rite and the dietary laws.

6 'Purities', covering categories of ritual purity and impurity.

The Mishnah is not simply a code, since it contains dissenting views mentioning the names and opinions of some 128 individual authorities who are known as *tannaim*. A *tanna* is a sage of the mishnaic period, the term coming from a root meaning 'to repeat'. Originally it seems to have referred merely to someone who had memorized the text without necessarily understanding what he knew, but eventually it became a title of honour and authority.

The Mishnah also does not touch upon some central rituals which would have been included in a code. Thus there is nothing about the laws relating to phylacteries (*tefillin*), the *mezuzah* parchment onthe doors of a house, the fringes (*tzitzit*) on the corners of the garment, the Torah scroll (*sefer torah*), or the liturgical formula of the *amidah* prayer which is at the centre of the daily services. The medieval authority Maimonides, in his commentary on the Mishnah (*Menahot* 4:1), explained that all these matters were sufficiently well known to ordinary Jews from regular practice not to make it necessary to include them in the text.

Thus the Mishnah is more like a textbook for the study of Jewish law than a code which seeks to lay down the halakhic norms. We cannot be sure what actually motivated Rabbi Judah the Prince and his colleagues to edit the mishnaic text, but they presented the Jewish scholarly world with an authoritative collection of the main halakhic views, and excluded much material which they did not regard as reliable. Since they severed the dependence of rabbinic learning on the Bible text, as found in *midrash*, the redaction of the Mishnah signified a breakthrough in religious consciousness.

The Mishnah acted as a stimulus to the process of gathering the material of the Oral Torah. Other collections of material similar in nature to that contained in the Mishnah have also survived. There is a work known as the *Tosefta*, which is regarded by some authorities as an early commentary on the Mishnah, but there are citations of mishnaic-style material in rabbinic literature known as *beraitah* (pl. *beraitot*), 'extraneous' material which had not been incorporated in the Mishnah.

The Mishnah was regarded as having originated with the oral traditions taught by Moses to the Israelites in explanation of the Pentateuch, and as such was a holy text. Indeed, the ethical section of the Mishnah, the 'Chapters of the Fathers', opens with the declaration:

> Moses received Torah from Sinai and handed it to Joshua, Joshua to the Elders, the Elders to the Prophets, and the Prophets handed it on to Men of the Great Assembly. They said three things: Be deliberate in judgement, raise up many disciples and make a fence around the Torah.

The implication of this is that the sayings of the sages about ethics, let alone those about *halakhah* and *aggadah* in other parts of the Mishnah, are aspects of the Torah which Moses received from God. Even the rabbinic enactments, most of which involved 'making fences round the Torah', were all part of the revelation at Sinai.

The study of the Mishnah was thought to help the souls of dead relatives to progress in their spiritual journey after death, the Hebrew letters of the word *mishnah*, when rearranged, spelling the word for 'soul', *neshamah*. A section of the Mishnah is thus studied in a house of mourning or on the anniversary of someone's death (*yahrzeit* in Yiddish). In the late Middle Ages one leading rabbi, Joseph Caro, was even possessed by the spirit of the Mishnah (known as a *maggid* or daemon), when he studied the mishnaic text with great devotion. This spirit conveyed messages to him from the heavenly world which Caro recorded in a diary published as *Maggid Mesharim*.

THE TALMUD

The intense study of the Mishnah in the academies of Palestine and Babylonia led to the compilation of the Palestinian Talmud in the fourth century CE and the Babylonian Talmud 100 years later. These two editions of the Talmud were known respectively as the *Yerushalmi* (i.e. 'Jerusalem', though, the Palestinian Talmud was not actually redacted there), and the *Bavli* (i.e. 'Babylonian'). The Bavli became the most authoritative rabbinic text of Judaism, since the Jewish community of Babylonia dominated the Jewish world for five or six hundred years after the completion of the Babylonian Talmud. Because of the particular interests of Babylonian Jewry, certain parts of the Mishnah, e.g., those dealing with the agricultural laws applicable essentially in the land of Israel, were not dealt with at any length in the Bavli, although they do occupy a large section of the Yerushalmi.

The two Talmuds differ in many substantial ways. The Bavli is more developed than the earlier version of the Talmud edited in Palestine, since the Babylonian academies in which the material was shaped were larger and of a higher calibre than their Palestinian counterparts. Folklore, angelology and magic play a larger part in the *aggadah* of the Bavli than of the Yerushalmi, reflecting the different cultural milieu. Babylonian civilization was heavily influenced by Persian religion, and Persian terms appear quite frequently in the Eastern Aramaic of the Bavli.

TALMUDIC STUDY

Since the Bavli was the principal subject of study in the Babylonian academies, it dominated Jewish thought in the post-talmudic period. So neglected was the Yerushalmi that the text has been preserved in a highly unsatisfactory condition, with many corrupt readings and textual variants. The Babylonian Talmud is in a much better state of preservation.

The Bavli is thought of as an ocean, and its study is like setting sail on a voyage of discovery. The more this talmudic ocean is explored, the more it reveals new landscapes of the mind and of the spirit to the traveller. Sages, after years of study and experience, are involved in the talmudic adventure just as much as young boys who begin to study the text for the first time. The sage will already have studied thousands of pages of the Talmud, perhaps even knowing much of it by heart. Yet he may well spend his mature years trying to reconcile contradictory interpretations of abstruse talmudic discussions.

The beginner, by contrast, must learn how to pronounce strange Hebrew and Aramaic words, and how to translate and interpret the many technical terms and colloquial phrases which convey the talmudic outlook. For instance:

'No one can make someone else an agent to commit a sin', i.e. everyone is responsible for his or her actions and no one can say in extenuation 'So-and-so told me to do this'.

'An individual's opinion is nullified by the opinion of all men', i.e. the *halakhah* deals with normal ways of behaviour and does not consider grossly eccentric behaviour in formulating law.

'The law of the kingdom is law', i.e. Jews must accept that the civil law, but not the religious law, of the land they live in has validity for them also.

'He who wishes to remove something already in the possession of his fellow must prove his case', i.e. the law puts the onus upon the person who wishes to change the *status quo* to bring evidence.

'Property that a law court declared ownerless (*hefker*) is indeed ownerless', i.e. for the sake of maintaining justice, a properly constituted Jewish law court can actually remove property from its owner.

'One may act effectively to benefit someone even if they are absent', i.e. where real benefit accrues to a person one may act on their behalf even without their express permission.

'Someone who is half slave and half free man', i.e. the slave of two partners who has been freed by only one of them. He inhabits an halakhic no-man's-land. A number of issues are tested against this case to show where the boundaries are of slavery, of freedom, of marriage and of ritual action in general.

'A person should allow himself to be killed rather than transgress', i.e. whereas the saving of life takes precedence over the commandments in normal circumstances, there are some commandments that one must not transgress even to save one's life, and some circumstances when a Jew must be prepared to die even for the sake of something relatively trivial.

In a *yeshivah* academy the Talmud is studied by groups of two students, *havruta*, who read the text together and argue out its interpretation at the tops of their voices. This high-resonance learning is meant to aid the memory and to allow the expression of emotion as well as intellect in the learning process. The study of the Torah is both learning and worship.

This all comes as quite a shock to those who enter the study hall (*bet ha-midrash*) of a *yeshivah* for the first time, particularly if they are used to an academic library. In the *yeshivah* the ocean of the Talmud generates rivers of sound flowing across the hall as the *havruta* groups join together in fours and sixes to discuss a particularly knotty problem with each other, and then sub-divide to return to paired study. There is the chanting and singing of the text, which sometimes involves the constant repetition of key phrases till their particular significance is grasped in context.

Much of the chanting, however, is not actually words from the text but interjections from the student: '*Oi oi oi*', '*Vai vai vai*'. 'What kind of a question is being asked here by *tosefot* (medieval commentators given to asking complicated questions)? *Nu nu nu.*' 'This is a difficult problem of Rabbi Akiva Eger (a pre-modern talmudic commentator). Difficult, so difficult. *Ai ai ai.*'

Together with the ability to analyse issues, and the improvisation of traditional Talmud tunes, a further prerequisite for Talmud study is knowing how to use one's thumb to follow the thread of an argument. The hand is swung round the thumb as axis, while at the same time the thumb is tilted now to the right now to the left. There is no explanation of what exactly the thumb adds to the debate but it is widely used even by those who are silently following someone else's exposition. The head nods in agreement and the thumb tilts as the argument develops.

121

RESPONSA

The prestige of the Bavli was guarded by the leaders of Babylonian Jewry in the post-talmudic period. These sages were known as *geonim* (*gaon* = 'excellence', henceforth Geonim). The Geonim were recognized as supreme halakhic authorities by most of Jewry. They replied to questions from all over the Jewish world about the meaning of obscure passages in the Talmud, as well as about practical matters such as rules of prayer, ritual and conduct. These terse geonic answers to inquiries initiated a whole genre of responsa (*she'elot uteshuvot*, literally 'questions and answers'), which soon became the most prolific source for the determination of the *halakhah*.

The vastness of this responsa literature came about because many rabbis penned letters to colleagues, discussing halakhic issues which raised novel points of law and seeking their colleagues' opinions. Although only a small fraction of this literature was intended for publication, responsa were collected together by pupils or members of the respondent's family and were eventually published. They reflect a wealth of social detail because of the need to discuss the realia lying behind particular problems. Part of this vast responsa literature is considered of only minor importance and rarely studied, while some collections of responsa are standard texts on the curriculum of most *yeshivah* academies.

All the major events of Jewish history are reflected in responsa literature. Thus wars and pogroms left hundreds of women, whose husbands had disappeared, as *agunot*, unable to remarry without solid proof of their widowhood. They turned to leading rabbis, seeking permission to remarry, and these rabbis had to investigate the precise circumstances under which death might have taken place before accepting that their husbands had died.

The major theological issues and movements which characterized Jewish life also find their reflection in responsa. Rabbis were asked questions on a great variety of topics. Can one study philosophy or is it a prohibited form of Gentile culture? Can one teach the Bible to Christians and Muslims? What is the status of Jews who have converted to another faith, and particularly of those who have been forcibly converted? Who can engage in the study of the mystical texts of *Kabbalah*, and what is one to do when the prescriptions of the *Kabbalah* conflict with the *halakhah* as laid down in the Talmud or in the codes? How can one know if the Messiah has arrived? Can one change the Ashkenazi prayer-book to bring it more in line with Sephardi practice favoured by the medieval kabbalists? Are members of the nineteenth-century Hasidic movement heretics? Can reforms be made to the synagogue liturgy, such as the introduction of shorter services, of choirs and organs, of vernacular prayers and a sermon to rectify the lack of decorum? Or are all such measures, which were favoured by early Reform Judaism, prohibited to traditional Jews?

CODES

Side by side with responsa, the *halakhah* was shaped by the codes of Jewish law which began to be produced in the geonic period. The most far-reaching of these law books is the great code of Maimonides (1136–1204), known as the *Mishneh Torah* ('Second Torah') or *Yad Ha-hazakah* ('The Strong Hand'), which not only covers the practical *halakhah* applicable to the life of the community and the individual, but also deals with theological ideas, with the dogmatic beliefs definitive of Jewish Orthodoxy, with laws relating to the Temple, as well as the laws of the messianic age.

Maimonides says in his introduction that his book summarizes all the laws contained in Talmudic literature:

> So that a person should not need to refer to any other work in the world concerning a law of the laws of Israel, but this book should be a collection of the whole Oral Torah ... For a person may firstly read the Written Torah and after that read this work and know from it the whole Oral Torah, and not need to read any other work in between them. (Introduction to the *Yad*)

His work was considered highly controversial because he seemed to claim that his was the final word on *halakhic* decision-making. He was criticized because he did not include any references to the sources from which he drew his conclusions, nor any indication of how he arrived at a conclusion in areas where there was considerably dispute among earlier authorities. Traditionalists also objected to his philosophical chapters, believing that they were more Aristotle than Moses, and refused to study the theological sections of the *Yad*.

The code which today is the most authoritative guide to normative *halakhah* is the *Shulhan Arukh* (literally 'Prepared Table'). This was written by R. Joseph Caro (1488–1575), a Sephardi authority who based his conclusions on the majority views of three of his predecessors, two of whom were Sephardim. The language which Caro used was borrowed to a large extent from Maimonides' code. An Ashkenazi halakhist from Poland, R. Moses Isserles (1525–72), composed glosses on the *Shulhan Arukh* reflecting the Ashkenazi position of which Caro had not given sufficient coverage. Isserles' glosses were known as the *Mappah* ('Tablecloth') and they were printed together with Carol's text. This combination of Sephardi and Ashkenazi viewpoints, coming soon after the introduction of Hebrew printing, made the *Shulhan Arukh* acceptable to wide sections of Jewry.

The fourfold division of material which Caro used was borrowed from the format of a previous code, the *Arbaah Turim*, on which he had written a learned commentary. His subject matter was thus divided up into the following:

1 *Orah haim* ('The Way of Life'), dealing with prayers, Sabbath and festival rituals.

2 *Yoreh deah* ('Teaching Knowledge'), containing laws of concern to the communal rabbi who has to decide matters concerning ritual slaughter, the dietary laws, mourning and menstruation.

3 *Even ha-ezer* ('The Stone of Helping'), dealing with marriage and divorce.

4 *Hoshen mishpat* ('The Breastplate of Judgement'), containing the laws of how a law court should function and the way people should behave in business.

Since the sixteenth century many commentaries and super-commentaries have been written on the *Shulhan Arukh*, and shortened or updated versions of the code have appeared. These provide easy reference for the layperson and include new technological and medical issues which affect *halakhic* behaviour in modern times. Unlike Maimonides' code, the *Shulhan Arukh* deals only with practical *halakhah* and ignores issues which are not germane to the life of the individual Jew or to the Jewish community and its institutions. The most popular simplified version of the *Shulhan Arukh* is the *Kitzur Shulhan Arukh* ('Shortened *Shulhan Arukh*'), written by Solomon Ganzfried

(1804–86) in Hungary, which has been translated into English and into a number of European languages.

The beginning of philosophy

Neither the Hebrew Bible nor the Talmud was particularly interested in doctrinal matters or in putting forward a coherent theology of Judaism. There are scattered references to the belief in one deity, to the prohibitions of worshipping others' gods or idols, to the authority of the revelation given to Moses and the prophets, to life after death and the resurrection of the body, to the divine justice which guides the world, punishing sinners and rewarding the righteous, and to the redemption to come in the messianic age. Particularly in the Babylonian Talmud and in midrashic literature, there are a myriad of folkloristic beliefs whose status as doctrine is never made clear.

The impetus for the development of Jewish philosophy came from Arabic translations of the writings of Plato and Aristotle, and it was essentially through the Muslim culture of the Middle Ages that Greek philosophy entered Jewish thought in a substantial way. In Muslim lands, where a more tolerant and intellectually liberal approach could be found than in Christendom, Jews were encouraged by the example of Islamic philosophy to apply Greek thought patterns to their own religion. This was partly out of necessity, because young, intellectually aware Jews were being attracted away from their own beliefs into the neutral territory which an interest in Greek thought had created. It was also to enable Jews to justify Jewish belief to philosophically minded Muslims and Christians.

Many of the early works of Jewish philosophy were written in Arabic, which was the lingua franca of the Jews in Muslim countries. The supporters of a philosophically orientated Judaism reshaped their religion, in line with the presuppositions of rationalism. They regarded the many superstitious practices of medieval Judaism as anathema. They also prevailed upon pietists, who drew no clear distinction between religious and superstitious rites, to regard certain abstract ways of thinking about God and the world as obviously correct and indeed mandated by the Bible.

The first major philosopher-theologian was Saadiah Gaon, who was born in Egypt in 882 CE and died as a leading scholar of Babylonian Jewry in 942 CE. Saadiah wrote *The Book of Beliefs and Opinions* in

125

Arabic to provide rational justification for traditional Jewish teaching and to counter heretical views then current in Babylonia. In this work he argued that while knowledge can be gained by philosophical investigation it can also be provided for those not inclined to philosophize from a reliable tradition. Revelation and reason are thus not in conflict but are two separate means whereby knowledge of the truth is provided. This led him to reinterpret the biblical and rabbinic teachings in rational terms, arguing that much of the language about God is not meant literally but allegorically or symbolically. This was not to make religion subservient to reason but to bring out the true meaning of religious teachings which denied that God had a material nature.

The greatest of Jewish philosophers, Moses Maimonides, who lived two centuries after Saadiah, disagreed with his philosophical approach, but said of him that his writings kept Torah alive and without him its true teachings would have disappeared from Israel. Saadiah was also a Hebrew poet of note and his religious poetry made its way into various parts of the liturgy.

Not all Jewish thinkers were enamoured of the philosophical reinterpretation of Judaism. Foremost among those who believed that rationalism, even rational religion, was no substitute for a living faith was Judah Halevi (1075–1141). Halevi was willing to speak in a philosophical idiom, but rejected the dominance of philosophy within Jewish theology. His main work translated into Hebrew with the title 'the *Kuzari*', was entitled in the original Arabic 'The Book of Argument and Proof in Defence of the Despised Faith'. In it he set out his semi-mystical understanding of the nature of Judaism, arguing against the claims of Christianity, Islam and Aristotelianism using rational methods.

The background of the book was the story of the conversion of the royal house of the Khazars to Judaism in the ninth century. The Khazars were a Turkic people living to the north of the Black Sea, who were caught between the conflicting claims of Christian and Muslim neighbours. In Halevi's *Kuzari* the Khazar king invites an Aristotelian philosopher and representatives of the three great monotheistic faiths – Christianity, Islam and Judaism – to present their teachings to him. The king is convinced that the Jewish religion, which underlies the other two and is clearly superior to mere philosophy, is in fact the true religion. In accepting it, the king also accepts that the philosophers' truth is only a limited perspective on revelatory truth.

Halevi argued that the Jewish people possess the unique gift of prophecy, which accounts for their status as a people chosen by God to be the bearer of divine revelation. Religious experience is superior to rational knowledge, though the latter is useful as an adjunct to religion. Aristotelianism is based on the experience of the human senses, while prophecy is based on a higher experience which comes from contact with the divine world. Whereas the philosopher-theologian can attain some theoretical knowledge of God, the prophet experiences him directly.

The teachings of revelation conveyed by the prophets set out the path of behaviour which brings a person to an experience of God. Just as the prophets are necessary for the Jewish people to perfect themselves in holiness, so the Jewish people, possessed of prophetic insight, are necessary to the nations of the world to help them draw near to divine experience. Israel is the heart of the nations, and its claim to religious truth is backed up by the testimony of the whole people at Mount Sinai when God revealed himself. The Christian and Muslim claims to prophecy are at best only supported by the private testimony of their religious founders.

MOSES MAIMONIDES

The most important medieval Jewish philosopher, Moses Maimonides (1136–1204), was also the leading rabbinic scholar of the post-talmudic period. It was said of him that 'from Moses till Moses there are none like Moses', i.e., that his intellectual stature could be compared only to that of the biblical Moses.

Maimonides wrote an Arabic commentary on the Mishnah, in which he set out the thirteen principal beliefs which he considered essential for Jewish doctrine. This was the first serious attempt from within Judaism to define the dogmatic base of the religion. The principal beliefs that Maimonides arrived at were:

1   The existence of a perfect Creator, who is the first cause and sustainer of what exists, and on whom all creatures are dependent.

2   That God, the cause of all that is, is one – not one as we might use the term in ordinary discourse, but one in a unique sense which has no comparison in everyday experience.

3   That the one God does not have a physical nature or any physical

attributes such as movement, or rest, or location. He therefore cannot be compared to any creature, and all language about him is simply analogous.

4   That the one God is the absolutely first being, preceding all other beings.

5   That human beings should worship and praise God alone, and not any of the lower beings of his creation such as angels or cosmic bodies which act only according to their nature without free will. Neither is it fitting to worship such beings as intermediaries in order to draw nearer to God.

6   That there are certain outstanding human beings, whose souls are perfected so that they achieve a spiritual level which enables them to receive prophetic revelation.

7   That Moses was the greatest of the prophets who preceded him and who succeeded him. His insight into divine knowledge was superior to that of all other persons, and he reached the level of the angels, having transcended human limitations. He was thus able to communicate with God directly without aid of the angels.

8   That the Torah was given by God through Moses, and it is all divine revelation. Anyone who claims that Moses composed part of the Torah himself is a heretic. The accepted interpretation of the Pentateuch found in the Oral Torah is also from God, so that traditional practice of the commandments is exactly as it was explained to Moses.

9   That since the Written Torah and the Oral Torah were both received from God, we may not add to them or detract from them.

10   That God knows the deeds of human beings and does not ignore what they do.

11   That God rewards those who keep the commandments of the Torah and punishes those who transgress its prohibitions.

12   That we should have a firm faith that the days of the Messiah will surely come, and will not be delayed. If the Messiah seems to tarry we should wait for him but we should not try to calculate the time of his coming by using hints found in Scripture. We must believe that he will be superior to all kings who have preceded him, and we should pray for his coming.

13 That there will be a resurrection of the dead. (Although Maimonides does not go into any detail about this belief in his list of principles, he later wrote an epistle on the subject since he was accused of doubting its importance.)

This programme of thirteen principles of faith was much criticized by later Jewish thinkers. Some objected to the very idea of reducing Judaism to a group of principles because this seemed to belittle the other beliefs of Judaism. Others subjected his particular list to philosophical scrutiny and concluded that he had chosen the wrong principles. Thus the fifteenth-century Spanish philosopher Joseph Albo, in his *Book of Principles*, argued for only three basic principles of Judaism: the existence of God; divine revelation; and divine reward and punishment. Despite the controversy surrounding Maimonides' thirteen principles, they were incorporated in the daily prayer-book in a simplified, and somewhat inaccurate, form in the *ani maamin* formulae and the *yigdal* hymn.

Modern movements within Judaism have also parted company with the Maimonidean formula for authentic Jewish belief. Conservative and Reform Judaism did not share Maimonides' traditional views on prophecy, revelation, the Messiah and the resurrection of the dead. The Reconstructionist Movement, a radical development of Conservative Judaism, in the supplement to its prayer-book includes thirteen criteria of Jewish loyalty, which are very different from Maimonides' original. They are preceded by the following words:

In view of the changed conditions in Jewish life, the criterion of loyalty to Judaism can no longer be the acceptance of a creed, but the experience of the need to have one's life enriched by the Jewish heritage. That experience should be formulated not in terms of dogmas but in terms of wants. The following wants supply the measure by which we may in our day test our loyalty to Judaism. (*Sabbath Prayer Book* (1945) New York: Reconstruction Foundation, p. 562)

Claude Montefiore, a founder of Liberal Judaism in Britain, wrote the following about Maimonides' articles of creed in his *Outlines of Liberal Judaism*:

The articles leave out, or are silent about, many 'articles of faith' which Liberal Judaism regards as essential . . . In addition to its omissions concerning the relation of God to man, the creed is also silent about the mission of

Israel and the relation of Judaism to the world at large. It is silent about the salvation of all men, of the ultimate redemption and enlightenment of the bad as well as the good. It omits other important matters too, such as the relation of religion to morality, the true service of God, the relation of faith to works, and of both to religion, the place of knowledge in religion, and so on.

MAIMONIDES' PHILOSOPHICAL WORKS

In philosophizing about the divinity, Maimonides gives his interpretation a decidedly Aristotelian colouring, and the personal God of the Bible and Talmud somehow gets lost among caveats and abstractions. In his code Maimonides had already declared the belief in the corporeality of the deity heretical. In response to this his most vociferous critic, R. David of Posquieres, commented:

> Why does he call such a person a heretic? For several people, greater and better than him, accepted such thoughts because of what they saw in Scripture and more than that from what they saw in the aggadic teachings which are misleading. (*Yad* Teshuva 3:7)

Maimonides' major philosophical work, *The Guide for the Perplexed*, originally written in Arabic but translated into Hebrew in his lifetime, caused even more controversy than his code and his Mishnah commentary. For the *Guide* Maimonides set out his understanding both of the nature of God and also of the commandments.

In explaining the function of ritual in his *Guide*, Maimonides related it to the pagan practices of the past and explained how Jewish practice was meant to wean Jews away from idolatry. It seemed to Maimonides' critics that, as a consequence, once the pagan background had disappeared there would be no need to keep the commandments. This was most obvious in Maimonides' explanation of the sacrifices. According to the *Guide*, sacrifices were the main method of divine service in biblical times for both Israelites and pagans. They were adopted and prescribed by the Torah so that people would not sacrifice to idols, but since the destruction of the Temple prayer has superseded sacrifice. Such a position is problematic because Maimonides himself, in his code, codified the laws of sacrifice, which would be reintroduced in the messianic age. Some traditionalists were so shocked by Maimonides' remarks on sacrifice in the *Guide* that they denied he wrote the work at all.

Intellectuals were forced to choose between Maimonides' philosophical reinterpretation of Judaism and the traditionalism of Halevi or of thinkers who eschewed philosophy altogether. Those who chose Maimonides found that they could take the philosophical adventure even further than their master and could understand the whole ritual side of Judaism as really a symbolic way of expressing purely philosophical truths. This angered the traditionalists even more.

After the death of Maimonides there was a strong reaction against the study of philosophy, which was banned by some of the leading rabbis and only allowed to those of outstanding piety and maturity. This anti-philosophic reaction forced Jewish philosophy on to the intellectual back burner for over three centuries. A philosophical revival took place in Judaism only in the period of the eighteenth-century Enlightenment, when Jews in Germany and Central Europe, under the influence of Moses Mendelssohn, began once again to explore a philosophical reinterpretation of Judaism.

MYSTICISM AND THE KABBALAH

Jewish mystical literature goes back at least as far as the early mishnaic period, if not back into the Bible itself. Prophetic visions of heaven became the subject of contemplation of mysticism in the tradition known as *maaseh merkabah*. The *Merkabah* mystics sought to undertake mystical journeys of the soul into the heavenly realm so that they could experience the vision of the divine throne. They were known as *yordei merkabah*, 'those who descend in the chariot', since the vision of heaven granted to the prophet Ezekiel involved the chariot in which the divine figure rode. These heavenly journeys are recorded in works known as *heikhalot* texts, which provide instructions on how to pass the fiery angels who guard the halls through which the adept passes.

There was also a more speculative tradition which dealt with the structures inherent in the divine creative process. This creation mysticism, known as *maaseh bereshit*, finds its earliest expression in the *Sefer Yetzirah* ('Book of Formation'). This book, which is ascribed to the biblical patriarch Abraham, surfaced about the third century CE. It was believed that the book could be used to control the creative powers residing within the world, since artificial humans or animals

131

could be created with the help of magical letter combinations referred to in the book.

The doctrine of ten *sefirot*, or semi-divine functions, which control the world, is first mentioned in the *Sefer Yetzirah*. In the Kabbalah (as the later mystical tradition is known) it developed into a substantial feature of Jewish mysticism, particularly in the *Sefer Ha-Zohar* ('The Book of Splendour', henceforth *Zohar*), which first appeared in thirteenth-century Spain. The publisher of the *Zohar* manuscript, Moses de Leon, claimed that he had come into possession of an ancient text recording the teachings of a famous second-century CE Palestinian master, Simeon bar Yochai. The reputed age of the teachings, and the power of their imagery, made the *Zohar* into the 'Bible' of the kabbalists. Parts of the work were eventually even incorporated into the prayer-book, and Jews influenced by kabbalistic teaching still chant sections on ritual occasions. The *Zohar* puts forward a mystical philosophy of Judaism in which the forces of evil are ranged against the working of the divine in the world and the commandments of Judaism are instrumental in preserving the divine harmony. The world emanates from the Godhead through the agency of the *sefirot*, and thus there is a divine underlay just below the surface of the mundane world. (See also Chapter 5.)

One of the most remarkable developments of the Kabbalah took place in Safed, North Palestine, in the sixteenth century, when Isaac Luria arrived from Egypt and taught a new system of Kabbalah to a small circle of mystical disciples. This new system implied that each individual Jew, through his religious activities, was furthering the messianic process. This process will be complete only when all the divine sparks trapped in the world are raised back to their divine status. The alienation of these sparks came about through a catastrophic upheaval which took place in the process of emanation and left the world needing rectification.

Lurianic Kabbalah generated messianic movements which raised the mystical theology of Judaism to the forefront of the popular consciousness. This popularization of mysticism eventually led to the Hasidic movement, founded in the mid-eighteenth century by Israel Baal Shem Tov (the Besht), a wandering folk healer and mystic. The Besht taught that God, the merciful father, could be found everywhere in all walks of life and in all activities, not merely in specifically religious contexts. Hasidism developed its own genre of sacred literature: works of a kabbalistic nature, story books full of wonderful tales about Hasidic Masters, and Bible commentaries which playfully drew lessons from words and images at a level of popular homiletics.

The prayer-book

Many of the popular elements from Jewish literature were gathered together in the different versions of the prayer-book (*siddur*) used by various communities. Originally, prayers were considered to be part of the oral tradition of Judaism and there was some resistance to writing them down. As the prayers grew from rather simple paradigms in talmudic times, it became imperative to commit them to writing and this was first done by the Geonim in Babylonia in the eighth to ninth centuries.

The elements which go to make up the fabric of these prayer-books come from the Pentateuch, the Prophets, the Book of Psalms, the mystical hymns of the Merkabah mystics, the *Zohar* and the many liturgical poets, *paytanim*. In the prayer-book there are references to the events of post-biblical Jewish history and especially the persecution of the Jews. There are martyrologies which include hymns remembering the Jewish martyrs of York, who burnt themselves alive as long ago as 1190 rather than be forcibly converted to Christianity. Some modern editions of these texts even include a dirge on the massacre of Jews during the Nazi Holocaust.

Inside the *siddur* are not only the fixed orders of public prayers, but also sections for Torah study and for private meditation, blessings for all sorts of occasions and table songs to be sung at home at the Sabbath meals. The prayer-book is also the repository of Jewish doctrine for the layperson and it includes poetic formulations of doctrine based on Maimonides' thirteen principles of faith.

The traditional prayer-book is mostly in Hebrew, with some few prayers in Aramaic, a related Semitic language. These were introduced at a time when Hebrew had become a literary language and ordinary people understood only Aramaic. Thus the *kaddish* prayer recited by mourners is in Aramaic. Today, with the rebirth of Israel and the revival of Hebrew as a spoken language, it is precisely the Aramaic portions of the prayer-book which are least understood. Some modern Israeli editions of the prayer-book include parallel Hebrew translations of the Aramaic.

133

There are translations of the prayer-book into all the major languages spoken by Jews in the diaspora. Conservative, Reconstructionist, Reform and Liberal versions of the prayer-book contain many more vernacular prayers than Orthodox ones and have eliminated those parts of the service which seemed too archaic. Orthodox Judaism has preserved even the most anachronistic prayers (e.g. those requesting the welfare of the exilarch, an institution long abandoned) on the grounds that they have become sanctified by use over the centuries.

Further reading

GENERAL

Alexander, P. S. (1984) *Judaism, Textual Sources for the Study of*. Manchester: Manchester University Press.
Unterman, A. (1981) *Jews, Their Religious Beliefs and Practices*. London: Routledge and Kegan Paul.
Unterman, A. (1991) *Dictionary of Jewish Lore and Legend*. London: Thames and Hudson.
Waxman, M. (1960) *A History of Jewish Literature*. New York: Yoseloff.

MIDRASH

Freedman, H. and Simon, M. (eds) (1939) *Midrash Rabbah*. London: Soncino.
Ginzberg, L. (1909) *The Legends of the Jews*. Philadelphia: Jewish Publication Society.

TALMUD

Cohen, A. (1949) *Everyman's Talmud*. London: Kent & Sons.
Steinsaltz, A. (1976) *The Essential Talmud*. London: Weidenfeld and Nicolson.

RESPONSA

Freehof, S. B. (1959) *The Responsa Literature*. Philadelphia: Jewish Publication Society.

Freehof, S. B. (1963) *A Treasury of the Responsa*. Philadelphia: Jewish Publication Society.

CODES

Goldin, H. E. (trans.) (1963) *Code of Jewish Law*. New York: Hebrew Publishing Company.

PHILOSOPHY

Guttman, J. (1964) *Philosophies of Judaism*. New York: Routledge and Kegan Paul.
Jacobs, L. (1964) *Principles of the Jewish Faith: An Analytic Study*. London: Vallentine Mitchell.

MYSTICISM

Scholem, G. (1941) *Major Trends in Jewish Mysticism*. New York: Schocken.
Sperling, H. and Simon, M. (trans.) (1934) *The Zohar*. London: Soncino.

PRAYER-BOOK

American Reform: (1975) *Gates of Prayer*. New York.
Conservative: (1985) *Siddur Sim Shalom*. New York.
Liberal: (1995) *Siddur Lev Chadash*. London.
Orthodox: (1990) *Authorised Daily Prayer Book of the United Hebrew Congregations of the Commonwealth* (Centenary edn). London.
Reform: (1984) *Forms of Prayer*. London.

5. Picturing God

Norman Solomon

Picturing God in words

Judaism allows no visual representation of God, no image or icon. The understanding of God is conveyed through verbal imagery and through reflection on experiences. As we cannot 'see' God, how do we learn to talk about him? How do we learn to use the word 'God' correctly?

In the following sections we explore several of the contexts in which, in traditional Jewish sources, the word 'God' or any of its equivalents has been used. This is a highly appropriate way to understand Jewish 'imagery' of God, for on the whole the Jewish sources do not theorize about the nature of God, but talk about situations in which God acts, or is perceived to be present.

At all stages there have been questionings, as if to say that talk about God is at best incomplete, inexhaustive, and often misleading. Already in biblical times there was unease about anthropomorphism, the use of human terms to describe God. Moses, sternly warning Israel against the manufacture of images, reminds them 'The Lord addressed you from the midst of the flame. You heard the sound of words, but saw no appearance, only a voice' (Deut 4:12). Deutero-Isaiah proclaimed 'To whom will you compare God; or what likeness will you compare with him?' (Isa 40:18). The most intense questionings were formulated by the medieval philosophers, who wrestled to interpret biblical anthropomorphism in the light of the firm denial to God of any bodily attributes.

Bible

The Hebrew scriptures present God through experience, both national and individual. We now review some of the biblical images of God, noticing what sort of experiences they refer to. The selection is not biblical theology *per se*, but focuses on those elements which most strongly influenced the formation of rabbinic Judaism.

The most decisive experience of God in Israelite/Jewish history was his self-revelation at Mount Sinai, as he proclaimed the Ten Commandments to the whole people. Why, asked the rabbis, did he open the Commandments with the statement 'I am the Lord your God'? Surely, his identity was evident to all?

> 'I am the Lord your God ... ' Why is this said? Since he revealed himself to them at the Red Sea as a mighty man of war, as it is said, 'The Lord is a warrior, the Lord is his name' (Exodus 15:3); then as an elder, replete with mercy, as it is said, 'They beheld the God of Israel, and beneath his feet was a pavement of sapphire, (and, referring to their redemption) blue as the very heavens ... ' (Exodus 24:10); and 'I kept looking, and then thrones were set in place and one ancient in years took his seat, his robe was white as snow and the hair of his head like cleanest wool (Daniel 7:9–10)' – so, to allow no pretext to the nations to say 'There are two powers', (he declared) 'I am the Lord your God; it is I who am on the sea and the dry land, in the past and in the future, in this world and in the next ... ' (*Mekhilta* on Exod 20:2)

Clearly, the rabbis understood that biblical talk about God consisted of images, not definitions. Each image (warrior, elder and so on) might correspond to some aspect of our experience of God's work, but no image, not even all the images together, could possibly exhaust the theme, nor does any image attempt to convey anything about God 'in himself'. Moreover, images do not have to be mutually consistent, for they are no more than pointers, from different locations, to the one ultimate which cannot be formulated in words.

The image of God at Sinai, God the 'lawgiver', is of a compelling presence; yet the voice is not stern, but that of a gentle and compassionate 'elder'. The *mitzvot* (commandments) of the Torah are the embodiment of his love for Israel. The 'Pharisaic' Psalm 119 encapsulates this equation of Torah and love. Nothing could be further from rabbinic Judaism than the Pauline concept of law as a burden (2 Cor 3:6), and the distorted image of God to which this gives rise.

God the Creator is majestically presented in the opening chapter of Genesis. Note the insistence on the 'rightness' of natural order, each species created in ascending order 'according to its kind'; likewise, at the Flood, Noah must save a viable population of each species.

Several psalms (29, 104) attest to God's wisdom in governing nature. That is, the experience of the 'harmony' of nature is translated into God-talk. The most powerful biblical testimony to the natural order as witness to God is Job 38 – 41. Nature is never confused with God, though. A comparison of Psalm 19 with the Egyptian 'Hymn to Ikhnaten' shows how the Psalmist reworked his Egyptian source to demote nature (the sun) from being God to being testimony to God.

God who made the world becomes God who governs it – the experience of history, particularly the Exodus, becomes a story of God:

Hear me, Jacob,
and Israel whom I called:
I am He; I am the first,
I am the last also,
With my own hands I founded the earth,
with my right hand I formed the expanse of sky; when I summoned them,
they sprang at once into being.
Assemble, all of you and listen to me;
which of you has declared what is coming,
that he whom I love shall wreak my will on Babylon
and the Chaldeans shall be scattered? (Isa 48:12–14)[1]

In determining the fate of nations, God is Warrior and Saviour (as God was not confused with nature, he is not confused with the Messiah):

'Who is this coming from Edom,
coming from Bozrah, his garments stained red?
Under his clothes his muscles stand out,
and he strides, stooping in his might?'
It is I, who announce that right has won the day.
I, who am strong to save ... (Isa 63:1–2)

These more violent images of God arise from the ascription to him of hatred of injustice and zeal against idolatry.

'Wherever you find God's power mentioned, you find also his

humility.'[2] Side by side with pictures of God as Almighty Creator and director of history are pictures of him as healer and comforter:

> The Lord is my shepherd; I shall want nothing.
> He makes me lie down in green pastures,
> and leads me beside the waters of peace;
> he renews life within me,
> and for his name's sake guides me in the right path.
> Even though I walk through a valley as dark as death
> I fear no evil, for thou art with me,
> thy staff and thy crook are my comfort.
> Thou spreadest a table for me in the sight of my enemies;
> thou hast richly bathed my head with oil,
> and my cup runs over.
> Goodness and love unfailing, these will follow me
> all the days of my life,
> and I shall dwell in the house of the Lord
> my whole life long. (Ps 23)

Elijah, the fearless prophet, scourge of kings and vanquisher of the prophets of Baal, discerned God not in the raging thunder but in the still, small voice:

> ... the Lord was passing by: a great and strong wind came rending mountains and shattering rocks before him, but the Lord was not in the wind; and after the wind there was an earthquake, but the Lord was not in the earthquake; and after the earthquake fire, but the Lord was not in the fire; and after the fire a low, murmuring sound. When Elijah heard it, he muffled his face in his cloak and went out and stood at the entrance to the cave. Then there came a voice: 'Why are you here, Elijah?' (1 Kgs 19:11–13)

To complete this section, here, with sample references, are some of the metaphors that contribute to the biblical picture of the relationship between God and people:

Metaphor	Comment
King and client state (Isaiah 43:15)	The suzerainty treaty as model 'covenant'
King and subject (Judges 8:23)	Individual allegiance in return for royal protection.

God and special people (Exodus 19; Amos 3)	A double-edged metaphor, of favour and responsibility
Shepherd and flock (Psalm 23)	
Master (mistress) and servant (Psalm 123:2)	
Owner and possession (Exodus 19:5)	
Lover and beloved (allegory of Song of Solomon)	
Husband and wife (Hosea 3)	
Bride and groom (Isaiah 62:5)	
Doctor and patient (Psalm 147:3; Exodus 15:26)	
Judge and plaintiff (Job 9:15)	
Father and child (Deuteronomy 14:1)	

Theologians often generate confusion by taking one or another of the metaphors too literally. A common candidate for preferential treatment is the covenant (king and client) relationship. So-called 'covenant theology' sets up 'the covenant' as an objective entity which defines people and obligations, and to which groups – Jews and Christians – can lay competing claims. 'Covenant' is not an objective entity. It is just one of several alternative biblical metaphors for the relationship between God and people, and no contradiction is involved in using it for different groups.

On Yom Kippur, just prior to an abject confession of sin, the congregation bursts into a song which celebrates several biblical metaphors:

For we are your people	and you are our God
We are your children	and you are our father
We are your servants	and you are our master
We are your congregation	and you are our portion
We are your inheritance	and you are our lot
We are your sheep	and you are our shepherd
We are your vine	and you are our keeper

140

We are your work	and you are our maker
We are your beloved	and you are our lover
We are your treasure	and you are our God
We are your people	and you are our king
We recognize you	and you have recognized us

Talmud

Like the Bible, the Talmud on the whole refrains from doctrinal formulations, and from definitions of God. Faith, *emunah*, is trust in God, not assent to propositions about his nature. Trust in God includes trust in the wisdom of his commandments. Faith and deeds are one (see Urbach, 1987; ch. 2).

The Talmud is on occasion provocatively anthropomorphic:

> Rav Judah said in the name of Rav: The day has twelve hours. For the first three, the Holy One, blessed be He, sits and studies the Torah. For the second three, he sits in judgment on the world; when he sees that it is deserving of destruction he rises from the throne of judgement and sits on the throne of mercy. For the third three, he sits and feeds the whole world, from the horns of the wild ox to the eggs of lice. In the fourth [period] he plays with Leviathan, as it is said, 'This Leviathan, which you have formed to sport with' (Psalm 104:26) ... (An alternative explanation) What does he do in the fourth [period]? He sits and teaches Torah to the small children in school. (Babylonian Talmud (BT), *Avoda Zara* 3b)

The literary history of this passage is complex; it combines images of God which occur separately in other contexts. As it stands in its final form, it utilizes images of God to emphasize four values which are central to rabbinic teaching. The first is that of learning: God himself, the giver of Torah, sets the example of loving engagement with it. The second is that of the balance of justice and mercy: vital as justice is, the world cannot survive without compassion. The third value is concern for all living things: if God spends his time sustaining the eggs of lice, how much more so should we take care of his creation. God's game with the Leviathan is his joyful anticipation of the coming of the Messiah, when justice, peace, enlightenment and happiness will prevail; but equally, the teaching of Torah to small children is a sign and guarantee of this paradise to come.

God is said to pray, and even to wear *tefillin* (BT *Berakhot* 7a, 6a).

He even 'wrapped himself in a prayer-shawl like a precentor and demonstrated to Moses the order of prayer for the forgiveness of sin' (BT *Rosh Ha-Shanah* 17).[3] The projection onto God of the way of life commanded for humans elicits innumerable pictures of God fulfilling his own *mitzvot* (commandments).

These homely images are counter-balanced by the use of special names and epithets coined by the rabbis to converse about God. Foremost among these is *shekhinah* (the 'dwelling', or 'presence'), a noun formed from the common biblical root *shakhan* ('dwell'), used in such phrases as 'they shall make me a sanctuary, and I shall dwell in their midst' (Exod 25:8). Ephraim Urbach correctly observes '*Shekhina* does not mean the place where the Deity is to be found ... but His manifest and hidden presence', and 'The concept of the *Shekhina* does not aim to solve the question of God's quiddity, but to give expression to His presence in the world and His nearness to man without, at the same time, destroying the sense of distance' (Urbach, 1987; pp. 40, 65). Less certain is Urbach's contention that the *shekhinah* is to be *identified* with God. This may sometimes be true, but it is a mistake to look for consistency in rabbinic usage over the long period involved.

The two common biblical names of God, the 'personal' tetra-grammaton, translated since the Septuagint by 'Lord', and the more general *Elohim*, are understood to refer to *middat ha-rahamim* (the Attribute of Mercy) and *middat ha-din* (the Attribute of Judgement) respectively (*Sifre Deuteronomy* 27).

Several additional expressions are used of God in the Talmud. *Ha-Maqom* ('the place' – 'the Omnipresent') is used by the early *tannaim* (second century), though it tended to be replaced later by *ha-Qadosh barukh hu* ('the Holy One, blessed be He'). *Rahmana* ('the Merciful'), presumably originally intended as an epithet for God, tends to be transferred to the Torah. *Gevurah* ('power'–omnipotence) indicates that God's word and power are unquestionable and unlimited; even his 'silence' is overpowering. *Ribbono shel Olam* ('Master of the Universe') occurs commonly in narratives as a term by which God is directly addressed; it appeals to his ability to respond effectively to claims on his justice (see Urbach, 1987; chs 4 and 5). Unfortunately, the unreliability of our texts makes it difficult to date precisely the nuances and changes in usage. But putting together the six non-biblical terms mentioned, we can see that the 'pictures' of God they convey stress six aspects of experience:

Shekhinah	God's nearness to humans
Ha-Maqom	His enveloping presence
Ha-Qadosh barukh hu	Holiness, blessedness
Rahmana	Compassion, especially as expressed through his gift of Torah
Gevurah	Power, through his revealed will
Ribbono shel Olam	His responsive control of the world

Each of these aspects is confirmed in liturgical formulations and through a wealth of remarks and anecdotes throughout rabbinic literature. Collectively, they contribute towards a 'picture' of God which reflects and interprets Jewish experience of the ultimate.

Translators: the Aramaic targums

No one knows for certain when regular Torah reading became a feature of synagogue worship. Tradition ascribes its institution to Moses (BT *Bava Qama* 82a; Jerusalem Talmud (JT) *Megillah* 4:1): as we might say, 'lost in the mists of antiquity'. Philo (*De Somniis* 127), Josephus (*Against Apion* 2:175) and the New Testament (Acts 15:21) all refer to regular public reading of the Torah. Though the Mishnah assumes regular reading of both Pentateuch and *haftara* ('completion': reading of the Prophets), the earliest explicit reference to fixed cycles of reading occurs in an anonymous, probably fourth-century, passage in the Babylonian Talmud. There the custom 'in the West' (the land of Israel) of reading the Pentateuch in a three-year cycle is contrasted with the Babylonian custom, now universal Jewish practice, of a one-year cycle (BT *Megilla* 29b).

Regular Hebrew reading in an Aramaic-speaking society necessitated translation. This was no casual process, but involved professional *meturgemanim* (translators), who would translate verse by verse as the Torah was read. Several Aramaic *targumim* (translations) are extant,[4] and still find liturgical as well as scholarly use. Many even today follow advice said to have been given by Joshua ben Levi to his sons in the third century to read the weekly Torah portion once in Hebrew and twice in translation (*targum*) (BT *Berakhot* 8b).

Every translator is an interpreter. Much rabbinic tradition is woven into the more discursive *targumim*, but even the more literal Onkelos found it necessary to deviate from the Hebrew text now and then to

143

avoid misleading his audience. He feared that too literal a rendering of the Hebrew text might cause people to have a wrong 'picture' of God. Frequently, Onkelos 'tones down' biblical anthropomorphisms, often by substituting *shekhinah* ('presence'), *yeqar* ('glory'), or *memra* ('word') for 'God'. 'I shall dwell in their midst' (Exod 25:8) becomes 'I shall set my *shekhinah* amongst them'; 'They beheld the God of Israel and beneath his feet was . . . ' (Exod 24:10) becomes 'They beheld the glory of the God of Israel and beneath his throne was . . . '; 'They heard the voice of the Lord God walking in the garden' (Gen 3:8) becomes 'They heard the sound of the *memra* of the Lord God walking in the garden'.

Moses Maimonides (1135–1204) seized on this as evidence that anthropomorphisms were to be interpreted figuratively. However, Moses Nahmanides (1194–1270) responded that not only was Onkelos manifestly inconsistent, if it really was his intention to avoid anthropomorphism, but the term *shekhinah* was actually a synonym for God, not the designation of some separate 'created glory'.[5]

Judaism and the visual arts

There is widespread misapprehension that since the Ten Commandments forbade the manufacture and possession of idols, Judaism has discouraged the visual arts. The discovery within the twentieth century of early synagogues, such as those of Capernaum and Beth Alfa in Israel or Dura-Europos on the Euphrates (in Syria), with its elaborate third-century frescos depicting biblical scenes, has demonstrated that Jews of the rabbinic period placed no ban on visual representation, even of the human form.[6]

Literary evidence supports the conclusion that the Jewish religious artists of Galilee and elsewhere were working within the parameters of what was eventually defined as *halakhah*, though not necessarily in accordance with the most restrictive interpretations. As we learn from the anecdote of Gamaliel in the bath-house of Aphrodite's temple, attitudes varied; Gamaliel himself found the statue unobjectionable since it was clearly intended as decoration, not for worship (Mishnah, *Avoda Zara* 3:4). The law developed through the Talmud and later tradition, and was defined by Joseph Caro (1488–1575) as follows:

It is forbidden to make a representation of anything in the heavenly region, such as ... angels, or a human form alone. This applies to a relief, but in sunken form, as in tapestry or wall painting, it is permitted. However, one may not make relief or sunken representations of sun, moon or stars unless this is for the purpose of instruction. Representations of animals, birds and fish, trees, plants and so on, may be made even in relief. Some say that representations of people and dragons are only forbidden if complete with all their limbs. (*Shulhan Arukh, Yore De'ah* 141:4–7)

In the unstable conditions of Jewish life, religious art has perforce been expressed most profusely in the decoration of artefacts such as the *kiddush* cup, the Passover dish, and the Hanukkah candelabrum, as well as in illuminated manuscripts. But the larger art forms, including stained glass windows and synagogue architecture, have also been practised when conditions allowed.

There is no direct representation of God. Kabbalistic Jews in countries where Christians cultivated icons went so far as to place cards with divine names before them as they prayed; these focus the mind on 'correct' aspects of God, but are not icons.

The early mystics: *Shi'ur Qomah*

The Mishnah (early third century) refers cryptically to *maaseh bereshit* (the 'work of creation') and *maaseh merkavah* (the 'work of the chariot'), esoteric studies of Genesis 1 and Ezekiel 1 respectively. The latter is developed in *Re'uyot Ezekiel* ('Visions of Ezekiel') and *Sefer ha-Razim* ('Book of Secrets'), and it is evident from several talmudic and midrashic sources that there were schools in the talmudic period in which these studies were cultivated. However, not homiletic speculation but active 'mystical ascent' characterizes the full-blown mysticism which arose when these elements were combined with the radical understanding of the Song of Songs as a self-portrait of God.

Scholarly consensus today is that the oldest Jewish mystical texts were composed not later than the second century, though the extant texts were subjected to later modification. Among the treatises preserved are those collectively known as the *hekhalot* literature. *Hekhalot* means 'palaces', and refers to seven palaces through which adepts ascend till they come face to face with the godhead. We do not know by what means people actually 'journeyed' – there has been speculation, though no evidence, that it involved the use of drugs – but

145

it is clear that a real experience, not a theoretical description, was the aim.

A short treatise called *Shi'ur Qomah* ('Measurement of Stature') actually ventures a description of *yotsrenu* ('our Creator' – God), as one might expect to behold him in the seventh palace. It lists God's limbs, their names and their measurements, drawing on the male imagery of the Song of Songs (especially 5:10–16); the Jewish interpretation of the Song as celebrating the love of God (the male lover) and Israel (the female beloved) was known to Origen, and must therefore go back at least to the second century. The Creator's limbs, according to this little book, are of the order of tens of millions of parasangs in length. Ten million parasangs are 180 billion handbreadths, and as each handbreadth is 'from one end of the world to the other' it may well be, as suggested by Joseph Dan,[7] that *Shi'ur Qomah* is actually trying to wean people away from an even more crudely anthropomorphic interpretation of the Song in terms of mere human size. The anthropomorphism of *Shi'ur Qomah* greatly embarrassed the more rationalistic Jewish thinkers of the Middle Ages. Maimonides, in reply to a correspondent who enquired whether *Shi'ur Qomah* was a Karaite work or 'of the deep secrets of the sages', was scathing in his brief reply: 'In sum, it would be a great *mitzvah* to erase and destroy all trace of this work, for "You shall not make mention of the name of other gods ... " (Exodus 23: 13); undoubtedly, whatever has measurements is "an other god".'[8] Others, misled by its pseudepigraphic attribution to the second-century rabbis Akiva and Ishmael, would feel constrained to 'explain it away' as ingeniously as possible.

Maimonides, the rationalist: denial of anthropomorphism

The Bible often speaks of God in human terms (anthropomorphism). We read, for instance, of God's 'mighty outstretched arm' intervening in history, or of his anger or pleasure, or of his taking an oath, or even changing his mind. But if God really has no physical form or dimensions, and is all-knowing and eternal, the creator who is himself beyond space and time, what sense can we make of such talk? The medieval Jewish philosopher Moses Maimonides devoted a large part of his *Guide for the Perplexed* to solving this question. All the biblical passages, he held, were metaphors, intended to convey deep truth to simple people. For instance, when the prophet speaks of 'The eyes of the Lord, which run to and fro through the whole earth' (Zech 4:10), he conveys in simple terms the idea that God's providence extends over everything on earth.[9]

If one cannot talk of God in human terms, are there any other ways of making positive statements about him? To the medieval philosophers, Jewish, Christian and Muslim, this was the problem of the 'attributes' of God. Are there attributes which may properly be ascribed to God? Can his 'essence' – that is, his real nature, rather than his dealings with us – be known? Though the Qur'an is far more reticent than the Bible, far less given to anthropomorphism, it does apply several attributes to God, such as 'merciful', 'mighty', 'protector' and so on. Muslim philosophers often distinguished between essential and inessential attributes, accepting the essential ones as real attributes of God, not mere metaphor. Maimonides, however, is adamant that one cannot attribute any qualities whatever to God, and progress towards understanding him comes only from denial of the attributes. Even the description of God as 'the First' is a metaphor, for 'first' can only properly be applied to objects which exist in time, and God is beyond time. To describe him as 'First', or as 'the Last', simply signifies that he is not subject to any change whatsoever (Maimonides, *Guide*, 1:57). This is how Maimonides expresses his thoroughgoing *via negativa*:[10]

... Know that the negative attributes of God are the true attributes; they do not include any incorrect notions or any deficiency whatever in reference to God, while positive attributes imply polytheism, and are inadequate, as we have already shown. It is now necessary to explain how negative expressions can in a certain sense be employed as attributes, and how they are distinguished from positive attributes. Then I shall show that we cannot describe the Creator by any means except by negative attributes ...

After this introduction, I would observe that ... God's existence is absolute, that it includes no composition, as will be proved, and that we comprehend only the fact that He exists, not His essence. Consequently it is a false assumption to hold that He has any positive attribute; for He does not possess existence in addition to His essence ... still less has He accidents, which could be described by an attribute. Hence it is clear that He has no positive attribute whatever. The negative attributes, however, are those which are necessary to direct the mind to the truths which we must believe concerning God; for on the one hand, they do not imply any plurality, and, on the other, they convey to man the highest possible knowledge of God; e.g., it has been established by proof that some being must exist besides those things which can be perceived by the senses, or apprehended by the mind; when we say of this being, that it exists, we mean that its non-existence is impossible. We then perceive that such a being is not, for instance, like the four elements, which are inanimate, and we therefore say that it is living, expressing thereby that it is not dead. We call such a being incorporeal, because we notice that it is unlike the heavens, which are living, but material. Seeing that it is also different from the intellect, which, though incorporeal and living, owes its existence to some cause, we say it's the first, expressing thereby that its existence is not due to any cause. We further notice, that the existence, that is the essence, of this being is not limited to its own existence; many existences emanate from it, and its influence is not like that of the fire in producing heat, or that of the sun in sending forth light, but consists in constantly giving them stability and order by well-established rule, as we shall show; we say, on that account, it has power, wisdom, and will, i.e., it is not feeble or ignorant, or hasty, and does not abandon its creatures; when we say that it is not feeble, we mean that its existence is capable of producing the existence of many other things; by saying that it is not ignorant, we mean 'It perceives' or 'It lives,' – for everything that perceives is living – by saying 'It is not hasty, and does not abandon its creatures,' we mean that all these creatures preserve a certain order and arrangement; they are not left to themselves; they are not produced aimlessly, but whatever condition they receive from that being is given with design and intention. We thus learn that there is no other being like unto God, and we say that He is One, i.e., there are not more Gods than one. (Maimonides, *Guide*, 1:59; Friedländer's translation, pp. 81–3)

What of the simple believer who does conceive of God as possessing positive attributes? What such a person believes in, says Maimonides, is not God at all, and therefore that person is in effect an atheist.

I do not merely declare that he who affirms attributes of God has not sufficient knowledge of the Creator, admits some association with God, or conceives Him to be different from what He is; but I say that he unknowingly loses his belief in God. (Maimonides, *Guide*, 1:60; Friedländer, p. 88)[11]

For all its apparent obscurity, the medieval debate on the attributes of God highlights the problems that still trouble us today when we try to make intelligible statements about God. If whatever we say about God is somehow wrong, can we really talk about God at all? And if we cannot talk about God, is the idea of God intelligible or communicable? Surely there must be some reference to our experience; to confine ourselves to abstract or negative terms detaches our understanding of God from the experience in which it is rooted.

Kabbalah

The influence of neo-Platonism on Jewish thought[12] brought to the fore the problem of how a perfect, unchanging God, whose nature could not be grasped in human terms, could have been responsible for the creation of the world, intervene in or even know its lowly affairs. If God is perfect and unchanging, one cannot ascribe to him intention, thought, word or action; these are processes in time, and necessarily involve change. Neo-Platonists solved this problem through the doctrine of emanation, according to which all that exists comes into being through successive emanations from the unchanging divine source. The One gives rise to the Many without itself changing.

Thirteenth-century Spanish Kabbalah drew heavily on the earlier *hekhalot* mysticism, but at the same time absorbed much of the philosophy of the intervening period. The classical exposition of this trend in Jewish mysticism is the *Zohar*, composed by Rabbi Moses de Leon towards the end of the thirteenth century but traditionally ascribed to the second-century teacher Shimon bar Yohai.[13] The *Zohar* interprets the emanations as the ten *sefirot* (sing. *sefirah*), the mediating channels or intelligences by which the material world is linked with the divine.

God himself is the *Ein Sof* ('without end' – infinite, absolute), about whom nothing can be said, and who cannot be grasped by any intellect. There can be no 'picture' of God. There can, however, be descriptions of the *sefirot*, and it is these which generate the rich imagery in mature kabbalistic writing.

The *sefirot* fall into three groups. The first triad corresponds to the 'world of thought' and consists of *keter* (the crown), followed by the masculine (active) potency of *hokhmah* (knowledge) and the feminine (passive) potency of *binah* (understanding). From the conjoining of masculine and feminine proceeded the second triad. The second triad corresponds to the 'world of soul' and consists of the masculine (active) potency of *hased* (love, kindness) and the feminine (passive) potency of *din* (judgement), which between them generate *tiferet* (beauty). The third triad corresponds to the 'world of material things'

149

and consists of the masculine (active) potency of *netsah* (victory, eternity) and the feminine (passive) potency of *hod* (glory), which between them generate *yesod* (the foundation). The tenth *sefirah* is *malkhut* (kingdom), the sum of the activity of the others.

Some of the *sefirot* have alternative names, and all function within a rich symbolic system. For instance, the first *sefirah*, *keter*, emanating from the infinite light of the *Ein Sof*, is also referred to as *attika* (the Ancient One), *nequdah rishona* (the first point), *nequda peshuta* (the simple point), *resh hivra* (the white head), *arikh anpin* (the slow to anger), *rum ma'alah* (the immeasurable height), or *ehyeh* (the 'I am'). The *sefirot* collectively comprise *Adam Qadmon* (the First Adam, or Primal Man), in whose image human beings are made. They are represented in the human body as follows:

keter	head
hokhmah	brain
binah	heart
hesed	right arm
din	left arm
tiferet	chest
netsah	right leg
hod	left leg
yesod	genitals
malkhut	complete body

Representations of the *sefirot* in the form of a tree or even a male human body are sometimes produced. But are these representations of God? Are the *sefirot* in some way the essence of God, and is knowledge of them theosophy, actual knowledge of God? This question is addressed in the *Zohar* itself:

> Should anyone ask: Is it not written 'You saw no image'? (Deuteronomy 4:15), he may answer 'The image I have seen is the one of which it is written "He shall see the very form of the Lord" (Numbers 12:8) and no other whatsoever, that he created and formed with letters.' That is why it says 'To whom will you liken me, who is compared with me?' (Isaiah 40:25) 'What likeness will you find for God or what form to resemble his?' (Isaiah 40:18)
>
> Even this image does not exist in its place, but when it descends to rule over creatures, and extends over them, it appears ... to each of them according to their (own) appearance, vision and shape ...

That is why he says, Though I appear to you in your own form, 'To whom will you liken me, who is compared with me?' (Isaiah 40:25). For before the Holy One, blessed be he, created form in the world, he was alone, without form or appearance ...

But after he had created the image of the chariot of supernal man, he descended there, and was named by that image ... that they might comprehend him through his attributes, how he would guide the world with mercy and justice, according to the deeds of men. For if his light would not extend over all creatures, how would they comprehend him, how would 'The whole earth is full of his glory' (Isaiah 6:3) be fulfilled?

Woe to anyone who compares him to any attribute, even of his own attributes, how much more so to any human attribute ... He is described insofar as he rules over the attribute ... but when he rises above it he has no measure, description or form.

[This is] Just like the sea, whose waters have no shape or form of their own, but take their form from the land over which they flow ... (*Zohar* II, 42b)

The primary interpretation of this passage is expressed by David R. Blumenthal:

God was unknown before creation, and that aspect of Him cannot be known even by exploring the meaning of His name or its letters. After Creation, however, He chose to reveal Himself to man and He made known His various Names and/or attributes. Finally, to identify His names and/or attributes with Him, with His essence, would be wrong, for they are only labels, expressions of an unknowable essence behind the word. (Blumenthal, 1978; p. 127)

So the picture is not of God himself for that would be, literally, unthinkable. The picture is of his attributes, an insight into the consciousness or creativity of God, not into his essence. If we consider the sefirotic system as an expression of our deep experience of reality, we find that it affirms as God-determined absolutes ten aspects of human experience, and explores their relationships both among each other and with the created world. Such a system makes possible 'anthropopathy', the attribution to God of human feelings and emotions; the biblical words denoting God's joy, anger, power, grace, loving-kindness and so on are literally applied to God, not in his essence as the *Ein Sof*, but in his conscious self-revelation as he interacts with his created world.

Liturgy

Instances of personal prayer, such as those of Abraham and Hannah, are found in the earliest biblical stories. Even when the national worship was centred on the Temple, sacrifice did not replace prayer, but supplemented it; if Ezekiel and Leviticus focus on the sacrificial aspects of Temple worship, Psalms is the supreme expression of its prayer. Trito-Isaiah, welcoming all humanity to the new Jerusalem Temple, declared in the name of God, 'My house shall be called a house of prayer for all peoples' (Isa 56:7).

Yet the liturgical framework for prayer as it exists today was set only in the second century. What 'picture' of God did Gamaliel II and his collaborators convey through their prayer formulations?

The balance between scriptural reading and actual prayer indicated a God (a) whose will could be known through his revealed word and (b) who might be approached, addressed, even pleaded with by each humble individual without the need for mediation through priest or sacrifice. This picture of a God who does not require intermediaries – priests, sacrifices, rituals – is a revolutionary achievement of rabbinic Judaism. Yet priesthood was not rejected in principle. Given the appropriate circumstances, priest, sacrifice and ritual might all contribute to the bond with God; but at the same time it was unambiguously affirmed that each man and woman could approach God directly in the sincerity of their own heart.

The twice daily scriptural reading was the *Shema*. Its first paragraph, Deuteronomy 6:4–9, has two themes, the loving acceptance of God's supremacy and of his commandments. The theme of the second paragraph (Deuteronomy 11:13–21) is reward and punishment. The third paragraph (Numbers 15:37–41) reinforced the experience of redemption, that God had brought Israel out of Egypt.

Shema was embedded in a group of blessings headed by a call to prayer, 'Bless the Lord who is to be blessed'. Two blessings preceded the *Shema*. The first praises God as creator of light and darkness, that is, as the one whose power is displayed daily through his orderly guidance of creation. The second declares his love of Israel, manifest through his revealing the Torah to them. Following *Shema*, the one morning or two evening blessings focus on God as redeemer and protector.

The main prayer at the three daily services is known by the rabbis simply as *tefillah* (prayer). It consists of nineteen (originally eighteen) short, thematic blessings. Each blessing has a 'seal', or ending, of the form 'Blessed are you, O Lord, who ... '. Most probably Gamaliel did no more than formulate themes and the structure of the whole, laying down precise wording for the endings but not for the themes.

The nineteen blessings commence with a set of three, standard for Sabbaths, festivals and weekdays (endings are those of the standard Orthodox prayer-books, sometimes abbreviated; themes are explained only where not obvious):

Ending	Theme
Shield of Abraham	God of the patriarchs (Abraham, Isaac, Jacob); past and future redeemer
Restore the dead to life	Power of life and death, dispenser of life-giving dew and rain
Holy God	

The second group varies according to occasion. On Sabbaths and festivals it consists of short readings for the day. On weekdays it consists of thirteen (originally twelve) petitions, couched in collective terms, but open to the inclusion of individual personal intercessions. The concluding formulae of the thirteen are:

Ending	Theme
Gracious giver of knowledge	
Who delights in repentance	
Who forgives sin	
Redeemer of Israel	Context – God who saves from the harsh conditions of life
Healer of the sick	
Who blesses years	Prayer for bountiful crops
Who gathers the dispersed of Israel	
Who loves justice	A reflection on injustice in the world

153

Who destroys slander and arrogance	Directed against treachery, arrogance, injustice and heresy
Stay and trust of the righteous	A prayer for welfare of the faithful including proselytes
Who rebuilds Jerusalem	
Who makes the horn of salvation flourish	For the 'restoration of David', that is, the coming of Messiah
Who hears prayer	General prayer for the acceptance of the preceding petitions

The concluding group of three blessings is standard for Sabbaths, festivals and weekdays:

Ending	Theme
Who restores the *shekhinah* to Zion (Jerusalem)	Petition that the full service of prayer and sacrifice be restored and accepted with love
Thanksgiving for God's 'daily miracles'	
Peace	

The attitude in which the *tefillah* is said contributes to the picture of God it instils in the worshipper. One stands, in a serious frame of mind, feet together, hands folded over heart, eyes closed, in humble submission before the Almighty, and facing the Temple site. Steps are taken forward at the beginning, backward as one 'departs' from the divine presence at the end. At various points one bows humbly. There is a sense of smallness and unworthiness in the presence of the infinite; yet this awe-inspiring infinite being is addressed as a loving, caring parent, who through ages past has concerned himself deeply in the story of Israel of which the worshipper is part.

Prayers for each festival or special occasion incorporate appropriate imagery of God. The Passover prayers, for instance, abound with references to God 'who brought us out of Egypt'; the image of God as 'redeemer' emphasizes his role in history and his concern for the poor and oppressed. The most powerful image is undoubtedly that reserved for the Ten Days of Penitence, spanning the period from the New Year to the Day of Atonement.

The *selihot* (prayers for forgiveness) services which precede New Year are formulated around the *shlosh esreh middot*, thirteen attributes of God based on Moses' prayer on behalf of Israel after the sin of the Golden Calf. These are the attributes:

Text of Exodus 34:6–7	*Attribute*[14]
Lord	The attribute of mercy extended before sin has been committed
Lord	The attribute of mercy extended after sin has been committed
God	in his pure attribute of mercy alternatively, the one with power (to forgive)
merciful	to the guilty, assuaging their punishment
gracious	even to the undeserving
patient (long-suffering)	granting opportunity to the sinner to repent
abundant in goodness	preferring to show mercy in judgement
and truth	incorruptible
keeping mercy to the thousandth generation	The attribute of mercy is far greater than that of justice (punishment is only to the third and fourth generation)
forgiving iniquity	sins committed deliberately but with malice
and transgression	sins committed in a rebellious spirit
and sin	accidental sin
by no means clearing the guilty, but visiting the sins of the fathers on the sons ...	This is also understood as an instance of God's compassion, for though he will not forgive unrepented evil, he hesitates to punish, waiting for generations; if the 'sons' abandon their fathers' sins, there is no punishment.

155

In a small but significant change, the ending of the third blessing of the *tefillah* during the Ten Days of Penitence becomes 'Holy King', instead of 'Holy God'. The 'king' metaphor for God presupposes the role of king as head of the Judiciary. Since this is a time for repentance, God is envisaged as a judge before whom all pass for judgement. Yet the king is very much a shepherd king, for the metaphor of sheep passing one by one before the shepherd also features in the liturgy of the day (derived from Mishnah, *Rosh HaShanah* 1:2). And the image of king is blended with the more tender image of father in the ancient prayer *Avinu Malkenu* ('Our father, our king!') featured twice daily through the penitential season.

As the Day of Atonement itself approaches, the twin images of father and king seem to move from the pole of judgement to that of forgiveness. The central blessing of the *tefillah* does indeed refer to a king, but a 'king who pardons and forgives our sins and the sins of his people the house of Israel, and each year makes our sins pass away ...' Liturgical poetry on the Temple liturgy of Atonement helps dramatize the move.

To complete this brief sketch of the way God is pictured in Jewish prayer, here are a few verses of the *Shir ha-kavod* ('Song of Glory') which is sung responsively at the end of the Orthodox Sabbath morning service. The poet, probably Judah the Pious of Regensburg (d. 1217), struggles with the philosophical problem of how to talk of the ineffable. His solution is the classical one that, though he can say nothing of God as he really is, he can freely draw on biblical and rabbinic imagery which sought to describe God's deeds.

> I will chant sweet hymns and compose songs for my soul yearns for You ...
> I declare Your glory, though I have not seen You; I portray You by imagery, though I have not known You.
>> Through the acts of Your prophets, by the speech of Your servants,
>> You gave a glimpse of the glory of Your majestic splendour.
> They described Your greatness and Your power from the display of Your mighty works.
>> They likened You, but not as You really are; they likened You in accordance with Your deeds.
> They represented You in countless visions; yet You are one In all the imagery.
>> They saw You as aged and also as youthful; the hair of Your head now grey, now black.

Aged in the day of Judgement, youthful in the day of battle; as a warrior
whose hands do battle for Him ...
With sparkling dew His head is covered. His locks with drops of the night
...
His glory rests on me; and mine on him; He is near to me when I call to
Him.
He is bright, he is ruddy; His clothes are red, as when He came from
treading the winepress in Edom.
He showed the *tefillin* knot to the meek Moses, when the Lord's likeness
was before his eyes.
He delights in His people, He glorifies the humble; He is enthroned by their
praises, He glories in them.[15]

Feminism

What religious Jewish responses are there to the changing awareness
of the role of the women's movement in society?

Hebrew, like English, separates its pronouns by gender. All nouns
have gender, and most verb forms vary by gender. It is linguistically
impossible to talk about God in Hebrew without committing oneself
on gender. Even the dodges, ugly but manageable in English, of using
'inclusive' language, avoiding pronouns, or coining neologisms such as
'godself', cannot work. However much we may insist that grammatical gender is not to do with sex, the fact remains that the constant and
consistent use of masculine language for God reinforces the concept of
male superiority, and male dominance in society. This is not lessened
by the theological certainty that it is nonsense to speak of God, who
has no physical form, as male or female in 'godself'.

As Clifford Geertz pointed out in his essay on 'Religion as a cultural
system', religious symbols function both as models *of* the community's
sense of reality and as models *for* human behaviour and social order.
So the question is not just whether we think of God as male or female,
but of how the ways we talk about God influence male and female
roles in society.

Genesis 1:27 runs 'So God created humankind in his own Image; in
the image of God he created him; male and female he created them'.[16]
This implies that in using our concept of God to model human
behaviour we should not distinguish between male and female. Consistent with this, the rabbinic formulation of the 'imitation of God'
incorporates virtues associated with female as well as male roles.

157

'After the Lord your God shall you walk' (Deut 13:5) is interpreted as *imitatio dei*:

> Said Rabbi Hama bar Hanina: How can a person walk after God? is it not written 'For the Lord your God is a consuming fire' (Deuteronomy 4:24)? But follow God's attributes. As He clothes the naked ... as He visits the sick ... comforts the bereaved ... buries the dead ... so should you. (BT *Sota* 14a)[17]

What is remarkable is the absence of distinctively male character-istics from those attributes of God we are called upon to emulate. It is God's care and compassion that we are exhorted to copy, not his vengeance and imposition of justice.

Are feminine images of deity, rather than just feminine attributes, to be found anywhere within the Jewish tradition? At least one verse speaks of our relationship with God as that of a slave-girl to her mistress:

> As the eyes of a slave follow his master's hand or the eyes of a slave-girl her mistress ... (Psalm 123:2)

But this is hardly auspicious. Images of slavery and royalty are today as problematic as those of male dominance. Scripture indeed says:

> On the day the Lord spoke to you out of the fire in Horeb, you saw no figure of any kind; so take good care not to fall into the degrading practice of making figures carved in relief, in the form of a man or a woman, or of any animal on earth ... (Deut 4:15–16)

The conscious search for God-imagery, even if not 'figures carved in relief', is an uncomfortable process for traditional Jews. Like Molière's M. Jourdain, astonished at the discovery that he had been talking prose all his life, we have suddenly realized that we were using images all along. The task now is to find the right images.

We have spoken above of the common rabbinic use of the term *shekhinah* for God. This noun, which means something like 'indwel-ling', certainly has feminine gender, but so do all abstract nouns in Hebrew. Although the abstract noun does not occur in scripture, it is obviously derived from the verb *shakhan*, 'to dwell', used in contexts such as 'They shall make me a sanctuary, and I shall dwell in their midst' (Exod 25:8). The difficult question (which we raised earlier in the name of Nahmanides), is whether it refers to God, or just to God's 'presence' in the world, that is, to some sort of emanation or radiant light from God.

> Said Rabbi Simon the son of Yohai: See how great is the love of the Holy One, blessed be He, for Israel, for wherever they have been exiled, the *Shekhinah* has accompanied them. (BT *Megilla* 29a)

Elsewhere, the *shekhinah* is said to have 'withdrawn' at the time of the destruction of the Temple, or even to be 'weeping in the inner houses' (BT *Hagiga* 5b).

It is highly unlikely that any of the rabbis who uttered these divergent statements about the *shekhinah* were thinking of it in gender terms. However, it is clear that they thought of the *shekhinah* as protecting and nurturing Israel. In this sense, it is legitimate for us today to draw upon this precedent for female imagery of God's relationship with people.

In the section on Kabbalah we referred to the masculine and feminine pairs of *sefirot*, for instance the masculine (active) potency of *hokhmah* (knowledge) and the feminine (passive) potency of *binah* (understanding) which engender the second triad. Such bisexual imagery affords a foothold within tradition for contemporary attempts to abandon exclusively male language, though in its original kabbalistic formulation it retains the concept of male dominance – male active, female passive.

If the availability of feminine imagery of God within Jewish tradition is limited, does it make sense to create new images? The attempt has been made by Jewish feminists. Rita M. Gross urges that, as a first stage, familiar forms of addressing God in prayer should be transposed to the feminine. For instance *ha-qedosha berukha hi* – 'the Holy One, blessed be She' – should be used in place of the current masculine form. Gross lists five basic goddess images that need translating into Jewish terms.

1 The 'coincidence of opposites' or 'ambiguity symbolism', close to the idea accepted in Jewish liturgy of God who creates both light and darkness.

2 Images of God the Mother, which must be joined with:

3 The goddess of culture in all its aspects, motherhood and culture being twin aspects of creativity.

159

4 The goddess as giver of wisdom and patron of scholarship and learning.

5 The assertion of sexuality as an aspect of divinity.

She sums up:

> Dimensions of deity that have been lost or severely attenuated during the long centuries when we spoke of God as if S/He were only a male are restored. They seem to have to do with acceptance and immanence, with nature and the cyclic round. Metaphors of enclosure, inner spaces, and curved lines seem to predominate. What a relief from the partial truth of intervention and transcendence; of history and linear time; of going forth, exposure and straight lines![18]

Views like those of Gross are strongly resisted, particularly in the Orthodox communities, where liturgical innovation of any kind is frowned upon and radical change is perceived as undermining authority. But the questions are being raised, experiments are taking place, and even the Orthodox are nervously toying with women's services and special forms of religious observance, as one sees in the growth of the *Rosh Hodesh* (New Moon) movement.

Modern and Holocaust theologies

Jews have been involved in virtually all the theological movements of the modern world. Spinoza unleashed the most radical questioning of traditional ideas on God. Did his identification of God with the natural order (*deus sive natura*) make him an atheist or, as Novalis had it, 'a man intoxicated by God'? Though he himself was excommunicated by the Jewish community, his deist philosophy influenced Moses Mendelssohn. At the time Mendelssohn was advocating a 'God of Reason', the new Hasidic movement in Eastern Europe was popularizing a modification of the kabbalistic theosophy described above. Jewish folk memory recalls a dispute between the Hasidic leader Shneur Zalman and Elijah, the Gaon of Vilna, as to the meaning of 'the whole earth is full of his glory' (Isa 6:3); this was a debate on the immanence or transcendence of God – was God in, or beyond, nature?

Evolution, existentialism, philosophy of language, postmodernism have all affected more recent Jewish thinking about God, yet perhaps no single event has presented as great a challenge as the Holocaust. The traditional 'picture' of God is that he is benevolent and all-powerful, a just and compassionate ruler of the world. If that is true, why did he not intervene to save innocent people, including a million and a half children, at the time of the Holocaust?

Of course, theologians, and indeed the Bible itself, have always worried about injustice in the world, about why the righteous often suffer and the wicked prosper. The whole book of Job is devoted to this problem. Contrary to Reform theologians such as Emil Fackenheim, the Holocaust did not raise a radically new problem on this score; it merely focused attention on a problem which has worried theists ever since Cain killed Abel.[19]

Richard Rubenstein pursued the vocation of Reform rabbi without worrying unduly about the presence of evil in the world, until a chance meeting with Heinrich Grüber, Dean of the Berlin Evangelical Church, in 1966. He was deeply shocked by Grüber's contention that 'For some reason, it was part of God's plan that the Jews died. God demands our death daily. He is the Lord. He is the Master; all is in His keeping and ordering' (Rubenstein, 1966, p. 54). Part of the shock lay in the fact that these words proceeded from the mouth of a man who was clearly not motivated by anti-Semitism. Rubenstein has been accused of denying the existence of God, but he strenuously rebuts this:

> No man can really say that God is dead. How can we know that? Nevertheless, I am compelled to say that we live in the time of the 'death of God'. *This is more a statement about man and his culture than about God* ... When I say we live in the time of the death of God, I mean that the thread uniting God and man, heaven and earth, has been broken. We stand in a cold, silent, unfeeling cosmos, unaided by any purposeful power beyond our own resources. After Auschwitz, what else can a Jew say about God? (Rubenstein, 1966; pp. 151–2)

And:

> I believe there is a conception of God ... which remains meaningful after the death of the God-who-acts-in-history. It is a very old conception of God with deep roots in both Western and Oriental mysticism. According to this conception, God is spoken of as the Holy *Nothingness*. When God is thus designated, he is conceived of as the ground and source of all existence. To speak of God as the Holy *Nothingness* is not to suggest that he is a void. On the contrary, he is an indivisible plenum so rich that all

161

existence derives from his very essence. God as the *Nothing* is not absence of being but superfluity of being.

Why then do we use the term *Nothingness*? Use of the term rests in part upon a very ancient observation that all definition of finite entities involves negation. The infinite God, the ground of all finite beings, cannot be defined. The infinite God is therefore in no sense a thing bearing any resemblance to the finite beings of the empirical world. The infinite God is nothing. At times, mystics also spoke of God in similar terms as the *Urgrund*, the primary ground, the dark unnameable abyss out of which the empirical world has come.

... whoever believes God is the source or ground of being usually believes that human personality is coterminous with the life of the human body. Death may be the entrance into eternal life, the perfect life of God; death may also end pain, craving, and suffering, but it involves the dissolution and disappearance of individual identity.

Perhaps the best available metaphor for the conception of God as the Holy Nothingness is that God is the ocean and we are the waves. In some sense each wave has its moment in which it is distinguishable as a somewhat separate entity. Nevertheless, no wave is entirely distinct from the ocean which is its substantial ground.[20]

Like the attenuated, psychological prop God, introduced by the Reconstructionist Rabbi Harold Kushner in his popular *When Bad Things Happen to Good People*, Rubenstein's God has little in common with the transcendent and omnipotent God of biblical tradition.

Orthodox theologians retain the image of God who is loving and omnipotent, and who intervenes in history on behalf of his people, Israel; it is we who have fallen short of his demands and been unfaithful to his Torah. But many object that to uphold this view in the wake of the destruction of six million Jews, among them the spiritual leadership of Jewry, promotes the image of a God whose demands are totally unreasonable and whose decisions as to when and how to intervene are arbitrary.

The image of God as hidden, or distant, was linked by the prophets of the exile to Israel's disobedience. Yet, as Samuel Balentine has shown, even in scripture God's hiding is not necessarily a judgement, but 'a subject for lament and protest as innocent suppliants charge that they have done nothing to warrant divine abandonment'.[21] The same ambiguity on the silence of God characterizes Holocaust theology.

In our view, it is possible to retain diverse, even contrary images of

God, as we have seen in both scripture and rabbinic tradition. The critical task is to relate these images to experience, not to define some entity from whose nature all the underlying experiences can be logically inferred. In terms of the *midrash* cited earlier, God appears sometimes as a warrior, sometimes as a gentle elder. To assert 'this is the same God' is to affirm the underlying unity of all experience, not the inferential integration of our descriptions of that experience. All our 'pictures' are pictures of the one God; to accord privilege to any one of them at the expense of the others is to commit idolatry.

Notes

1   Biblical quotations in this chapter are taken from the New English Bible.
2   Rabbi Yohanan (third century CE) in BT, *Megilla* 31a.
3   The text of this prayer, the 'thirteen attributes' of Exodus 34, is given in the section on liturgy (p. 153).
4   For an introduction see John Bowker (1969) *The Targums and Rabbinic Literature*. Cambridge: Cambridge University Press. Much research has been completed since that date, and several *Targumim* have been translated into English. T. & T. Clark of Edinburgh are publishing a series of the Aramaic Bible; vol. 6, *The Targum Onkelos to Genesis*, by Bernard Grossfeld, appeared in 1988 and has an excellent introduction.
5   Ramban (Moses Nahmanides) on Genesis 46:1. See above (p. 142) for reference to Urbach's account of the use of the term *shekhinah* in rabbinic literature.
6   Popular works on Jewish art include Roth (1971); Sed-Rajna (1985); and catalogues of the main Jewish museum collections, especially those of the Israel National Museum in Jerusalem.
7   Joseph Dan, 'The religious experience of the Merkavah' in Arthur Green (ed.) (1989) *Jewish Spirituality: From the Bible Through the Middle Ages*. London: SCM Press, p. 296.
8   5694/1934 *Maimonides: Responsa*, ed. A. H. Freimann. Jerusalem, p. 343.
9   Maimonides, *Guide*, I:44: (1963) *The Guide of the Perplexed by Moses Maimonides*, trans. Shlomo Pines, intro. by Leo Strauss, 2 vols. Chicago: University of Chicago Press.
10 The *via negativa* (negative way), the doctrine that one cannot affirm anything of the transcendent God, only deny attributes, may be traced back to the Christian Pseudo-Dionysius in the fifth century, and has had many Christian and Muslim, as well as Jewish, adherents.

11 I have substituted 'unknowingly' for Friedländer's pre-Freudian 'unconsciously'.

12 On medieval Jewish philosophy, including neo-Platonism, see Colette Sirat (1985) *A History of Jewish Philosophy in the Middle Ages.* Cambridge: Cambridge University Press and Editions de la Maison des Sciences de l'Homme.

13 For a detailed analysis of the literary history of the Zohar see Scholem (1941) , ch. 5 and Isaiah Tishby's introduction to his Hebrew translation of *Zohar* texts (1961) *Mishnat ha-Zohar.* Jerusalem; trans. David Goldstein as Lachower and Tishby (1989).

14 These interpretations are largely culled from Babylonian Talmud, *Rosh Ha-Shana* 17a and *Yoma* 36b, *Mekhilta* on Exodus 34, *Targum Onkelos,* and Obadiah Sforno's commentary.

15 *Authorised Daily Prayer Book,* Centenary edn, ed. Lord Jakobovits (1990). London, pp. 420–2.

16 The New English Bible text, which I have used, actually has 'man' here. I have emended this to 'humans', as this is a more accurate interpretation of the Hebrew term *Adam.* The New English Bible was published before the rise of feminism.

17 See Maimonides, *Mishneh Torah: Hilkhot Deot* 1:6 for a reconstruction of this passage.

18 Rita M. Gross, 'Steps towards feminine images of deity in Jewish theology' in Heschel (1983), pp. 234–47.

19 For a fuller exposition of this argument see Norman Solomon (1991) *Judaism and World Religion.* Basingstoke: Macmillan and New York: St Martin's Press, ch. 7.

20 Richard L. Rubenstein (1970) *Morality and Eros.* New York: McGraw-Hill, pp. 185–6.

21 Samuel E. Balentine (1983) *The Hidden God.* Oxford and New York: Oxford University Press, p. v.

References

Heschel, S. (ed.) (1983) *On Being a Jewish Feminist.* New York: Schocken Books.

Lachower, F. and Tishby, I. (eds), trans. D. Goldstein (1989) *The Wisdom of the Zohar* (3 vols). Oxford: Oxford University Press for Littman Library of Jewish Civilisation.

Maimonides, Moses, trans. S. Pines, intro. Leo Strauss (1963) *Guide of the Perplexed* (2 vols). Chicago and London: University of Chicago Press; also (1904) *The Guide for the Perplexed,* trans. M. Friedländer (2nd edn). London: Routledge and Kegan Paul.

Roth, C. (rev. edn B. Narkiss) (1971) *Jewish Art: An Illustrated History*. London: Vallentine Mitchell.

Rubenstein, R. (1966) *After Auschwitz*. Indianapolis: Bobbs-Merrill.

Scholem, G. G. (1941) *Major Trends in Jewish Mysticism*. Jerusalem: Schocken Books.

Sed-Rajna, G. (1985) *Ancient Jewish Art: East and West*. Secaucus, NJ: Chartwell Books Inc.

Urbach, E. E. trans. I. Abrahams (1987) *The Sages*. Cambridge, MA and London: Harvard University Press.

6. Human nature and destiny

Sybil Sheridan

> Rabbi Simeon said 'When the Holy One, blessed be He, came to create Adam, the ministering angels formed themselves into groups and parties, some of them saying "Let him be created" whilst others urged "Let him not be created" ... ' (*Bereshit* [Genesis] *Rabbah* 5:6)

This famous *midrash*[1] sets out a basic dilemma that runs through much of Jewish thought.

> Love said 'Let him be created because he will dispense acts of love'; Truth said 'Let him not be created, because he is compounded of falsehood'; Righteousness said 'Let him be created because he will perform righteous deeds'; Peace said 'Let him not be created because he is full of strife'.

Since there was no clear majority in favour or against the creation of humanity, God took Truth and threw it to earth; thus explaining the verse in Psalm 85: 'Truth springeth out of the earth; and righteousness hath looked down from heaven.'

Another version has it:

> While the ministering angels were arguing with each other and disputing with each other, the Holy One, blessed be He, created him. Said He to them: 'What can ye avail? Man has already been made!'

This theme runs through much of rabbinic literature. Humanity is host to a bundle of contradictions and it is unclear whether we should celebrate or deplore this event of creation. However, since Judaism does not demand strict conformity in thought, there is by no means only one interpretation available. Nevertheless, the underlying theme tends to be optimistic. Despite people's evil ways, they remain ever

166

with the possibility of reconciliation with God. All God's creation is seen as 'good' (Gen 1), but on the sixth day, after the creation of man, 'God saw everything that He had made, and behold, it was very good' (Gen 1:31).

The biblical accounts of the creation of humankind

> And God said, 'Let us make man in our image, after our likeness. They shall rule the fish of the sea, the birds of the sky, the cattle, the whole earth and all the creeping things that creep on earth.' And God created man in His image, in the image of God He created him; male and female He created them. (Gen 1:26–27)

> The Lord God formed man from the dust of the earth. He blew into his nostrils the breath of life, and man became a living being . . . The Lord God took the man and placed him in the garden of Eden, to till it and tend it. (Gen 2:7, 15)

Jewish tradition sees the two accounts of creation as one continuous narrative. Rather than contradicting each other, they offer different insights into the nature of God's creation. In the second chapter of Genesis, God fashions a person out of the earth. The Hebrew is *adam*, a generic word denoting all humanity, while the Hebrew for earth is *adamah*. *Adam* is an 'earthling' taken from the earth. The connection also shows humanity's purpose in God's world; *adam* is to tend the earth – to look after God's garden; 'to dress it and keep it'.

In the first chapter, all creatures that live on the land are formed out of the earth in a similar fashion.

> God said, 'Let the earth bring forth every kind of living creature: cattle, creeping things and wild beasts of every kind.' And it was so. (Gen 1:24)

Moreover, human beings and animals were created on the same day. This was understood in the *midrash* to mean that people resemble animals, not only physically, but 'He eats and drinks like animals, procreates like animals and dies like animals' (*Bereshit Rabbah* 14:3). The origins of humanity are, therefore, totally creaturely.

However, this is only half the story. Genesis 2:7 continues to describe how God breathed the breath of life into the nostrils of the creature 'and he became a living being'. Two closely related Hebrew terms in this sentence offered the rabbis of the *midrash* a clue to the uniqueness of humanity: *nefesh*, translated into the English here as 'being', and *neshamah*, rendered as 'breath'. Both terms are used to mean 'soul', but while *nefesh* is a term used also of animals (Gen 1:24), *neshamah* is not. *Nefesh* is the anima found in all creatures. *Neshamah* is what is described in Genesis (1:26–27) as the image of God in humanity.

Image of God in humanity

God's announcement that he will make humankind in his own image has resulted in a variety of interpretations. However, they all share one overriding principle: they are at pains to avoid any implied anthropomorphism – or, rather, 'deomorphism' – in the verse. Whatever can be made of the statement, it is not to mean that humans resemble God physically. The medieval rabbis had great difficulty with the anthropomorphic language of the early chapters of the Bible and this is reflected in the quotations that follow.

According to *Bereshit Rabbah* 14:3, the image of God makes *adam* like the angels.

> He stands upright, like the ministering angels, he speaks, he understands, he sees like the ministering angels.

Other rabbinic interpretations offer a range of suggestions. According to one such (*Sifre* to Deuteronomy 1:13), animals are imbued with a natural or instinctive intelligence which enables them to function according to their needs and nature, but without forethought. This is known as *hokhmah*: wisdom. Human beings also possess *hokhmah*, but in addition have *binah*: understanding, the ability to make connections, the faculty of reason. Upon *binah* the whole creativity and productivity of humankind depends.

Another interpretation is that humanity mirrors on earth the activity of God in the universe. In his commentary on the verse 'Let us make man in our own image', Shabatai Donnolo, a tenth-century physician and philosopher, wrote:

> This image and likeness of which the Blessed One spoke is not the form of the appearance of the Countenance, but the form of the work of God and

His activity in the universe. As God is supreme and rules over man and over all the world, beneath and above, so is man; as God knows and discerns things that happened and foresees things to come, so Man, whom God has granted wisdom to know; as God supplies and gives food to all flesh, so does man sustain all the members of his household, his attendants, and his animals, and as the Creator built the world and laid the foundations of the earth, stretched the heavens and gathered the waters together, so man is able to build, to found, and to call and gather together, to sow, to make grow, to plant and to do ... and 'in most things man is likened in small measure to God, in accordance with the limitations of the strength and the short span of the life which God has given him.[2]

The contemporary philosopher Isidore Epstein (1954) makes a further distinction between 'image' and 'likeness'. On the basis of medieval rabbinic commentary, he suggests that the image of God delineates the objective elements of God's nature – the attributes that define the divine essence, such as unity, eternity, omnipresence, omnipotence, omniscience and incorporeality. The likeness of God, on the other hand, delineates the subjective aspects of God's character, as it impresses itself on his creatures through his activity in the universe. These attributes are commonly associated with the list of thirteen described in Exodus 34:6–7:

> The Lord! the Lord! a God compassionate and gracious, slow to anger, abounding in kindness and faithfulness, extending kindness to the thousandth generation, forgiving iniquity, transgression, and sin; yet He does not remit all punishment but visits the iniquity of parents upon children and children's children, upon the third and fourth generations.

With regard to 'image', the human *neshamah* can be seen as replicating some, but not all, of the objective attributes of God's essence. The human soul is a unity, incorporeal, omnipresent and eternal; but it is not omniscient or omnipotent. It is through the *neshamah* that humans come to an understanding of what God is. In the words of Saadiah Gaon:[3]

> Though his body is small, his soul is longer than heaven and earth, for through it, he reaches even what is above them and the cause of them, the creator itself.

Regarding 'likeness', the human character can emulate most, but not all, of the subjective attributes of God. Humankind has the capacity to be merciful, gracious, long-suffering and abundant in truth. But the punishment of the guilty is a task reserved for God alone.

With the capacity to emulate the subjective attributes of God comes the notion of *imitatio dei* – that a person not only can, but should, imitate God and act as God in the world. The biblical basis for this is Leviticus 19:1.

> And the Lord spoke to Moses, saying: Speak to the whole Israelite community and say to them: You shall be holy, for I, the Lord your God, am holy.

There are many expressions of this concept in rabbinic Judaism, for example, in the *Midrash Tanhuma* (*Toledot* 12):

> 'After the Lord you shall walk' (Deut 13:5). How can man walk after God? Is He not a consuming fire? What is meant is that man ought to walk after the attributes of God. Just as the Lord clothes the naked, so you shall clothe the naked. Just as He visits the sick, so you shall visit the sick. Just as the Lord comforted the bereaved, so you shall comfort the bereaved; just as He buried the dead, so you shall bury the dead.

The creation of woman

The discrepancies in the two accounts regarding the creation of woman have given rise to a great deal of literature regarding the nature of both sexes, their relationship and their purpose.

In the first chapter of Genesis, male and female are created equally. 'In the image of God created He him; male and female created He them' (Gen 1:27). The nature and purpose of man and woman is, therefore, identical. In the second chapter:

> The Lord God said: 'It is not good for man to be alone; I will make a fitting helper for him.' ... So the Lord God cast a deep sleep upon the man; and, while he slept, He took one of his ribs and closed up the flesh at that spot. And the Lord God fashioned the rib that he had taken from the man into a woman; and He brought her to the man. (Gen 1:18, 21–22)

Here, the creation of woman is clearly different from that of man.

Moreover, the purpose for woman's creation is distinctive. Woman was created because man could not find a suitable companion among the animals. The subsequent verses show clearly that her role is to be man's sexual partner.

Midrash, in elaborating on this account of creation, shows something of the prevailing view of women held in the period.

> He considered well from what part to create her. Said He: 'I will not create her from his head, lest she be swell headed; nor from the eye, lest she be a coquette; nor from the ear, lest she be an eavesdropper; nor from the mouth, lest she be a gossip; nor from the heart, lest she be prone to jealousy; nor from the hand, lest she be light-fingered; nor from the foot, lest she be a gadabout; but from the modest part of man, for even when he stands naked, that part is covered (i.e. with flesh)'. (*Bereshit Rabbah* 18:3)

Other rabbis were more concerned with reconciling the two accounts, however. The first account was seen by many as the prototype for all humanity. *Adam* is the generic word for all mankind, and it is only after the woman *ishah* is created – that the male of the species is specified and called *ish*. To some, the first person was the perfect image of God, a heavenly model upon which the earthly one was based. The mystical tradition made much of *Adam kadmon* – primordial *adam* – as a purely spiritual entity that contains the divine emanations of God. Others saw the first person as human, but containing both male and female; either a hermaphrodite that later became two people, or a double-faced being who was then split into two.[4]

A later *midrash*[5] quotes a tradition that the first man had two wives. The original, Lilith, was created equally with him and refused to be dominated sexually by him. He therefore divorced her and God made Eve out of the man's rib, so that her natural longing would be to be part of him. Though from a minor and most probably heretical source, this idea has received much prominence in recent years through the women's movement, for whom Lilith has become a significant symbol.

The biblical text itself says less about the subordination of woman than it does about the purpose of her creation as partner to man and, even more importantly, about her role in bearing children. The matriarchs stand as the supreme and ideal examples of womanhood, while in rabbinic literature, the childless prophets Deborah and Hulda are sharply criticized.[6]

One popular rabbinic tradition sees God, man and woman as equal partners in the creation of children. 'There are three partners in man; the Holy One, blessed be He, his father and his mother' (BT *Niddah* 31a). The father and mother provide all the physical attributes for the child, while God,

> The Holy One, blessed be He, gives him the spirit and the soul, beauty of features, eyesight, the power of hearing and the ability to walk, understanding and discernment.

There are numerous tales of rabbis attempting to create people. Such creatures, known as golems, were apparently moderately successful. They could move about and obey orders, but could not speak, or think independently. Without woman, and without God's breath of life, a real human being cannot be formed.

The purpose of humanity's creation

> God blessed them and God said to them: 'Be fertile and increase, fill the earth and master it; and rule the fish of the sea, the birds of the sky, and all the living things that creep on the earth.' (Gen 1:28)

In both Genesis accounts, humanity is viewed as the crown of God's creation. Through intelligence and creative energy, people learn to control the earth. They are not entirely subject to the fortunes and failures of nature; and the regular rhythm of the changing seasons is exploited for the growth of crops and the enhancement of life. Though they are physically defenceless, the unique power that is humankind's makes them the match of any animal, but the early chapters of Genesis make it clear that one is not to kill God's creatures.

> God said, 'See, I give you every seed-bearing plant that is upon all the earth, and every tree that has seed-bearing fruit; they shall be yours for food.' (Gen 1:29)

In the second accounts God sets *adam* in the garden of Eden to 'dress it and keep it' (Gen 2:15). As well as the pinnacle of creation, humanity here becomes a partner with God in the maintenance of that creation. God's continued presence is required to prevent the world returning to chaos, but humankind's involvement determines what kind of a world it becomes. Humanity's purpose is to work.

> 'For the Lord thy God hath blessed thee in all the work of thy hand'. (Deut 2:7) ... If man does work, he receives the divine blessing; if not, he loses it. (*Midrash* to Psalm 22)

In this passage, work is taken literally, and God's blessing upon humanity is dependent upon this. But in many texts, work means more than physical labour.

> The Holy One, blessed be He, said to him: 'Up to now, I alone was engaged in work, now you too must also be engaged in it.' (*Zohar Hadash* on Gen 5)

This mystical text understands work as mirroring God's activity. Humanity's acts of kindness and compassion are as necessary to the world's continued existence as is the tending of the plants in the garden.

Other passages include the worship of God as part of this maintenance plan, based on Isaiah 43:2, which says 'This people I formed for myself that they might tell my praise'. Above all, humanity's purpose is to do God's will as expressed in the biblical commandments.

Free will

> In a supreme act of self-limitation, the Absolute God gave man freedom of moral choice. He could will to do right and wrong, obey or disobey his maker. It was heaven's greatest gift to man, he was not an automaton.[7]

This freedom of humanity to act independently of God has often puzzled philosophers, for how does this coincide with God's omnipotence? Today, after the experience of the Holocaust, there is a tendency to move towards a view of the limited power of God, but though the question was addressed by the early rabbis, such a view was out of the question. The problem of reconciling free will with determinism was discussed but never fully resolved. 'All is foreseen, yet free choice is granted man' (*Mishnah Avot* 3:19) remains the classic formulation. The two elements stand side by side, without any attempt

173

to reconcile them. The statement continues: 'The world is judged by goodness, yet all depends on the abundance of work' (*ibid.*). It was accepted that God was in full control, but the preoccupation of the rabbis was with what God required human beings to do – to exercise free will for the good of the world.

Goodness is one of humanity's basic qualities. At the close of the sixth day of creation God 'saw everything that he had made and behold, it was very good' (Gen 1:31). A person's duty is to maintain this, yet it is possible to choose to refrain from doing so. In the Talmud it is said that before conception, the sperm is laid before God, who decrees all its qualities except one.

> 'Sovereign of the universe, What shall be the fate of this drop? Shall it produce a strong man or a weak man, a wise man or a fool, a rich man or a poor man?' Whereas 'wicked man' or 'righteous one' he does not mention, in agreement with the statement of R. Hanina. For R. Hanina stated: 'Everything is in the hands of God except the fear of God.' (*Niddah* 16b)

Humanity can, through exercising the moral choice for good, fulfil its destiny as the crown of God's creation; or, through exercising the choice for bad, sink to the level of the animals among whom human beings were formed.

The garden of Eden

> And the Lord God commanded the man, saying: 'Of every tree of the garden, you are free to eat; but as for the tree of knowledge of good and bad, you must not eat of it for as soon as you eat of it, you shall die.' (Gen 2:16–17)

The freedom of humanity to disobey was exercised for the first time in the garden of Eden. Adam ate of the fruit, and guilt, suffering and death were its consequences. Although all humanity is a victim of those consequences, the notion that all people have been tainted by that first wrongful act is not part of Judaism.

There is no idea of 'original sin' – rather, Adam and Eve stand as a paradigm for what happens to each person in his or her life. Every individual stands independently in relationship with God, with the same injunction to obey his commands and the very same possibility to disobey.

> The person who sins, he alone shall die. A child shall not share the burden of a parent's guilt, nor shall a parent share the burden of a child's guilt; the righteousness of the righteous shall be accounted to him alone, and wickedness of the wicked shall be accounted to him alone. (Ezek 18:20)

What did change with this act were the circumstances in which humanity lives. Eating of the fruit brought knowledge of good and evil, right and wrong. Moral choice was extended beyond that of obedience and disobedience; a fully-fledged sense of ethical conduct now comes into play. Whereas at creation *adam* was given wisdom – *hokhmah* – and understanding – *binah* – he now acquires knowledge – *daat*.

This knowledge, coupled with freedom of choice, results in great power, for evil as well as for good. To limit this now dangerous power, *adam* is denied access to the tree of life and the possibility of immortality. A new element impedes the divine injunction to work that of drudgery. Pain is introduced – life will never be the same again.

The medieval philosophers understood the tale allegorically. Moses Maimonides,[8] for example, saw the tree of life as embodying pure wisdom, and the tree of knowledge as practical wisdom. Adam, who was the embodiment of intellectual perfection, chose to follow his instincts rather than pure reason. He gave up the pursuit of facts for that of values; of truth and falsehood for good and evil; of physics and metaphysics for ethics and politics. Other philosophers consider that it is the gross animal nature of humankind that let Adam down. Capable of the highest intellectual perfection, he chose to gratify his senses instead.

But despite the gloominess of this view of humanity, there is always a chance to go back to the golden age of Eden. Humankind, who through folly was driven out, by virtue, can return. Eden is paradise, the walled garden containing the delights of heaven and awaiting the righteous who will enter it after death.

Modern philosophers tend towards a different track, however. While on one level the story seems to be an aetiological myth that harks back to a golden era lost to humanity, on another, there is something strangely positive about it. The childhood of Eden is replaced by the adulthood of life outside the garden. A harder life, true, but one with infinitely greater possibilities – greater potential for good, and for personal and universal fulfilment. This gives rise to the question whether God actually wanted Adam to disobey him. 'Did he fall or was he pushed?' is a recurring question.

Origin and nature of evil

The problem of evil in the world is one that has occupied Jewish thinkers from the Bible onwards. While the Torah emphasizes the message 'Do good and prosper; do evil and suffer', the reality has always been very different. The question of suffering of the righteous arises in the story of Abraham and Sodom (Gen 18: 23–33), and runs throughout the Prophets and Writings, culminating in the story of Job. It has also dominated the thought of generations of rabbis and remains even today one of the major philosophical issues.

The rabbis of the first centuries of the current era lived in a world where dualism was a popular philosophy. Since this threatened the unity of God, they were at pains to emphasize that God was the source of evil, as described in Isaiah:

I form light and create darkness,
I make weal and create woe –
I the Lord do all these things. (45:7)

But this is not to mean that God is himself evil, rather, that he creates evil for the world.

Satan appears quite frequently in the Hebrew Bible, and is regarded as an agent of God. The word means 'adversary' and is descriptive of a job, rather than a personality. God's angels perform this function when necessary, for example, in the story of Job where, in order to show the extent of his loyalty to God, it is necessary that Job suffer.

Later Judaism developed an elaborate demonology, and in particular the notion of fallen angels, but the emphasis on God's unity remained so strong that it appears that even these remain, to a certain extent, in his power.

Whether God physically created evil or, as other texts suggest, simply allowed evil to exist, it is somehow considered necessary to the world. The early rabbis described humanity as having two desires or inclinations: a good, *yezer (yetser) ha-tov*, and an evil, *yetser ha-ra*. These are constantly in juxtaposition, and human inconsistency is seen as the result of one or the other momentarily gaining the upper hand. Nevertheless, the *yetser ha-ra* is much the stronger, and a person's life is a constant battle against it.

> R. Isaac stated 'The [Evil] Inclination of a man grows stronger within him from day to day as it is said, "Only evil all the day" (Gen 6:5)'. R. Simeon b. Lakish stated 'The Evil Inclination grows in strength from day to day and seeks to kill him as it is said, "The wicked watches the righteous and seeketh to slay him" (Ps 37:32); and were it not that the Holy One, blessed be He, is his help, he would not be able to withstand it . . . ' (BT *Sukkah* 52a–b)

The *yetser ha-ra* is variously identified with the sexual instinct, physical appetite, aggression and ambition. However, of itself, it is not altogether evil. *Bereshit Rabbah* 9:7 suggests:

> But for the Evil Desire, no man would build a house, take a wife and beget children; and thus said Solomon: 'Again I considered all labour and all excelling in work, that it is a man's rivalry with his neighbour.'

There is a legend that the Men of the Great Assembly[9] once caught the *yetser ha-ra* and were about to put it to death when God intervened saying that if there were no evil inclination, the world itself would die.

But necessary though it may be to the world, it must be overcome in humanity. Each individual must engage in a constant and continuing struggle to overcome the evil inclination that will last throughout life. But the *yetser ha-ra* can be overcome through obedience to God's will.

> In the time to come, the Holy One, blessed be He will bring the Evil Inclination and slay it In the presence of the righteous and the wicked. To the righteous, it will have the appearance of a towering hill, and to the wicked it will have the appearance of a hair thread. Both the former and the latter will weep; the righteous will weep saying, 'How were we able to overcome such a towering hill!' The wicked also will weep saying, 'How is it that we were unable to conquer this hair thread!' (BT *Sukkah* 52a)

Sin and wrongdoing

The result of the *yetser ha-ra* gaining control is that humankind sins. In the Bible there are about twenty different words for 'sin', each of

177

which applies to different types of wrongdoing. The most popular are the three *het*, *pesha* and *avon*. They are often used together – as among God's attributes in Exodus 34:7 – but they have distinctive meanings nevertheless.

The word *het* comes from a Hebrew root meaning 'to miss the mark', and so comes to mean 'to fall'. It is used in the Bible to signify the failure of relations between two individuals, for example, between Jacob and Laban (Gen 31:36), and also the failure in obligation to God, as in the infringement of the ban (Deut 20:16ff.) in Joshua 7:11. It is often translated as 'offence' or 'transgression'.

Pesha means 'breach' and suggests a more deliberate act of disobedience. Though used occasionally for relations between individuals, it is more usually associated with humankind's reaction to God's demands, for example, Amos 2:4. This is the word most usually translated as 'sin', but 'disobedience' or 'rebellion' are closer to the meaning.

The root of the word *avon* means 'crooked' or 'bent'. It suggests some deviation from the good, but not necessarily deliberate; rather it is part of the human condition that we should strive against, for example, Psalm 38:7. It is translated traditionally as 'iniquity'; but the term 'wrong' or 'wrongdoing' fits well here.

For the Bible the main concern with these faults is that they break the special relationship God has with humanity. When persons do wrong, they fail to honour their part of the bargain made with God, known as the covenant, and the fear is that God, in response, will stop helping and protecting his people.

> And when you announce all these things to that people, and they ask you, 'Why has the Lord decreed upon us all this fearful evil? What is our iniquity and what the sin that we have committed against the Lord our God?' say to them, 'Because your fathers deserted me – declares the Lord – and followed other gods and served them and worshipped them; they deserted Me and did not keep My instruction. And you have acted worse than your fathers, every one of you following the wilfulness of his evil heart and paying no heed to Me.' (Jer 16:10–12)

On the whole, though not entirely, the Bible is concerned with the sins of Israel as a people. Individual responsibility, and concern for individual sin and how it affects society, were ideas developed by the early rabbis. The Mishnah and Talmud[10] are full of discussions on what exactly constitutes sin, its effects, its punishment, and the possibility and means of forgiveness.

The term favoured by the rabbis for sin is *avera*, which comes from a root meaning 'to pass over', and suggests ignoring or rejecting God's will. Sins were divided into two categories: sins of omission and sins of commission, the latter being the more serious. The rabbis also distinguished between 'light' and 'heavy' sins, recognizing that in some circumstances, some of the lighter precepts could be transgressed – in fact should be – to save life, for example. But three sins were considered so serious that people must lose their own life rather than commit them. These were murder, idolatry and sexual crimes such as incest and adultery.

The rabbis carefully delineated the various punishments for sin, but rather than punishment, what God desires most of all is the repentance of the sinner.

> Moreover, if the wicked one repents of all the sins that he committed and keeps all My laws and does what is just and right, he shall live; he shall not die. None of the transgressions he committed shall be remembered against him; because of the righteousness he has practised, he shall live. Is it my desire that a wicked person shall die? says the Lord God. It is rather that he shall turn back from his ways and live. (Ezek 18:21–23)

Repentance and atonement

If sin is seen as turning away from God, either by deliberately breaking his laws, or by default because of humankind's inherent weakness, then repentance is the turning back to him. In the Bible the word used is *shuv* or 'turn' – the turning of the heart or mind back towards God in a new relationship with him. In rabbinic literature, this becomes *teshuvah*; 'returning': coming back to God and restoring the bond between them. The importance of *teshuvah* is seen in a famous passage, where a lower scriptural authority is overridden by a higher one until the words of God himself override them all.

> They asked of wisdom: What is the punishment of the sinner? Wisdom replied: 'Evil pursues the sinner' (Prov 13:21). They asked of prophecy: What is the punishment of the sinner? Prophecy replied: 'The soul that sinneth, it shall die' (Ezek 18:4). They asked of Torah: What punishment of

the sinner? Torah replied: 'Let him bring a sacrifice and it will atone.' Then they asked of the Holy One, Blessed be He: What punishment of the sinner? He replied, Let him repent and bring atonement. (JT *Makkot* 2:6)

All people can do *teshuvah*. No sin is so great that penitence is impossible, and God will help all he can in the process.

A king had a son who had gone astray from his father a journey of a hundred days: his friends said to him 'Return to your father'; he said 'I cannot.' Then his father sent to say 'Return as far as you can, and I will come to you the rest of the way.' So God says 'Return to Me and I will return to you'. (*Pesikta Rabati*)

Originally, repentance required a public confession of the sin and a sacrifice; later, fasting and prayer replaced the sacrificial element. If the wrong is against a person, the wrongdoer must confess and ask forgiveness of that person as well as make restitution, and resolve never to commit the same offence again. Then the wrongdoer can approach God and the wrong will be pardoned – literally 'covered over' in the Hebrew. It is then as if the sin had never been committed, the slate has been wiped clean. For sins against God, the same processes of confession, restitution and resolve never to do wrong again are involved.

Teshuvah can be made at any time:

R. Eliezer said: Repent one day before you die. His disciples said 'Who knows when he will die?' 'All the more, then, let him repent today, peradventure he will die tomorrow. The result will be that all his life will be spent in penitence.' (*Midrash* on Ps 90:12)

However, the weeks leading up to the Day of Atonement, Yom Kippur, are the main period for repentance, with an elaborate liturgy to assist in the process. It begins in the month preceding the New Year with *selihot* prayers requesting God's pardon. The New Year, Rosh Hashanah, is known as the Day of Judgement. On this day, one popular image has it, God looks into the deeds of humankind in the past year and passes judgement. Those who have been totally good are inscribed in the Book of Life, while those who have been thoroughly wicked are inscribed in the Book of Death. For those – the majority – who have been neither completely good nor bad, God suspends judgement until Yom Kippur some ten days later. Those Ten Days of

Penitence are the time when Jews are expected to repent of their wrongs in order to be granted atonement.

The confession is central to the Yom Kippur service. At the time of the Temple and its sacrificial cult, the High Priest would confess on behalf of himself and his family, then for the priesthood, and, finally, for all Israel. Since the destruction of the Temple, each individual Jew confesses for himself or herself, but within the communality of the people of Israel. Thus the public confession that is made repeatedly during the day is for crimes that may not have been committed by the individuals concerned. Nevertheless, through this, it is understood that God forgives his people – till the next time.

The covenant

The history of the world, and particularly of the Jewish people, is perceived through the Bible as one of a constant cycle of wrongdoing, repentance and forgiveness. After Adam, humanity quickly descended into the depths of corruption and violence. Saved through Noah from total destruction, it soon returned to evil. Then one man, Abraham, and the nation that he founded, Israel, became the agents of God's design on earth. Constantly rebelling, refusing to obey God's dictates, this nation suffers punishment, and exile. Restoration and forgiveness come only when they change their ways and return to God.

The idea of a covenant – an agreement between God and individual human beings or nations of help and obligation, and sealed by a sign, or ceremony – is central to Jewish understanding of humankind's relationship with God. The first covenant in the Bible is that made with Noah (Gen 9:8–17) and with all living creatures, swearing God will never again wreak such total destruction as wrought by the flood. The sign is the rainbow, and the implication is that human beings, in return, must live better lives than before.

However, humanity continues much as before, and this leads to the choosing of one man rather than all humankind for the furtherance of God's purpose on earth. That man is Abraham, and the covenants made with him (Gen 15, 17) relate to the giving of land – the land of Israel – and the promise of fathering a great nation. The reciprocal obligation, on the part of Abraham's descendants, is to circumcise their sons on the eighth day after birth, as a sign of the relationship between God and his people.

181

The covenant that is central to Judaism, however, is that made with Moses on behalf of the people of Israel on Mount Sinai (Exod 19 – 24:11). There, God established himself as the only God of Israel, and Israel became his special people, mutually bound in a series of intricate laws and obligations that are developed through the rest of the Torah, are expanded in rabbinic literature, and have become the overriding focus of Jewish practice to this day.

> If you follow My laws and faithfully observe My commandments, I will grant your rains in their season, so that the earth shall yield its produce and the trees of the field their fruit. Your threshing shall overtake the vintage, and your vintage shall overtake the sowing; you shall eat your fill of bread and dwell securely in your land . . . I will establish My abode in your midst, and I will not spurn you. I will be ever in your midst; I will be your God, and you shall be My people. (Lev 26:3–5, 11–12)

The covenant clearly establishes God as Israel's King. As his subjects, his people not only owe him sole allegiance, but are obligated to behave as fitting representatives of their Lord.

> Now then, if you will obey Me faithfully, and keep My covenant, you shall be My treasured possession among all the people. Indeed, all the earth is Mine, but you shall be to Me a kingdom of priests and a holy nation. (Exod 19:5–6)

If Israel fails to keep God's commands, then appropriate punishment follows, seen largely in the barrenness of the land, its conquest, and ultimately the exile of its people.

The rest of the biblical narratives demonstrate how easily Israel fell into breaking the covenant, in particular, in the worship of other gods. The major events of Israelite history, namely, the destruction of the two Temples and the two exiles that followed[11] are understood to be the result of God's response – by breaking his obligation to provide the people with the land of Israel. The prophets look to a future age, however, and a new covenant:

> But such is the covenant I will make with the House of Israel after these days – declares the Lord: I will put My Teaching into their inmost being and inscribe it upon their hearts. Then I will be their God, and they shall be My people. No longer will they need to teach one another and say to one another, 'Heed the Lord' for all of them, from the least of them to the greatest, shall heed Me – declares the Lord. For I will forgive their iniquities, and remember their sins no more. (Jer 31:33–34)

Later Judaism perceived that this will happen with the coming of the Messiah, and the people of Israel will finally be restored in perfect covenant with their God.

The chosen people

Inextricably bound up with the idea of covenant is that of Israel's election by God to be his special representative on earth.

While in biblical times many tribes would have their particular god, such a relationship would be a natural one without the complications of theology. There was no idea of a god choosing his particular people. Yet God's specific choosing of Israel is central to Jewish theology. Moreover, the choice was reciprocal.

> Joshua said to the people, 'You are witnesses against yourselves that you have by your own act chosen to serve the Lord!' 'Yes we are!' they responded. (Josh 24:22)

Another difference for Israel was that their god was the God of all peoples, and the obligation on the part of Israel was towards all nations.

> Thus said God the Lord,
> Who created the heavens and stretched them out,
> Who spread out the earth and what it brings forth,
> Who gave breath to the people upon it
> And life to those who walk thereon:
> I the Lord, in My grace, have summoned you,
> And I have grasped you by the hand.
> I created you, and appointed you
> A covenant people, a light of nations –
> Opening eyes deprived of light,
> Rescuing prisoners from confinement,
> From the dungeon those who sit in darkness. (Isa 42:5–7)

In a strange way, the particularism of the notion of a chosen people gives rise to a universalism of vision. God chooses his people to serve his purpose in furthering the destiny of all humanity. By following God's commandments – *mitzvot* – Israel is contributing to the perfecting of the world.

> By three things is the world sustained: by the Law, by the Temple service, and by deeds of loving-kindness. (*Pirkei Avot* 1:2)

This, probably the most famous passage in the Mishnah, attributed to Simeon the Just, indicates the centrality of this notion. Of the three things essential to the maintenance of the world, two are exclusively Jewish activities, while the third, though a universal principle, is clear in this context to refer to Jewish obligation only.

The people of Israel were also required to witness to God's nature and being in the universe. Through them the world would turn to God. This did not mean converting to Judaism, but turning to the worship of the one true God. Many today would claim this to have happened through the spread of Christianity and Islam – two religions that owe their roots to Judaism. So in this way, too, the particularism of the chosenness of Israel can be seen as leading to universalism.

Nevertheless, through the centuries there has been some considerable embarrassment at what appears to be an exclusivistic view of the nature of the universe and humankind's place in it. The medieval rabbis were at pains to stress that Israel was chosen for service, not privilege, and that greater responsibility lay upon the Jew, therefore, than the non-Jew. The Jew had to observe all the commandments, or *mitzvot*, of the Torah – calculated as 613 – while the non-Jew had to observe only seven to be accounted a righteous person.

These seven are known as the *mitzvot* of the sons of Noah, harking back to the Noachide covenant with Noah, and are usually understood to relate to idolatry, blasphemy, sexual sins, murder, theft, eating a limb from a living animal and establishing courts of justice. Moreover, the greater responsibility of Israel meant the greater the punishment for erring: 'You only have I known of all the families of the earth; therefore I will visit upon you all your iniquities' (Amos 3:2).

Finally, the rabbis found some justification for Israel's chosenness in the notion that other nations had been selected first, but refused to accept the role.

Before God gave Israel the Torah, He approached every tribe and nation, and offered them the Torah, that hereafter they might have no excuse to say 'Had the Holy One, blessed be He, desired to give us the Torah, we should have accepted it'. He went to the children of Esau and said 'Will ye accept the Torah?' They answered Him, saying 'What is written therein?' He answered them: 'Thou shalt not kill.' Then they all said: 'Wilt Thou perchance take from us the blessing with which our Father Esau was blessed? For he was blessed with the words "By thy sword shalt thou live". We do not want to accept the Torah.' Thereupon He went to the children of Lot and said unto them 'Will ye accept the Torah?' They said 'What is written therein?' He answered: 'Thou shalt not commit unchastity.' They said 'From unchastity we spring; we do not want to accept the Torah'. Then He went to the children of Ishmael and said: 'Do ye want to accept the Torah?' They said 'What is written therein?' He answered: 'Thou shalt not steal.' They said, 'Wilt Thou take from us the blessing with which our father was blessed? God promised him "His hand will be against every man". We do not want to accept Thy Torah.' Thence he went to all the other nations, who likewise rejected the Torah saying: 'We cannot give up the law of our fathers, we do not want Thy Torah, give it to Thy people Israel.' Upon this, he came to Israel and spoke to them 'Will ye accept the Torah?' They said to him 'What is written therein?' He answered: 'Six hundred and thirteen commandments.' They said 'All that the Lord has spoken, we will do and be obedient[12]'.

While embarrassment with the notion of Israel's being chosen continues to exist, there is no sign that the idea will ever lose its central importance. Jewish prayers are full of references to it, for example, in the sanctification of a Festival.

Blessed art Thou, O Lord, our God, King of the Universe, who has chosen us from among all peoples and exalted us above all nations and hallowed us by Thy commandments.[13]

However, although Israel may be perceived as the agents of God in the world, the ultimate redemption that is expected will extend to all peoples.

Messiah

Redemption will come in the messianic age, a future era when the world will be perfected and all humanity will come to know God. While Judaism allows for the possible perfection of humanity by itself, there exists, alongside that, a notion of a future divine intervention in the world that will stop the bloodshed and restore the world's people to the state of bliss that was theirs in the Garden of Eden.

The Bible contains both ideas. The prophets Nahum, Habakkuk, Malachi and Joel describe a messianic age brought about by the people's change of heart, while Isaiah, Micah, Jeremiah and Zechariah look to a messianic figure who will be the ideal leader, executing

185

justice and righteousness in the name of the Lord, once he has redeemed his people.

> And a throne shall be established in goodness
> In the tent of David,
> And on it shall sit in faithfulness
> A ruler devoted to justice
> And zealous for equity. (Isa 6:5)

Depending on the period in history, or the particular circumstances of the period, either one or the other idea has been the more popular.

The term *messiah* comes from a Hebrew word meaning 'to anoint'. In the Bible, kings and high priests were anointed with oil to indicate divine sanction of their office. One non-Jewish King is also called *messiah*: Cyrus, the Persian ruler who allowed the return to Jerusalem of the exiled Jews in Babylonia (Isa 45:1). He fulfils the function of messiah in that he acts as an agent of God, carrying out his divine purpose.

The apocalyptic literature of the centuries that followed the Prophets developed an elaborate plan of exactly how the messianic age would come about. This included miraculous 'signs': cataclysmic events, such as earthquakes, wars, famine and floods known as the 'birthpangs of the Messiah'; the return of Elijah, who, according to biblical tradition, never died (2 Kgs 2:11), and, according to later tradition, would announce the imminent arrival of the Messiah; the 'trumpet of the Messiah' – the blowing of the heavenly *shofar* as at the revelation on Mount Sinai (Exod 19:19); the 'ingathering of the exiles', when all Jews will return to the promised land; the reception of proselytes; the final apocalyptic war between the forces of good and evil ('the war of Gog and Magog': Ezek 38–39); the 'Days of the Messiah', when he rules the earth with righteousness (Isa 9:1–6 and others); the renovation of the world, where it is restored to its original pristine glory; the Day of Judgement; the bodily resurrection of the dead; and finally, the world to come.

All these ideas had an enormous effect on subsequent literature, though nothing like a fixed and totally accepted doctrine ever emerged. Some rabbis concentrated on trying to calculate the time of the Messiah's arrival, others on his identity, others on the qualities the Messiah would show.

Over the centuries, at times of great persecution, messianic figures have arisen, only to be regarded, after their failure to change the world materially, as false messiahs. In our age, some Hasidim[14] declare the Messiah is in our midst, but that it is up to the Jews of the world to observe Judaism correctly, before he will reveal himself.

This theory connects that of divine intervention with the idea of human ability and responsibility to perfect the world. Hasidic theology is based on that of the sixteenth-century kabbalists, and in particular Isaac Luria,[15] who proposed the notion of the divine sparks. According to this doctrine, the divine light that emanated from the Godhead was too strong to be contained in the lower reaches of the heavens, and by some cosmic catastrophe, the vessels that held it shattered, and the light fell as sparks to earth. To effect the repair of the cosmos, it becomes the duty of the Jew to lift up those sparks and restore them to heaven, through piety and observance of the *mitzvot*. In this view, humanity can redeem not only itself and the world, but also the entire cosmos, and even the Godhead itself, by its own efforts alone.

The main champion of a messianic age without a messiah is Progressive Judaism.[16] Influenced by the belief, prevalent in the early decades of the twentieth century, that humanity was indeed moving into a new era of peace and universal friendship, it rejected the notion of a personal messiah in favour of a messianic age, based on the writings of the prophets. Though this optimism was shattered by the Holocaust and has resulted in a reappraisal, the majority of Progressive Jews still believe humanity can, by its own efforts, change the world. If God intervenes at all, it is by changing the hearts of human beings, not by sending a leader or by miraculous or apocalyptic events.

After death

The idea of an existence after death is central to Jewish belief, though again, there is no one consistent idea found in the various developments of Jewish thought.

The Bible has no clear description of what life after death is like, though references to *Sheol*, a dark, shadowy underworld, run through the prophetic books, most notably in the story concerning Saul and the witch of En Dor in 1 Samuel 28:8. It has been suggested that this was

187

part of a popular faith that was frowned upon by the religious authorities as being part of pagan culture.

The one biblical passage upon which the beliefs of later Judaism seem to be based is Daniel 12:2.

Many of those that sleep in the dust will awake, some to eternal life, others to reproaches, to everlasting abhorrence.

Alongside the notion of a Messiah, during the time of the Second Temple two distinctive ideas emerged: the immortality of the soul, and the bodily resurrection of the dead. The problem is that they are in some sense contradictory and much of rabbinic literature on the subject is, therefore, inconsistent.

R. Jacob said: This world is like a vestibule before the world to come: prepare thyself in the vestibule that thou mayest enter into the banqueting hall. (*Pirkei Avot* 4:16)

It is not clear whether the world to come is to be enjoyed on earth or in heaven. The ideas expressed in rabbinic literature suggest the following sequence. On death the soul leaves the body and remains for a year in Sheol as a sort of purgatory. Then the wicked enter Gehinnon where they suffer unremitting punishment, while the righteous enter into the delights of the Garden of Eden, a place where the sages of all generations discuss scripture while their wives sit at their feet. With the coming of the Messiah comes universal redemption; the souls return to dust, where they are reconstituted with their bodies, and the righteous enter the world to come, where:

there is no eating nor drinking nor propagation nor business nor jealousy nor hatred nor competition, but the righteous sit with their crowns on their heads feasting on the brightness of the divine presence. (BT *Berakhot* 17a)

The medieval philosophers were concerned by the contradictions and tried hard to resolve them. Saadiah Gaon did so by implying two resurrections and suggesting that punishment for the wicked was eternal. Moses Maimonides virtually ignored the idea of a physical resurrection, putting forward the idea of the soul's immortality in the active intellect, with heavenly bliss as the knowledge of God and Gehinnon as the annihilation of the soul. Kabbalistic mysticism took yet another idea found in rabbinic Judaism, that of *gilgul* or the

188

transmigration of souls, to suggest that the sinner is one that has not fulfilled its soul's destiny and that soul must return in other bodies till such time as it does so.

While it appears that, theologically, the idea of the immortality of the soul took precedence over that of resurrection, in popular religion, where it was (mistakenly) perceived as being more authentically Jewish, resurrection became the overriding belief. The few sentences that Maimonides wrote on resurrection became a principle of faith,[17] while his lengthy treatises on the soul are ignored.

The main prayer of Judaism, the Eighteen Benedictions, or *Amidah*, contains the following paragraph:

> Thou sustainest the living with lovingkindness, revivest the dead with great mercy, supportest the falling, healest the sick, freest the bound, and keepest thy faith with them that sleep in the dust. Who is like unto thee, Lord of mighty acts, and who resembleth thee, O King, who orderest death and restorest life and causest salvation to spring forth? Yea, faithful thou art to revive the dead. Blessed art thou, O Lord who revivest the dead.[18]

This prayer, which owes its origins to the Pharisees, who were in conflict with the Sadducees over this matter, is said three times daily, and four times on Sabbaths and festivals. So the belief is still strongly present in Judaism, although today, many deny its literal import. The current trend seems not to speculate, but to say, with Maimonides, that to try to grasp the nature of the hereafter is 'like a man who is blind trying to grasp the nature of colour'.[19]

Notes

1 Homiletical interpretations of the Bible composed by rabbis in the early centuries of the current era. See Chapter 4, p. 114.

2 Quoted in Epstein (1954), p. 210.

3 Saadiah Gaon (Babylonia, 882–942 CE), one of the greatest and most influential Jewish thinkers. See Chapter 4, p. 126.

4 *Bereshit Rabbah* 8:1.

5 *Alphabet of Ben Sira*, c. tenth century CE.

6 'Eminence does not become a woman. There were two eminent women in the Bible ... their names are hateful' (*Deborah* means 'hornet', and *Hulda* 'weasel'): *Megillah* 14a.

7 Steven T. Katz (1977) *Jewish Ideas and Concepts*. New York: Schocken Books, p. 102.

8   Moses Maimonides (1135–1204; b. Spain), foremost philosopher combining Aristotelian principles with classic Jewish teaching. See Chapter 4, pp. 127–31.
9   Leaders of Israel during the Persian period from Ezra to 'Simeon the Just' (probably the High Priest Simeon II, 219–199 BCE).
10 Mishnah: codification of rabbinic law compiled in Palestine 200 CE; Talmud: rabbinic commentaries on the Mishnah, written in Palestine and Babylon c. third-sixth century. See Chapter 4, pp. 117–19.
11 Temple destruction in 586 BCE, followed by the Babylonian exile, and in 70 CE by the Romans, followed by the general dispersion which, despite the establishment of the state of Israel in 1948, is perceived as still continuing.
12 Quoted in Louis Ginzberg (1909) *The Legends of the Jews*. Philadelphia: Jewish Publications Society, vol. III, p. 80.
13 J. H. Hertz (1976) *The Authorised Daily Prayer Book*. London: Bloch, p. 808.
14 Hasidism emerged in seventeenth-century Poland as a popularist quasi-mystical sect in reaction to the excessive scholasticism of the rabbinic Judaism of the time. On the death of its founder, the movement organized itself into different sects, each following a particular charismatic 'rebbe', of whom the Lubavitch are the best known.
15 Isaac Luria (1534–1572), the foremost mystic of the most influential school of Kabbalah, centred on Safed in Galilee.
16 Following on the Enlightenment and the emancipation of the Jews of Europe in the eighteenth century, there was a reformation of Judaism that sought more contemporary interpretations of Jewish tradition in the light of modern secular thinking. In England today, this is represented by two movements: Liberal Judaism and Reform.
17 Maimonides' 'Thirteen Principles of Faith', based on his commentary *Mishnah Sanhedrin* 10:1, are printed in all Orthodox prayer-books. *The Authorised Daily Prayer Book*, p. 248. See pp. 127–9 above.
18 *Authorised Daily Prayer Book*, p. 135.
19 Maimonides, commentary on the Mishnah; *Sanhedrin* 10:1.

References and further reading

Cohen, Arthur A. and Mendes-Flohr, Paul (eds) (1987) *Contemporary Jewish Religious Thought*. New York: Charles Scribners.
Cohen, S. S. (1971) *Jewish Theology*. Assen: Royal Vangorum.
Eisenstein, I. (ed.) (1966) *Varieties of Jewish Belief*. New York: Reconstructionist Press.
Epstein, I. (1954) *The Faith of Judaism*. London: Soncino.

Heschel, A. J. (1955) *God in Search of Man*. New York: Jewish Publication Society.

Jacobs, L. (1973) *A Jewish Theology*. London: Darton Longman and Todd.

Kohler, K. (1968) *Jewish Theology*. New York: Ktav.

Schechter, S. (1961) *Aspects of Rabbinic Theology*. New York: Ktav.

Scholem, Gershom G. (1971) *The Messianic Idea in Judaism*. New York: Schocken.

Articles in the *Encyclopaedia Judaica* (1972). Jerusalem: Keter Publishing House.

7. Women in Judaism

Alexandra Wright

Introduction

Judaism is the religious culture of the Jewish people. The central teaching of Judaism is the belief in one God and the duty to love God. This affirmation is found in the Hebrew scriptures (Deut 6:4–5) and repeated in the Jewish liturgy in the daily morning and evening service:

> Hear, O Israel: the Eternal One is our God, the Eternal God is One. And you shall love your Eternal God with all your heart, with all your soul and with all your strength ...

Belief in and love of God are borne out in another teaching essential to Judaism: 'You shall love your neighbour as yourself' (Lev 19:18). Love of God and love and respect for one's fellow human beings characterize the religion of the Jewish people. The laws, practices, rituals and customs that have evolved over a very long period of time are considered to be the means whereby one strives for the ideal relationship with God and with God's creatures.

The Hebrew Bible

The earliest stage in the history of the Jewish people is told through a collection of narratives found in the Hebrew Bible. It is the story of the migrations of a family and its descendants. That family, and later community, had entered into a covenant with God, obedience to

192

which gave the Israelite community a special status in the eyes of their God (Exod 19:5–6). The essence of the covenant was its laws: prescriptions governing all aspects of the life of the individual, the family and the community of Israel.

The women of the Hebrew Bible are both the subjects of legislation, for example on slavery or divorce, and also, themselves, subjects of narratives or historical accounts. While it is difficult to generalize about the position of women in such a diffuse work of literature, it is perhaps possible to say that the women of the Hebrew Bible enjoy a particular status both privately and publicly in the domains which they inhabit. The matriarchs of the book of Genesis, Sarah, Rebekah, Leah and Rachel, are portrayed not only in their domestic roles as wives and mothers, but also as individuals whose lives contributed to the course of Jewish history. Deborah, in the book of Judges, and the prophetesses Miriam and Huldah represent women who occupied important leadership roles in ancient times, while the 'virtuous woman' in the book of Proverbs (chapter 31) represents the idealization of a woman who works hard for her household, who enters into negotiations to buy and sell, who is charitable, kind, wise and respected because of the work she undertakes.

There are, too, other role models in the Hebrew Bible, from whom contemporary women have drawn inspiration: Hagar, the single mother who is made homeless by the father of her child and his wife; Tamar, the daughter of King David, who is raped by her brother (2 Sam 13); Yael, in the book of Judges, whose courage and fearlessness are imitated by Judith in the Apocrypha; and Ruth, whose loyalty to her mother-in-law Naomi is held up as an example of a woman who forsook her own people to join the culture and religion of her new family. The five daughters of Zelophehad (Num 27) provide an interesting example of women whose influence brought about a change in the inheritance law, which subsequently allowed women to inherit property from their father if there were no sons. In the mythical narrative of the garden of Eden, the first woman, Eve, plays a crucial role in Jewish tradition, not as catalyst of a 'fall' – a concept which is foreign to Judaism – but as a woman who desired wisdom (Gen 3:6) and whose role in these chapters is somehow inevitable, if not ordained in the divine scheme of things.[1]

The heterogeneity of the Hebrew Bible, its contradictions, the diversity of its literary genres and the different stylistic uses of the Hebrew language reflect a wide variety of portrayals of, and attitudes to, women, not to mention the constantly changing circumstances of Israel's history.[2]

Intertestamental literature

It is not possible to say with any certainty at what point the corpus of books of the Hebrew Bible became canonized, that is to say, a recognized, authoritative collection which excluded other literature. There is a little evidence that suggests this might have begun happening as early as the second century BCE. From this period and earlier, until the second century CE, the Jewish literature of the Greek and Roman world, the non-canonical literature of Judaism, conveys the developments that were taking place in the Jewish community. Again, it contains different literary genres: apocalypses, narrative fiction, testaments and history, not to mention the works of Josephus and Philo. The centuries that produced this literature witnessed great religious turmoil and upheaval, and culminated tragically for the Jewish people in the destruction of the Temple in Jerusalem in 70 CE and the end of the Jewish commonwealth and Jewish independence. Some of the narratives and Wisdom literature of this period reflect an attitude to women and their position in society, but there are, too, epitaphs and inscriptions and other archives that offer us a more reliable source for a picture of women's lives in the diaspora world of late antiquity.

Excavated inscriptions from this period demonstrate that women held titles of leadership and seemed to take a more active part in synagogue life than they were destined to do at a later date. Certain women are described as *archisynagogissa* ('head of synagogue') and *presbytera* ('elder' or 'member of council').

The Dead Sea Scrolls provide a remarkable insight into community life and biblical interpretation during this period. Indeed, some of the interpretation by the parties of the Pharisees, Sadducees or Essenes is decidedly idiosyncratic. For example, the Pentateuch gives no direct ruling on whether a niece may marry her uncle. Pharisaic and rabbinic Judaism legitimizes this union on the basis of the silence of the Torah, and even praises it as a particularly generous act comparable to the loving-kindness shown to the poor and needy (BT *Yevamot* 62b). However, the Qumran Essenes regarded the union as 'fornication':

Moses said 'You shall not approach your mother's sister [i.e., your aunt];

she is your mother's near kin' (Lev 18:13). But although the laws against incest are written for men, they also apply to women. When therefore a brother's daughter uncovers the nakedness of her father's brother, she is (also his) near kin.[3]

Rabbinic Judaism

Until the Pharisaic revolution had marginalized almost completely expressions of non-rabbinic Judaism, Jewish life in the ancient Hellenistic and Roman world was characterized by its heterogeneity. The destruction of the Temple, the centre of almost continuous Jewish worship and sacrifice since the days of King Solomon, was a catastrophe for the Jews, but it was not unmitigated. The Pharisaic movement, hardly a new movement within Judaism, was to determine the pathway of Jewish history. In the last decades of Jewish independence, the Pharisees, a scholar class of Jews, had lived side by side with other sects within Judaism, notably the Sadducees, the men of the Temple. Yet there was hardly any consonance in the views of these two movements. Even as the Temple was going up in flames, Pharisaic leaders such as Johanan ben Zakkai, were suggesting that service to God could be performed as effectively in the synagogues or houses of study as within the Temple.

The Pharisees saw themselves as guardians and interpreters of the teachings of the Torah (the Five Books of Moses). But those teachings did not derive exclusively from the Pentateuch. By the side of this body of written teaching, there evolved a corpus of oral teaching. These prescriptions were more detailed, defining how the written law was to be carried out and enforced. Its authority was considered to be as great as the authority of the Written Torah, for it was believed to be part of the revelation that had been received on Mount Sinai. The Oral Torah expands and defines, it resolves conflicts inherent in scripture, provides for new situations and interprets the Written Torah.

The teachers of the first and second centuries (tannaim), notably R. Akiva and R. Meir, had begun the work of codifying the Oral Law, but it was left to R. Judah the Prince, towards the end of the second century CE, to complete their labours. The completed work of codification is known as the Mishnah ('teaching'). It contains six orders, each order being concerned with a different aspect of Jewish life. One complete order is devoted to the legal status of women (Nashim).

Pharisaic literature is not exclusively legislative or prescriptive. Its counterpart is richly interpretative, containing legendary embellishments on the narratives of the Torah, and different theological preoccupations and viewpoints. The generic terms that are used to classify these two kinds of literature are *halakhah* (literally 'the way', law) and *aggadah* (lore). Both genres are found in the literature of the Talmud. Discussions about women in the Mishnah and Talmud are numerous. Both deal with the legal status of women in the private and public domain, but both also deal with attitudes to women. One of the difficulties in studying this material is that the discussions are recorded by the rabbis and teachers of Jewish colleges of learning in Palestine and Babylonia. There is sparse mention of individual women, and such allusions are scarcely corroborated in other material. Mostly, we find references to women generally, and occasionally a caustic or indeed affectionate remark from one man about his mother, or his wife or daughter.

The Talmud is a very diffuse work. It does not present discussion systematically as does the Mishnah, on which it is based. It presents discussions in the form of a stream of consciousness. Its exponents pick up allusions and frequently introduce a different branch of discourse. For this reason, it was always necessary for the scholars of subsequent generations to make further clarifications of the law and to respond to new situations.

The Gaonic period (from the seventh century), and certainly the Middle Ages of the Islamic world and central and northern Europe, offer us further evidence for the life of women and their domestic and public roles. It is clear that Jews were often influenced by the cultures in which they lived, so that there sometimes existed a wide disparity between women in the Islamic world, for example, and more independent women of central Europe.

The discovery of a *genizah* (literally 'storing'; a repository of documents) in Cairo at the end of the nineteenth century has provided scholars with remarkable historical information concerning the preoccupation of Jews of Israel and Egypt from the ninth to the twelfth centuries. Again we are fortunate to learn more about the status and position of women in this period from some of the documents preserved.

The major literary sources of this period are medieval codes of Jewish law, reflecting both Sephardi and Ashkenazi practices, and the responsa literature, a genre of literature which has continued until the present day. The responsa literature addresses itself to individual questions posed by different communities concerning the daily religious life of individuals. Entire sections are devoted to the laws concerning women: their education, betrothal and marriage, their occupations, their duties and responsibilities towards their families and the boundaries that were set around their religious involvement in the community.

Rare are the testimonies of women themselves until the modern period. A notable exception is Glueckel of Hameln (1646–1724), whose autobiography offers a rare insight into the personal lives of women. Glueckel, a widow, had considerable commercial success, and we learn that women were certainly not excluded from the world of economics or commerce.

Emancipation

The emancipation of European Jewry in the early nineteenth century had an immense influence on the intellectual and social life of the Jewish people. Women and men were faced with two choices: to retain the traditional practices and beliefs of Judaism, or harmonize their religion with their civic emancipation and thus gain from their compatriots recognition as full citizens. In response to this choice, two distinct religious movements arose in the nineteenth century: Orthodoxy and Reform. Attitudes towards women and the extent to which women are accorded full equality within these movements are shaped by the theological premise on which each movement is based, and in particular by the attitude to the authority of Written and Oral Torah.

The role of women in Judaism today is largely determined by the religious and intellectual environment in which one has grown up. The Progressive Jewish movements of Israel and the diaspora accord equality to women in religious life, which means that women are permitted to lead services, become rabbis and assume those rituals that have been regarded as being exclusively for men. The Orthodox movements do not restrict women in their choice of secular career, but draw a distinction between secular and religious life. The nature of equality is different. While women may conduct services, read from the Torah and accept as binding certain obligations that were traditionally perceived to be exclusively male obligations, they may do

197

these things for themselves and for each other, but not for a mixed congregation.

Contemporary scholarship dealing with the place of women in Jewish life has been enhanced considerably by feminist studies of all periods of Jewish history. The student today is beginning to claim an easier access to the lives of Jewish women of the past than has hitherto been possible. We no longer need to rely on the androcentric sources that offer us only one insight into women's lives. The work of scholars such as Bernadette Brooten and others is offering us a completely new way of looking at women and their place in Judaism.

Beginnings

The commandment to seek out a partner for companionship and procreation derives from the book of Genesis.

> Therefore shall a man leave his father and his mother, and shall cleave unto his wife and they shall be one flesh. (Gen 2:24)

> And God blessed [the man and the woman] and God said to them: 'Be fruitful and multiply, and replenish the earth.' (Gen 1:28)

The birth of female children is not mentioned at all in the Hebrew Bible, whereas the importance of securing a male heir is given great emphasis. While the narrator of the book of Genesis mentions the birth and naming of each of Jacob's sons, the arrival of Jacob's daughter, Dinah, is not commented on at all. During the slavery in Egypt and the multiplication of the Israelites there, the Hebrew midwives are instructed by Pharaoh to kill all male babies and allow female children to survive. These details are indicative of the attitude towards, and position of, women in ancient Near Eastern society. The woman does not appear to be important to Israelite lineage. Cultic and national identity is passed through the male line.

The biblical laws surrounding childbirth also indicate that the boundaries in which women existed were materially different from those defined by and for men. A woman was rendered ritually unclean after the birth of her children, seven days and then a further 33 days for her male child, and for a female child fourteen days and then a further 66 days (Lev 12:1–5).[4] Like many other primitive religions, the ancient form of Judaism surrounded pregnancy, birth and menstruation with many taboos and a system of strict order which defined what was considered ritually clean and ritually unclean. This was not an isolated system, but part of a larger definition of margins connected with what was considered to be holy or polluting, whether of the body or to do with the sanctuary or other areas of holiness and defilement.

A minority of Jewish women today observe these laws of isolation. For others, the emphasis is laid upon the act of welcoming the child into the covenant. For boys, this is done with the ritual of circumcision at eight days old, at which ceremony the boy is also given his Hebrew name. For girls, the ceremony is combined with an act of thanksgiving by the parents in the synagogue at no specifically defined time after the birth of the child. The elements of such a service include both the mother's and the father's expression of gratitude and thanksgiving that they have been brought through an anxious time:

> I love the Eternal One who has heard my supplications.
> Who has heeded me and whose name I will call upon all my days.
> How can I repay the Eternal One for all the divine benefits wrought unto me?
> I will offer You the sacrifice of thanksgiving and call upon the name of the Eternal One. (from Psalm 116)

The child is then given her Hebrew name. The hope that she will grow up to become a full and loyal member of the House of Israel is expressed, and God's blessing is invoked upon her life. In synagogues where women cannot be called up to recite prayers aloud, the father alone is called up without the child and given the honour of reciting the blessing over the Torah on the Sabbath following his daughter's birth.

Education

The study of the Torah is considered to be the most important of all the commandments incumbent upon the Jewish individual. The Torah here indicates the whole of Jewish tradition as transmitted through the great works of Jewish literature – the Bible, the Mishnah, the Gemara,[5] medieval codes, and so forth. This commandment derives from Deuteronomy 6:7, in which each generation is commanded to teach diligently to their children the words of the Shema: 'Hear O Israel: The Eternal One is our God, the Eternal God is One.' Study is considered

199

to be a form of worship leading to the observance of the command-ments, and it is with that aim in mind that the rabbis made *talmud torah* (study of the Torah) central in the life of the Jew.

In traditional Jewish law (*halakhah*) the obligation to teach one's child falls on the father. Furthermore, the obligation is binding if the child is a son, but it is not binding if that child is a daughter. Women's exemption from study derives from a passage in the Mishnah and the talmudic commentary on it (BT *Kiddushin* 29a). The exemption of women does not mean that women may not study. Indeed, in another discussion from the Talmud (BT *Sotah* 20a), there is a disagreement between the second-century tannaitic teacher ben Azzai and his con-temporary R. Eliezer. While ben Azzai is of the opinion that a man is under the obligation to teach his daughter Torah, R. Eliezer counters with the statement 'Whoever teaches his daughter Torah, teaches her nonsense'. While R. Eliezer's statement received some modification in the Gemara (BT *Sotah* 21b), it was to be responsible for perpetuating the ignorance of women until more enlightened scholars realized the importance of rearing women in Jewish classical texts.

Rachel Biale makes this point in relation to an interesting paradox which emerges from the legal obligation of the father to teach his son Torah and the more popular image of the mother's influence in the home:

> It is interesting to contrast the text of *Kiddushin* 29a which places the responsibility of preparing a child for a proper Jewish life as an adult on the father, with the popular image of the traditional Jewish woman. The image one encounters time and again in literature, memoirs, and sentimental and polemical writings glorifying the role of women in traditional Judaism points to the woman as the bearer of tradition in the home, and as the one who passes the heritage to her children. The relation between the image and the historical reality is an elusive problem ... but it is important to note that the image is grounded in popular ethos, perhaps magnified by senti-mentalism, and is not based on the requirements of the *Halakhah*. (Biale, 1984, p. 30)

Just to underline this dichotomy between the *halakhah* and the experiential reality, one should record that the talmudic period knew of a number of exceptionally learned women who were singled out for their piety and knowledge. Beruriah, the wife of the second-century teacher Rabbi Meir, is one example; Imma Shalom, the wife of Eliezer ben Hyrcanus and sister of Rabban Gamaliel of Yavneh, is another.

Rachel, the wife of Akiva, valued learning in her husband and was said to have sold her hair to allow her husband to go and study.

These women follow in the footsteps of earlier examples of learning and leadership. Deborah's role as judge and prophetess is an important one in the Hebrew Bible (Judg 4 – 5). She is the only one of the twelve judges in the book of that name of whom it is said that she presides as a judge over the people. Her male counterparts all appear to be local military heroes and leaders. Her role as prophetess is not explicated, but we do know that it was a prophetess, Huldah, whom King Josiah consulted at the time when a book of law was found in the Temple in the sixth century BCE.

Observance of the commandments required knowledge of the commandments. Some practical knowledge of the basics of Jewish law was inevitably necessary. *Halakhah* prescribes three positive commandments to be undertaken specifically by women and, of course, women were obligated to observe all negative prohibitions, such as the observance of the Sabbath and the dietary rules. The three positive commandments are: the lighting of the Sabbath candles, the separation of the dough of the *hallah* (the Sabbath bread) and *niddah* (the laws of menstruation). Knowledge of these laws prepared a girl for the domestic role she was to undertake in adulthood. They symbolized her responsibility for the household and as regulator of sexual relations between her and her husband.

The difference of opinion that existed among talmudic scholars over the subject of women and learning has continued right into the twentieth century. While R. Eliezer's opinion, that in teaching a woman Torah one is teaching her nonsense, is certainly not adhered to, there has, until recently, been an inequality between the education of women and that of men. It is very much the social and economic status of a family that determines whether a woman is to receive either secular or religious education. Pomona Modena, a member of the eminent Modena family of Ferrara in seventeenth-century Italy, is a model of female scholarship. She was well versed in the Talmud. On one occasion, Rabbi David of Imola addressed a detailed responsum to her, on a point of Jewish law which only a scholar could have understood.

Bathsheba Modena, a relation of Pomona and an ancestress of the famous Leone da Modena, was an inspired poetess. She was, according to one of her grandchildren, constantly engaged in study, had considerable acquaintance with the *Zohar*, the medieval mystical commentary on the Torah, was an expert in the writings of Maimonides and undertook regular study each week. There is also some evidence to suggest that she had considerable influence on the intellectual development of the *conversa* Dona Gracia Nasi. Another outstanding woman of this period was Benvenida Abarbanel, the niece of Isaac Abarbanel, whose family had left Spain in 1492 to live in Naples. She was an educated woman who had established a good relationship with the Duchess of Tuscany and had managed to postpone a decree of expulsion of the Jews from southern Italy in 1541. After the death of her husband, Samuel, she took over his business concerns, attained important trade privileges and lived the life of a pious and charitable woman, whose home was a centre of study and culture. Immanuel Aboab, the chronicler, described her as 'one of the most noble and high-spirited matrons who have existed in Israel since the time of our dispersion; such was the Senora Benvenida Abarbanel – pattern of chastity, of piety, of prudence and of valour'.

Not all Jewish women benefited from such a fine education. In Eastern Europe, there existed certainly among the more wealthy Jews a view which endorsed secular education for girls but which neglected Jewish learning at such an advanced level. Such learning was certainly valued, but for men, not for women. It was not unusual for a wealthy man to consider a match for his daughter to a young talmudic scholar whose breadth of knowledge would hardly match his own daughter's accomplishments in language and the arts.

Contemporary Jews agree on the importance of education for both girls and boys. In the United States of America, where the majority of Jews reside, and in Israel, universities provide programmes for men and women who wish to undertake Jewish studies at a higher level of learning. The training of women for the rabbinate in the Progressive tradition, and the importance ascribed to religious education within Orthodoxy today, have also ensured a high level of learning and Jewish scholarship among women. In addition, women scholars are throwing new light on traditional subjects and unearthing new topics for discussion which reveal a higher degree of involvement by women in public Jewish life than was hitherto imagined. The influence of women's research on the contemporary practice of Judaism, particularly among women, has been far-reaching.[6]

Courtship and marriage

THE HOME

The institution of marriage and the establishment of a family have played a crucial part in ensuring the survival of Judaism. While the synagogue plays a critical role in safeguarding the institution of communal prayer and observance, and adult study, the home is the place in which the child first experiences and learns about his or her Jewish heritage. The Sabbath is welcomed every Friday evening in the home with the lighting of the candles, traditionally performed by the woman of the household. Several festivals are marked prominently in the home, notably Pesach (Passover), with the *seder* (a service and meal taking place round the table at home), and Sukkot, where a *sukkah* (booth) is built. Food and meal times play an important part in helping the Jew to define his or her identity.

Blessings both before and after the meal make the Jew conscious of the people's relationship to God and obligations to their fellow human beings; and the dietary laws remind the Jew of both *tsaar baaleiy hayyim*, the ethical principle that prohibits cruelty to animals, and the distinctiveness of the Jewish people. These major observances all take place within the confines of the home. Though marriage may not be considered ideal for everyone in today's society, it has the potential to provide a safe context in which to bring up children and to teach them the moral values of truth and compassion which Judaism prizes so highly.

MONOGAMY AND POLYGYNY

Curiously, the Bible furnishes no prescriptions regarding the actual ceremony or act of marriage. There are plenty of accounts of marriages and partnerships, but no record of how such unions were performed. We learn from the stories of Abraham and Sarah and Hagar, Jacob, Leah and Rachel, David and Solomon, that it was not unusual in biblical times for men to acquire more than one partner and to father children through those partners. Polygyny was permitted even during the talmudic era, though women were permitted to have only one husband. However, though the Talmud goes as far as speculating on the maximum number of wives a man may have, the legislation as well as the speculation seems to have been academic. We do not know of one rabbi in the entire Talmud (out of approximately 2,800 mentioned) who was polygynous.

In the Middle Ages, Christianity forbade polygyny, and Jews living under Christian rule developed an aversion to, and embarrassment about, the law permitting it. The ban against polygyny is attributed to Rabbenu Gershom (960-1028), though there is evidence that such a ban had already been accepted in many communities even before his time. The ban was introduced in the form of a *takkanah*, a new ruling, which was a departure from biblical and talmudic law. It was backed by the threat of excommunication by the community and its leading rabbis. Not all Jewish communities accepted this ban. In Islamic countries, where polygyny was permitted, some Jews still married more than one wife. Indeed, when the Jews of Yemen were brought to the newly formed state of Israel in 1948, some men arrived with more than one wife. Even though Israel prohibited polygyny, these Yemenite Jews were permitted to maintain their polygynous marriages.

Family life

The narratives of the Hebrew Bible possess a tangible, human dimension. We do not see the portrayal of an ideal state of marriage. The conflicts and jealousies as well as the happier aspects of family life are portrayed in the narratives about Jacob and his family and many others. The account of the courtship and marriage of Isaac to Rebekah shows us that the woman possessed a certain degree of freedom in deciding whom she was to marry. Indeed, the consent of the bride remained an important principle in rabbinic Judaism. Rebekah's role is clearly as companion to her husband – we are told that Isaac was comforted by her after the death of his mother. From the story of Jacob and Rachel, we learn about the affection and devotion that can exist between a husband and wife. Jacob laboured for fourteen years, the price he paid for Rachel to become his wife, and we are told 'It seemed but a short time for the great love he had for her'.

While lineage was passed down through the patrilineal line in biblical times, the role of the woman in marriage is not wholly a passive one. The matriarchs, Sarah, Rebekah, Leah and Rachel, are spirited individuals in their own right. Both Sarah and Rebekah are instrumental in pushing forward the younger of their husband's two sons, Isaac and Jacob respectively, who are to occupy the centre of the stage in the unfolding biblical drama. In other words, these women are used as instruments of the divine plan. In Genesis 38, the story of Tamar, daughter-in-law of Judah, one of Jacob's sons, interrupts the narrative of Joseph to illustrate the institution of levirate marriage and to underline the prominence of the tribe of Judah in the history of Israel.

Yibbum (Levirate marriage)

The law of *yibbum* is prescribed in Deuteronomy 25:5–10:

> If brethren dwell together and one of them die, and have no child, the wife of the dead shall not be married abroad to one not of his kin; her husband's brother shall go in unto her, and take her to him to wife, and perform the duty of a husband's brother unto her [*v'yib'mah*]. And it shall be, that the first-born that she bears shall succeed in the name of his brother that is dead, that his name be not blotted out of Israel. And if the man does not wish to take his brother's wife, then his brother's wife shall go up to the gate to the elders, and shall say: 'My husband's brother refuses to raise up unto his brother a name in Israel; he will not perform the duty of a husband's brother to me.' Then the elders of his city shall call him, and speak to him; and if he stand and say: 'I do not wish to take her'; then his brother's wife shall draw near to him in the presence of the elders, and undo his shoe from his foot, and spit in his face; and she shall answer and say: 'So shall be done unto the man who does not build up his brother's house.'

What lies behind the principle of levirate marriage and other institutions which were preserved by rabbinic Judaism, such as *agunah* (see above, pp. 75 and 122)? Under Jewish law, a girl belonged to her father. Marriage represented, on one level, the acquisition of a bride by the groom from her father. The only way she 'acquired herself', i.e., gained her independence, so to speak, was through divorce, which had to be granted to her by her husband, or on the death of her husband. Although a husband 'acquired' a wife, by 'taking' her, using the biblical and mishnaic vocabulary, she was not his property. He could not sell her, for example. The act of acquisition was to forbid her to all other men. She was to become exclusively the wife of her husband.

THE DEVELOPMENT OF MARRIAGE LAWS

How did a man 'acquire' a wife? The opening pages of the mishnaic tractate *Kiddushin* provide us briefly with the fundamental laws of marriage:

> A woman is acquired in three ways and acquires herself in two. She is acquired by money, by deed, or by intercourse. And she acquires herself by divorce or by the death of her husband. A childless widow is acquired by intercourse and acquires herself by *halitzah* (taking off the shoe) or by her brother-in-law's death.

The sum of money involved in this transaction was negligible; the act was symbolic rather than real. Its function was to designate one particular woman to be the wife of her husband. The Mishnah also cites a second way of effecting marriage: 'by deed'. This 'deed' actually refers to the bill of divorce which releases a woman from marriage. The Gemara deduces that since a divorce document can release a woman from marriage, it must also effect her marriage. The third way to effect the marriage was simply through intercourse. However, though both the Mishnah and the Palestinian Talmud (JT *Kiddushin* 1:1) state the validity of any of these three ways of marriage, the talmudic discussion that follows on the mishnaic passage reveals certain changes, and a level of disapproval of betrothal simply by intercourse. There is a measure of discomfort, as well, with the idea that betrothal can be effected through the almost negligible sum of a *perutah*. Eventually, these simple requirements developed and became more demanding, to the extent that the third-century Babylonian *amora* would punish anyone who became betrothed 'in the market place, or by intercourse, or without prior engagement, or who annulled a divorce ... ' (BT *Kiddushin* 12b).

The talmudic literature reflects, therefore, a change from a fairly simple code of sexual morality to a much stricter one. The biblical code consists of primary rules relating to incest (Lev 18), perversion and adultery, laws concerned with rape and seduction and a few others.[7]

MODESTY

Rabbinic morality reflects a preoccupation with a woman's modesty. The practice of a minority of very pious married women today of covering their hair stems from the belief that a woman's appearance in public with uncovered head constituted immoral behaviour. The Palestinian Talmud (JT *Sotah* 16b) records that the school of Shammai, who recognized no cause for divorce other than adultery, believed that a wife's appearance in public without a head covering constituted legitimate cause for divorce. In other words it was compared to unfaithfulness.

In the sixteenth century, women started wearing a *sheitel* (wig) to cover their hair. It was worn by the bride at her marriage and throughout her married life. However, the practice was not universal. Many women rebelled against what was now an outmoded fashion and went bare-headed. Oriental Jewish women continued to use a veil, as had been used since ancient times. Although the wig is still used by pious women today, for example by the Hasidic sects, the majority of women do not cover their hair.

Rabbinic standards of modesty with respect to exposure and dress were extremely rigorous, though it was frequently the prevailing cultural attitudes that influenced Jewish responses. In the ancient Orient, for example, women wore a veil over the head and a woman of dignity would draw it down over her face. The Palestinian tradition of covering one's face continued through the Middle Ages. However, this practice was not widely accepted among the Jews of Babylonia, and the legislators during the Gaonic period in Babylonia and later on in Europe speak of the veiling of a woman's face as unusual.[8]

SEXUALITY AND *NIDDAH*

Two responses characterize the classical Jewish attitude towards women's sexuality. One is governed by the laws of *niddah* (menstruation). Contact with a menstruant woman was taboo, not only in Judaism, but also in other ancient cultures. Marital sex is strictly regulated by the laws of *niddah*, forbidding husband and wife contact during and after the period of a woman's menstruation and intensifying sexual contact during a period which is conducive to conception. The second attitude is characterized by legislation which prescribes what might be permitted in terms of sexual relations between a husband and wife. While *halakhah* might permit relative freedom in sexual practices, this often created a tension with a more ascetic general attitude towards sexuality. Maimonides summarizes this tension clearly:

> A man's wife is permitted to him. Therefore, whatever a man wishes to do with his wife he may do. He may have intercourse whenever he pleases and he may kiss any organ he wishes. And he may have intercourse in a natural or unnatural manner as long as he does not expend semen to no purpose. And nevertheless, the pious way is not to act lightly in this matter, and to sanctify himself during intercourse, as we have explained in the Laws of Knowledge. And he ought not to deviate from the common practice, for this thing [intercourse] is really only for procreation. (Maimonides, *Mishnah Torah, Issurei Bi'ah* 21:9)

What Maimonides recognizes is a certain latitude in the practical aspects of the *halakhah*, while demanding a certain degree of piety in a man's sanctification of the act of sexual intercourse. There is little doubt that this kind of legislation was directed towards the male partner, whose 'extroverted sexuality' required harnessing to the sexual rhythms of his wife. Biale points out the contrast in perceptions of male and female sexuality:

> Male sexuality is seen by the rabbis as the greater threat to familial and social structures. Male sexuality is active and egocentric, and always in danger of 'running wild'. It must be restrained through the controls of marriage, procreative duties, responsibility towards the woman, and a powerful taboo on male homosexuality and masturbation.
>
> Female sexuality is seen very differently ... Women are portrayed as sexually introverted and passive ... Though her sexuality is hidden, it is as powerful as a man's obvious eroticism, or even greater: 'A woman's passion is greater than that of a man'. (*Bava Metzi'a* 84a) (Biale, 1984, p. 122)

The biblical laws of *niddah* required a woman to remain 'unclean' for seven days, to correspond with her menstrual discharge. At the end of that period she was to bring a burnt offering to make expiation for her discharge (Lev 15:19–33). Post-biblical *halakhah*, however, required her to remain impure for up to fourteen days, a maximum of seven of menses plus a subsequent period of seven 'white days', free of bleeding. The end of this period was marked by *tevilah* (immersion) in a *mikveh* (see p. 00), which indicated permission to resume sexual relations between husband and wife.

After the destruction of the Temple in 70 CE, a shift took place in the laws of *niddah*, from a focus on purity and impurity to a sexual prohibition. Originally, it appears that the laws of *niddah* were designed to keep a woman away from the Temple and from sacred objects only. The laws were not intended to interfere with her daily life and work. Later on, however, the restrictions of the *niddah* applied to the private realm of husband–wife relations. The laws of *niddah* do not exclude a woman from attending the synagogue or taking a part in communal life, though some women voluntarily used to exclude themselves from the community during menstruation. The separation of husband and wife during the period of a woman's menstruation and immersion in a *mikveh* can be a powerful affirmation of a woman's sexuality. Though not all Jewish women observe these laws, many regard them as a way of renewing the marital relationship and preserving the purity of the family. Other women have evolved new rituals to mark the onset of menstruation or menopause, placing these important events in women's lives in a religious context.

VIRGINITY

Virginity was always highly esteemed and marriage required chastity of both sexes. During the Second Commonwealth we are told of specific times of the year when courting took place:

> There never were in Israel greater days of joy than the 15th of Av and Yom Kippur. On these days the daughters of Jerusalem used to walk out in white garments, which they borrowed in order not to shame anyone who had none. The daughters of Jerusalem came out and danced in the vineyards exclaiming at the same time 'Young man, lift up your eyes and see what you choose for yourself'. The beautiful among them called out 'Set your eyes on beauty for the quality most to be prized in woman is beauty'; those of them who came of noble families called out 'Do not set your eyes on beauty but set your eyes on [good] family'. For 'Grace is deceitful and beauty is vain; but a woman that fears the Eternal One, she shall be praised' (Proverbs 31:30). 'Look for [a good] family, for woman has been created to bring up a family.' The homely ones among them called out 'Carry off your purchase in the name of Heaven, only on one condition – that you adorn us with jewels of gold'. (M *Taanit* 4:8)

THE MARRIAGE CEREMONY

The marriage service today combines what were originally two separate ceremonies; betrothal and marriage. These two rituals were separated, usually by a year, the marriage being established when both husband and wife came to live together. Some time in the Middle Ages the two ceremonies were combined into one for different reasons. The waiting period provided a number of problems. Betrothal was not engagement; it required an annulment through divorce to cancel it. The problem of the waiting period was dealt with in different ways by different communities. In Alexandria, for example, it was common to add a clause to the *ketubah* (the marriage contract) which was written during the *kiddushin* (the betrothal). If the groom did not take the bride home to begin their married life within a year, then the betrothal would be void. Other practices were to write an agreement making the *kiddushin* dependent on the *nissuin* (marriage) taking place, usually within a year. In Babylonia, no such conditions were attached to the *kiddushin*; instead the family took great care to protect the bride during the waiting period. Eventually the two ceremonies were merged into one.

The ceremony reflects both the contractual element of a marriage between a man and a woman, not, as already stated, in the sense that a man acquires the woman as his property, but in the sense that marriage mirrors the divine covenant that exists between God and the Jewish people. In non-Orthodox marriages, both bride and groom declare their intention to be loyal to each other and recite the betrothal formula: 'Behold you are betrothed to me [by this ring] according to the law of Moses and Israel.' In Orthodox marriages only the man recites this formula.

Marriage is a profoundly solemn and religious occasion. It takes place beneath the *huppah* (wedding canopy), which symbolizes the new home and family unit of the couple. The essence of marriage is the holiness of the union between a man and wife. Each is, so to speak, dedicated to the other, and yet they are at the same time, part of a larger family, of the community of Israel.

Post-biblical Judaism made a number of provisions protecting a woman's rights. One was a clause in the *ketubah* in which the groom promises to make substantial payments to his wife in the event of a divorce. This only partly mitigated, and mitigates, the fact that under Orthodox Jewish law men possess the unilateral power to divorce their wives. We have already mentioned the ban attributed to Rabbenu Gershom against polygyny; in addition, there was another ban which forbids a man to divorce a woman against her consent.

What is interesting to note, once again, is the dichotomy that exists between the prescriptive position of woman, and the historical and experiential reality of women. The status of women as defined in Jewish legislation, their characters and beliefs about them, as collected in the counterpart of *halakhah*, *aggadah* (Jewish lore), reflect the preoccupations of men rather than of the women themselves. Though to be married was considered an ideal to the extent that a man without a wife was thought to live without blessing, the overriding concern of legislation is both to protect and to control the woman, particularly in the public domain – which was reserved for men.

Women and work

Much of women's work took place indoors, where they could be relaxed, hiding in their own apartments. Spinning, weaving, washing, cooking, baking and grinding flour were the jobs undertaken by women in the seclusion of their homes. One remark reflects this cloistered existence, saying of the woman that 'she is banished from people and confined to prison' (BT *Eruvin* 100b). However, there was cultural progress, and as the rabbis raised the level of cultural awareness in their own generations, so the position of women improved. Sometimes a wife supported her husband and worked for the family; she farmed or traded, she attended public lectures, visited the house of study, participated in synagogue services, attended weddings and funerals and could have her own social life.

In the sphere of the home, women did possess, and still do possess, a certain degree of knowledge and authority. Though legislation often marginalizes the status and position of women in religious life, it does not often reflect the reality of the woman's position in the home, or indeed in the community. The three positive commandments of lighting the Sabbath candles, separating the dough from the Sabbath bread and the law of the *niddah*, symbolize the traditional woman's role in the home and the power that she possesses in relation to her domestic and private life.

It is not surprising to note that the position of contemporary women – their freedom to work, to express themselves, to take a full part in the public sphere – has been adopted by many Jewish women. Though there remains a minority for whom traditional Jewish law is divinely ordained, by far the majority see their Jewish tradition as engaging in a dynamic dialectic with contemporary society and its influences. The influence of modern movements such as feminism has been considerable in recent years and has played a particularly important part in helping to educate women to take an equal role in synagogue life, as we shall see.

Divorce and *agunah*

While irretrievable breakdown of marriage is recognized in Judaism and divorce permitted, the rabbis of the Talmud acknowledged the tragic aspect of divorce in the statement that when a man divorces his first wife, the very altar sheds tears (BT *Gittin* 90b). Biblical laws of divorce are not systematic or detailed:

> A man takes a wife and possesses her. She fails to please him because he finds some indecency about her, and he writes her a bill of divorcement, hands it to her, and sends her away from his house; she leaves his household and becomes the wife of another man, then the second man rejects her, writes her a bill of divorcement, hands it to her, and sends her away from his house; or the man who married her last dies, then the husband who divorced her first shall not take her to wife again, since she has been defiled – for that would be abhorrent to the Lord. You must not bring sin upon the land which the Lord your God is giving you as a heritage. (Deut 24:1–4)

These verses appear to characterize that tension in Judaism which, on the one hand, accepts divorce but, on the other, sees it as profoundly regrettable. A man and a woman who have become divorced from each other are not permitted to remarry each other, because they have been 'defiled' – or rather the woman has been 'defiled' by a second man. This ambivalent attitude towards divorce is also borne out by legislation that forbids a priest to marry a divorcee (Leviticus 21), though priests were not forbidden to divorce their wives.

Despite these vestiges of anti-divorce legislation, post-biblical *halakhah* accepts divorce as legitimate. The *get*, which is the bill of divorcement given by a man to his wife, essentially releases her from the marriage and permits her to take another man should she wish to remarry. The grounds for a divorce to take place are given in the Bible as 'some indecency' (*ervat davar*), but inherent in this simple formulation are multiple problems which are the subject of Talmud (BT *Gittin* 90a–b):

> The School of Shammai held that a man should not divorce his wife unless he has found her guilty of some sexual misconduct, while the School of Hillel say that he may divorce her even if she has merely spoiled his food. Rabbi Akiva, he may divorce her even if he simply finds another woman more beautiful than she.

Each of these opinions is substantiated by a scriptural verse, quoted in support of each of the three opinions.

However, the legislation on divorce does not stop there. Two important factors were introduced to protect a woman from being divorced against her will and leaving her without any financial support. One was the medieval ban, traditionally ascribed to Rabbenu Gershom, which was introduced as a counter to the talmudic statement that a woman may be divorced with her consent or without it (BT *Yevamot* 12b). The new law made a divorce given to a woman against her will null and void. The second factor was the *ketubah* (the marriage document), introduced much earlier, which outlined the obligations of the husband towards the wife and included financial arrangements in case the marriage ended through divorce or the husband's death.

Despite the complexity of divorce legislation which developed in the post-biblical period, a woman remained vulnerable. She still could not initiate a divorce, and, more seriously, if her husband refused to grant her a divorce, she could find herself in the position of being an *agunah* (chained woman).

The *agunah* is a woman who is not free to remarry. If her husband has disappeared, or is presumed dead, or refuses to grant her a religious divorce, if she remarries she is deemed to be an adulteress and her children will be *mamzerim* (offspring of an illicit union). This is the most serious problem that confronts Orthodox Jewish courts today. Particularly in the wake of the Shoah (Holocaust), the position of *agunot* is an intolerable and tragic one. Non-Orthodox Judaism has found methods to circumvent this law and permit *agunot* to remarry.

Synagogue, prayer and the commandments

Judaism teaches that God guides humanity. This guidance is presented in terms of the *mitzvot*, the commandments. Orthodox Jews understand the *mitzvot* to have originated at Mount Sinai. Progressive Jews see the *mitzvot* as the religious responses of individuals and generations to the economic, social and political conditions of their era. They see those responses continuing even today, with the need for a certain elasticity in the way they respond to the changing circumstances of their time. However, the principles of Judaism do not change: the strict search for truth, the need for justice to be tempered by compassion, absolute equality for men and women of all races, creeds and nations – these are the certainties with which one starts when formulating an answer to the question: What is it that God requires of us?

Traditional Judaism acknowledges a structure of 613 commandments which are variously derived from the Torah. Several attempts were made, especially in the Middle Ages, to list these commandments, 365 negative commandments and 248 positive commandments. The great majority of the *mitzvot* apply equally to both women and men. This is especially true of the negative commandments. But there were exceptions, and these fall into two categories: those *mitzvot* which are specifically linked to gender, such as circumcision for a man and the laws of menstruation for a woman; and commandments which are not directly related to biological differences, but which are, nevertheless, gender based.

Women's exemption from certain laws derived from a principle which was laid down in the Talmud (BT *Kiddushin* 33b). Women were exempt from all positive commandments that are time-bound. Exemption here does not mean prohibition; it means that women are permitted to observe those positive commandments which are linked with a specific time if they wish to take the duty upon themselves, but they do not have to. So, for example, women are exempt from the obligation to dwell in the *sukkah* on the Feast of Tabernacles. They do not have to hear the *shofar* on the New Year and Yom Kippur; they are exempt from the obligation of wearing *tzitzit* ('fringes') or *tefillin* ('phylacteries'). This is not a general rule, for there are exceptions. Women must observe the commandment to eat unleavened bread at Pesach, even though this is a positive commandment linked to a specific time. Also there are certain commandments which are positive and not time-bound from which women are exempt, such as study of

214

the Torah (see above), procreation[9] and redemption of the first-born son. Though women were permitted to perform all these commandments, the reality was that they did not take on these *mitzvot* until recently, when the *halakhah* began to be studied by women, who discovered a range of observances that had been closed to them for a variety of reasons.

The reasons justifying female exemption from these laws were for the most part domestic. David ben Joseph Abudarham, a medieval commentator, explains the reason for the exemption of women from timebound positive *mitzvot* as due to a basic conflict between the commands of God and the demands of a husband:

> The reason women are exempt from time-bound positive *mitzvot* is that a woman is bound to her husband to fulfil his needs. Were she obligated in time-bound positive *mitzvot*, it could happen that while she is performing a *mitzvah*, her husband would order her to do his commandment. If she would perform the commandment of the Creator and leave aside his commandment, woe to her from the husband! If she does her husband's commandment and leaves aside the Creator's, woe to her from her Maker! Therefore, the Creator has exempted her from his commandments, so that she may have peace with her husband.

It would appear that women were exempt from commandments which fell outside the domestic sphere; commandments to do with prayer, study, reading from the Torah are all duties which fall within the realm of a man's religious existence, according to the *halakhah*. Therefore, the exemption of women is not a legal-logical principle, according to Rachel Biale, but a social-cultural one. Biale's commentary to the passage from Sefer Abudarham quoted above shows an astute understanding of the position of women in relation to their men-folk:

> The rivalry between God and husband over female obedience is not merely a picturesque way of explaining the exemption of women from certain *mitzvot*. Indeed it seems to underscore a profound point, though I am not sure it was one intended by the author of Sefer Abudarham. The *halakhic* and religious position of women is strained by a tension between two views of women. God, in the 'rivalry' of our text, holds a fundamental theological and ethical position which recognizes no stratification of human beings, no inferiority of women to men. All persons are of equal value, spiritually and morally, and all human life is equally sanctified. On the other hand, the husband represents an attitude grounded in daily life and

social reality, where there are distinctions of religion, class, learning and of course, gender. Women are inferior to men in economic power, social standing, legal rights, and religious role and importance. While in ultimate moral and spiritual terms a woman's life is equal to a man's, her concrete, day-to-day life is marked by subservience to men. This tension appears in Genesis in the two creation myths. In one account woman is created equally with man 'in God's image,' and in the other account is created to meet man's needs. (Biale, 1984)

This tension in the woman's position in Jewish law is reflected in terms of her obligation to pray. While women are obligated to pray, they are exempt from reciting the twice-daily recited affirmation of belief, the *Shema*, because it is a positive commandment which is linked to a specific time, namely the evening and the morning. We see here that women shared a secondary role in religious life, together with slaves and minors. The result of this specific exemption was that women exempted themselves generally from the act of public, communal prayer and women's prayer became associated with an act of private, personal worship. Various prohibitions compounded this division between 'men's prayer' and 'women's prayer'. Women were not permitted to be counted in a *minyan* (the quorum of ten men required for any act of public worship). Though they were legally permitted to read from the Torah, they did not do so on account of the 'honour of the congregation'. The fear was that if a woman was called to read she would show up the male members of the congregation who perhaps did not possess the technical skill required to be able to read from the Torah. The segregation of women from men in synagogue was another factor in reducing the participation of women in synagogue services.

Orthodox scholars today are divided in their response to the question of whether women may take a full part in public ritual and prayer. In the United States of America, Orthodox rabbis do allow women to conduct their own services, read from the Torah and assume those responsibilities which were originally in the domain of male worship. However, women are still not permitted to undertake those duties on behalf of men. In Great Britain, the role of the women is greatly restricted. Women are not allowed to conduct their own services on the premises of a synagogue, but only in a private home.

The non-Orthodox movements do permit full participation of women in services, with a few exceptions. Women may don *tefillin* if they so wish, they may wear a *tallit* for morning services, they pray equally with men and can lead the services on behalf of a mixed congregation. Women have been ordained as rabbis since 1972 in the United States of America and since 1975 in Great Britain. Women are also permitted to assume roles of leadership and act as witnesses, which Orthodox *halakhah* prohibits. Such changes are a classic example of Judaism responding to the religious needs of the Jewish woman in contemporary society, without losing sight of those prophetic principles of strict justice and truth which are the pillars on which the religion is founded and which sustain its existence.

Notes

1 I am grateful to Rabbi Rachel Montagu, who underlined this point in a sermon in which she said that the work of a gardener is not as long-term as the work of *tikkun olam* ('repair of the world').

2 For further reading on women in the Bible see Phyllis Trible 'Depatriarchalizing in Biblical interpretation' in Koltun (1976); Phyllis Trible (1984) *Texts of Terror*. Philadelphia: Fortress Press; and Trible (1978).

3 *Cairo Damascus Rule* v, 7–9; *Temple Scroll* LXVI, 16–17. For a clear description of the Jewish sects in this period and the historical context see Hyam Maccoby (1989) *Judaism in the First Century*. London: Sheldon Press; Geza Vermes (1987) *The Dead Sea Scrolls in English* (rev. edn). Harmondsworth: Penguin, which provides helpful introductory essays on the history and religious ideas of the Qumran community.

4 Rachel Biale in Biale (1984) suggests that 'the birth of a female, who will one day herself menstruate and give birth, is seen as "doubly bloody" and doubly impure'.

5 The term 'Gamara' is synonymous with Talmud.

6 For a discussion on the subject of literature for women from the Middle Ages onwards, and in particular pious paraphrases of the Hebrew Bible into Yiddish, see Brayer (1986) *A Psychohistorical Perspective*, vol. 2, pp. 114–19.

7 See Epstein (1948).

8 *Ibid.*, ch. 2.

9 While one might assume that the biblical injunction 'Be fruitful and multiply' (Gen 1:28) is addressed to both men and women, since both participate in the procreative act as equal partners, the *halakhah* makes procreation the duty of the man only. Rachel Biale's explanation for this rabbinic exegesis that goes against the plain meaning of the Torah is helpful here: 'Why do [the rabbis] go to such lengths to exempt women

from the duty of procreation? I believe that there are two primary reasons. The first is a general sentiment regarding procreation. It seems that the rabbis took it as self-evident that women had a natural desire to bear children. Men, on the other hand, were seen as torn between familial "instincts" and other powerful motivations such as learning and economic activity. For men it was necessary to mandate procreation as a duty to assure that other activities did not take precedence. For women it was seen as unnecessary, and perhaps "unnatural". The second reason may have been to allow contraception in some circumstances' (pp. 202–3).

References and further reading

Biale, Rachel (1984) *Women and Jewish Law*. New York: Schocken.

Brayer, Menachem M. (1986) *The Jewish Woman in Rabbinic Literature*. New York: Ktav.

Epstein, Louis (1948: reprinted 1967) *Sex Laws and Customs in Judaism*. New York: Ktav.

Heschel, Susannah (ed.) (1983) *On Being a Jewish Feminist*. New York: Schocken.

Koltun, Elizabeth (ed.) (1976) *The Jewish Woman*. New York: Schocken.

Trible, Phyllis (1978) *God and the Rhetoric of Sexuality*. Philadelphia: Fortress Press.

8. Attitudes to nature

Norman Solomon

It is widely recognized today that people are destroying the environment on which living things depend for their existence. It is not at first
sight clear what the problems facing the earth's environment have to
do with religious beliefs. After all, the only belief necessary to motivate
a constructive response is a belief in the desirability of human survival,
wedded to the perception that human survival depends on the whole
interlinking system of nature. Moreover, the discovery of which
procedures would effectively solve the problems of conservation is a
technical, not a religious, one. If scientists are able to offer alternative
procedures of the same or different efficiency, the religions may feel
that the ethical or spiritual values they espouse should determine the
choice. However, few choices depend on value judgements alone, and
no judgement is helpful which is not based on the best available
scientific information.

These considerations will be borne in mind as we examine the
relevance of traditional Jewish sources to our theme. In the following
pages we offer a structured guide to the main traditional Jewish
sources which relate to the great environmental problems of our time
(concluding with a model Jewish statement on nature). Judaism did
not 'stop' with the Bible or the Talmud; it is a living religion, constantly developing in response to changing social realities and
intellectual perceptions. At the present time, it is passing through one
of its most creative phases; however, within the limited scope of this
chapter only a few references can be made to the contemporary
literature.

Traditional Jewish thought is expressed in several complementary
genres. The most distinctive is *halakhah*, or law, but history, myth,
poetry, philosophy and other forms of expression are also significant.

Our focus here is not on the contributions made by individual Jews, for instance scientists and economists, to the modern ecological movement – this would make an interesting study in itself – but on the religious sources, which demonstrate the continuity between traditional Jewish thought and a range of contemporary approaches.

Attitudes to creation

GOODNESS OF THE PHYSICAL WORLD

'God saw that it was good' is the refrain of the first creation story of Genesis (1:1 – 2:4), which includes the physical creation of humankind, male and female. The created world is thus testimony to God's goodness and greatness (see Pss 8, 104, 148; Job 36:22 – 41:34).

For the ordinary Jew, this goodness of creation is encapsulated in the blessing to be recited on seeing the first blossoms in spring:

> You are blessed, Lord our God and ruler of the universe, who have omitted nothing from your world, but created within it good creatures and good and beautiful trees in which people may take delight. (Prayer Book)

The second 'creation' story (Gen 2:5 – 3:24) accounts for the psychological make-up of humankind. There is no devil, only a 'wily serpent', and the excuse of being misled by the serpent does not exempt Adam and Eve from personal responsibility for what they have done. Bad gets into the world through the free exercise of choice by people, not in the process of creation, certainly not through fallen angels, devils, or any other external projection of human guilt; such creatures are notably absent from the catalogue of creation in Genesis 1.

Post-biblical Judaism did not adopt the concept of 'the devil'. In the Middle Ages, however, the dualism of body and spirit prevailed, and with it a tendency to denigrate 'this world' and 'material things'. The Palestinian kabbalist Isaac Luria (1534–72), taught that God initiated the process of creation by 'withdrawing' himself from the infinite space he occupied. This theory stresses the 'inferiority' and distance from God of material creation, but compensates by drawing attention to the divine element concealed in all things. The modern Jewish theologian who wishes to emphasize the inherent goodness of God's creation has not only the resources of the Hebrew scriptures on which to draw, but a continuous tradition based on them.

The Bible encompasses three realms: of God, of humankind and of nature. It does not confuse them. Its 'creation spirituality' articulates 'original blessing' rather than 'original sin' – 'God saw all that he had made, and it was very good' (Gen 1:31) – and this includes all creatures, culminating with humans. As Aaron Lichtenstein remarked at a conference on Judaism and Ecology at Bar Ilan University (Tel Aviv), 'Our approach is decidedly anthropocentric, and that is nothing to be ashamed of'.[1]

'Hierarchy in creation' below (p. 224) discusses the hierarchy within nature itself.

BIODIVERSITY

I recall sitting in the synagogue as a child and listening to the reading of Genesis. I was puzzled by the Hebrew word *leminehu*, 'according to its kind', which followed the names of most of the created items and was apparently superfluous. Obviously, if God created fruit with seeds, the seeds were 'according to its kind'!

As time went on I became more puzzled. Scripture seemed obsessive about 'kinds' (species). There were careful lists and definitions of which species of creature might or might not be eaten (Lev 11 and Deut 14). Wool and linen were not to be mixed in a garment (Lev 19:19, Deut 22:11), ox and ass were not to plough together (Deut 22:10), fields (Lev 19:19) and vineyards (Deut 12:9) were not to be sown with mixed seeds, or animals cross-bred (Lev 19:19) and, following the rabbinic interpretation of a thrice repeated biblical phrase (Exod 23:19, 34:26; Deut 14:21), meat and milk were not to be cooked or eaten together.

The story of Noah's Ark manifests anxiety that all species should be conserved, irrespective of their usefulness to humankind – Noah is instructed to take into his ark viable (according to the thought of the time) populations of both 'clean' and 'unclean' animals. That is why the 'Inter-stellar Ark' is the model, among those concerned with such things, for gigantic spaceships to carry total, balanced communities of living things through the galaxy for survival or colonization.

The biblical preoccupation with species and with keeping them distinct can now be read as a way of declaring the 'rightness' of God's pattern for creation and of calling on humankind not only not to interfere with it, but to cherish biodiversity by conserving species.

Scripture does not, of course, take account of the evolution of species, with its postulates of (a) the alteration of species over time and (b) the extinction (long before the evolution of humans) of most species which have so far appeared on earth.[2] Yet at the very least these Hebrew texts assign unique value to each species as it now is, within the context of the present order of creation; this is sufficient to give a religious dimension, within Judaism, to the call to conserve species. Opinions differ as to how significant this is with regard to genetic manipulation, particularly the transfer of genes across species, as occasionally done in the production of 'GM foods'.

Pereq Shirah

Pereq Shirah (the 'Chapter of Song') affords a remarkable demonstration of the traditional Jewish attitude to nature and its species. No one knows who composed this 'song', though it may have originated among the *hekhalot* mystics of the fourth or fifth centuries.

More significant than its origin is its actual use in private devotion. It has been associated with the 'Songs of Unity' composed by the German pietists of the twelfth century, who undoubtedly stimulated its popularity. At some stage, copyists prefaced to it exhortatory sayings which were erroneously attributed to talmudic rabbis, for instance: 'Rabbi Eliezer the Great declared that whoever says *Pereq Shirah* in this world will acquire the right to say it in the world to come.'

As the work is printed today, it is divided into five or six sections:

1 the physical creation (this includes heaven and hell, Leviathan and other sea creatures)
2 plants and trees
3 creeping things
4 birds
5 land animals (in some versions this section is subdivided).

Each section consists of from ten to 25 biblical verses, each interpreted as the song or saying of some part of creation or of some individual creature. The cock, in the fourth section, is given 'seven voices', and its function in the poem is to link the earthly song, in which all nature praises God, with the heavenly song.

We shall see 'Hierarchy in creation' below (p. 224) how the philosopher Albo (1380–1435) drew on *Pereq Shirah* to express the relationship between the human and the animal; yet *Pereq Shirah* itself draws all creation – even the inanimate, even heaven and hell themselves – into the relationship, expressing a fullness which derives only from the rich diversity of things, and which readily translates into the modern concept of biodiversity.

STEWARDSHIP OR DOMINATION?

There has been discussion among Christian theologians as to whether the opening chapters of Genesis call on humans to act as stewards – guardians – of creation, or to dominate and exploit the created world. There is little debate on this point among Jewish theologians,[3] to whom it has always been obvious that when Genesis states that Adam was placed in the garden 'to till it and to care for it' (2:15) it means just what it says. As Rav Kook (1865–1935)[4] put it:

> No rational person can doubt that the Torah, when it commands people to 'rule over the fishes of the sea and the birds of the sky and all living things that move on the earth', does not have in mind a cruel ruler who exploits his people and servants for his own will and desires – God forbid that such a detestable law of slavery [be attributed to God] who 'is good to all and his tender care rests upon all his creatures' (Ps 145:9) and 'the world is built on tender mercy' (Ps 89:3).[5, 6]

In the twelfth century the great Jewish Bible scholar Abraham ibn Ezra commented as follows on the words of Psalm 115:16, 'The heavens are the heavens of the Lord, and he gave the earth to people':

> The ignorant have compared man's rule over the earth with God's rule over the heavens. This is not right, for God rules over everything. The meaning of 'he gave it to people' is that man is God's steward (*paqid* – officer or official with special responsibility for a specific task) over the earth, and must do everything according to God's word.

So perverse is it to understand 'and rule over it' (Gen 1:28) – let alone Psalm 8 – as meaning 'exploit and destroy' that many Christians take such interpretations as a deliberate attempt to besmirch Christianity, and not a few Jews have read the discussions as an attempt to 'blame the Jews' for yet another disaster in Christendom. The context of Genesis 1:28 is indeed that of humans being made in the image of God, the beneficent creator of good things; its meaning is, therefore, very precise: that humans, being in the image of God, are summoned to share in his creative work, and to do all in their power to sustain creation.

HIERARCHY IN CREATION

'God created humans[7] in His image ... male and female he created them' (Gen 1:27). In some sense, humankind is superior to animals, animals to plants, plants to the inanimate. There is a hierarchy in created things.

The hierarchical model has two practical consequences. First, as we have seen, is that of responsibility of the higher for the lower, traditionally expressed as 'rule', latterly as 'stewardship'. The second is that, in a competitive situation, the higher has priority over the lower. Humans have priority over dogs so that, for instance, it is wrong for a man to risk his life to save that of a dog, though right, in many circumstances, for him to risk his life to save that of another human. Contemporary dilemmas arising from this are described below in the section which discusses ethical problems relating to conservation.

The Spanish Jewish philosopher Joseph Albo (1380–1435) placed humans at the top of the earthly hierarchy, and discerned in this the possibility for humans to receive God's revelation (*Sefer Ha-Iqqarim*, Book III, ch. 1). This is just a mediaeval way of saying what we have already remarked. God's revelation, as understood by Albo and Jewish tradition, is the Torah, from which we learn our responsibilities to each other and to the rest of creation.

According to Albo, just as clothes are an integral part of the animal, but external to people, who have to make clothes for themselves, so are specific ethical impulses integral to the behaviour of particular animals, and we should learn from their behaviour. 'Who teaches us from the beasts of the earth, and imparts wisdom to us through the birds of the sky?' (Job 35:11); as the Talmud puts it: 'R. Yohanan said, If these things were not commanded in the Torah we could learn modesty from the cat, the ant would preach against robbery, and the dove against incest' (BT *Eruvin* 100b). The superiority of humans lies in their unique combination of freedom to choose and the intelligence

224

to judge, without which the divine revelation would have no application. Being in this sense 'higher' than other creatures, humans must be humble towards all. Albo, in citing these passages and commending the reading of *Pereq Shirah* (see above, p. 222), articulates the attitude of humble stewardship towards creation which characterizes rabbinic Judaism.

Rav Kook, drawing on a range of classical Jewish sources, from Psalm 148 to Lurianic mysticism, beautifully acknowledges the divine significance of all things (the immanence of God):

> I recall that with God's grace in the year 5665 [1904/5] I visited Jaffa in the Holy Land, and went to pay my respects to its Chief Rabbi [Rav Kook]. He received me warmly ... and after the afternoon prayer I accompanied him as he went out into the fields, as was his wont, to concentrate his thoughts. As we were walking I plucked some flower or plant; he trembled, and quietly told me that he always took great care not to pluck, unless it were for some benefit, anything that could grow, for there was no plant below that did not have its guardian[8] above. Everything that grew said something, every stone whispered some secret, all creation sang.[9]

CONCERN FOR ANIMALS

Kindness to animals is a motivating factor for general concern with the environment, rather than itself an element in conservation. Kindness to animals features prominently in the Jewish tradition. The Ten Commandments include domestic animals in the Sabbath rest:

> Remember to keep the sabbath day holy ... you shall not do any work, you, your son or your daughter ... your cattle. (Exod 20:10 NEB)

Early in the third century the rabbis formulated the 'seven Laws of the Children of Noah', which was an attempt to define the religious obligations of humankind in general, for all people are descended from Noah. The laws, unknown in this form in sources earlier than the third century, are: Do not blaspheme, do not worship idols, do not murder, do not commit adultery, do not steal, do establish courts of justice, do not eat 'a limb torn from a living animal'. The last covers cruelty to animals, evidently understood as a major human responsibility.[10]

Pious tales and folklore exemplify this attitude.

A calf was about to be slaughtered. It ran to Rabbi (Judah the Patriarch, about the year 200), nestled its head in his robe and whimpered. He said to it 'Go! This is what you were created for!' As he did not show it mercy, heaven decreed suffering upon him. One day Rabbi's housekeeper was sweeping. She came across some young weasels and threw them and swept them out; he said 'Let them alone! Is it not written "His mercies extend to all his creatures" (Psalm 148:9)?' Heaven decreed 'Since he is merciful, let us show him mercy'. (BT *Bava Metzia* 85a, slightly adapted)

The folk tale of the Rabbi and the Frog, a long and strange tale of how the rabbi was rewarded for his kindness to the amphibian, illustrates popular Jewish thought in the Middle Ages on this matter.[11]

Causing pain or distress to animals

In rabbinic law this concern condenses into the concept of *tsaar baalei hayyim* ('distress to living creatures').[12] The third-century Babylonian Rav ruled that one should feed one's cattle before breaking bread oneself (BT *Berakhot* 40a); even the Sabbath laws are relaxed somewhat to enable rescue of injured animals or milking of cows to ease their distress. Recently, concern has been expressed about intensive animal husbandry, including battery chicken production (Shochet, 1984). Likewise, many rabbinic responsa have been published on the restraints to be placed on experimentation on animals; clearly, experimentation is not allowed for frivolous purposes, but it is necessary to define both the human benefits which might justify animal experimentation and the safeguards necessary to avoid unnecessary suffering to animals. (See Bleich, 1989, for a review of the halakhic literature on animal experimentation.)

Meat eating

The Torah does not enjoin vegetarianism, though Adam and Eve were vegetarian (Gen 1:29). Restrictions on meat eating perhaps indicate that it is a concession to human weakness; among the mediaeval Jewish philosophers of the Iberian peninsula, Joseph Albo (1380-1435) wrote that the first people were forbidden to eat meat because of the cruelty involved in killing animals (*Sefer Ha-Iqqarim* 3:15). Isaac Abravanel (1437–1508) endorsed this in his commentary on Isaiah, chapter 11 and also taught in his commentary on Genesis, chapter 2, that when the Messiah comes we would return to the ideal, vegetarian state. Today the popular trend to vegetarianism has won many Jewish adherents though little official backing from religious leaders.[13]

Although the Torah does not insist on vegetarianism, it places considerable restraints on the eating of meat: only the meat of certain animals may be eaten, certain parts may not be eaten at all, the blood must be drained, and there are regulations as to how the animals should be slaughtered. *Shehitah*, the method of slaughter, is by a single sharp cut across the trachea and oesophagus; this may be performed only by a qualified religious expert, and nowadays there are special pens and procedures to ensure that the animal suffers the minimum of psychological distress as well as the minimum pain. Since in any case the animal very swiftly loses consciousness, generally before the onset of pain from the sharp cut, this is a very humane process.

From time to time voices are heard suggesting that *shehitah* is cruel to animals, but the criticisms often concern inessential aspects of *shehitah* such as the form of casting-pen used, rather than *shehitah* itself. Nevertheless, there is at least a theoretical problem for Jews of what to do should it be demonstrated that the *shehitah* process is to some extent cruel; there would be a contradiction between two equally clear demands of Torah, that meat not be eaten unless *shehitah* has been correctly performed, and that one should not practise cruelty to animals. Since the only cruelty which could conceivably be demonstrated would be minor, it is probable that the decision reached would be that *shehitah* be continued, and the procedures improved as far as possible; otherwise, Orthodox Jews would be forced to be vegetarians. Judaism does not recognize cruelty to animals as an absolute value (see 'Animal versus human life' below, pp. 236–7); any *prima facie* instance must be evaluated as to its seriousness and then balanced against alternatives.

Judah Tiktin[14] cites the kabbalist Isaac Luria (1534–72) as saying 'Happy are they who are able to abstain from eating meat and drinking wine throughout the week'. This has been cited as support for vegetarianism, but is irrelevant. The context is that of abstaining from meat and wine on Mondays and Thursdays (the traditional penitential days), a custom akin to the once widespread Roman Catholic practice of not eating meat on Fridays. The goal is self-denial, or asceticism, not vegetarianism, as may be inferred from the fact that the very same authorities endorse the eating of meat and the drinking of wine in

227

moderation as the appropriate way to celebrate the Sabbath and festivals. There have, indeed, been some holy men whose asceticism has led them to abstain entirely from eating meat and drinking wine – Rabbi Joseph Kahaneman (1888–1969) for instance – but this provides no basis in principle for vegetarianism.

Hunting

On 23 February 1716 Duke Christian of Sachsen-Weissenfels celebrated his fifty-third birthday with a great hunting party. History would have passed by the Duke as well as the occasion had not J. S. Bach honoured them with his *Hunting Cantata*. The text by Salomo Franck, secretary of the upper consistory at Weimar, is a grand celebration of nature and its priest, Duke Christian, with no sense that hunting sounds a discordant note, and the cantata includes one of Bach's most expressive arias, 'Schafe können sicher weiden' ('Sheep may safely graze').

Hunting, it has been argued, enhances appreciation of nature. Moreover, the hunter does not oppose conservation; he destroys only individual prey but has an interest in preserving the species. Conditions of Jewish life in the past millennium or so have rarely afforded Jewish princes the opportunity to celebrate their birthdays by hunting parties. But it has happened from time to time and has led rabbis, the best known being Ezekiel Landau (1713–93) of Prague, to voice their censure.

Professor Nahum Rakover,[15] Deputy Attorney General of Israel, sums up the *halakhic* objections to 'sport' hunting under eight heads:

1 It is destructive/wasteful (see subsection 'Cutting down fruit trees' below, p. 231).

2 It causes distress to animals (see 'Causing pain or distress to animals' above, p. 226).

3 It actively produces non-kosher carcasses (since the prey, even if a kosher animal, will not have been slaughtered lawfully).

4 It leads to trading non-kosher commodities.

5 The hunter exposes himself to danger unnecessarily.

6 It wastes time (which should be devoted to study and good deeds).

7   The hunt is a 'seat of the scornful' (Ps 1:1).[16]

8   'Thou shalt not conform to their institutions' (Lev 18:3) (i.e. hunting is contrary to the Jewish ethos).

From this we see that although Jewish religious tradition despises hunting for sport, this is on ethical and ritual grounds rather than in the interest of conservation.

The land and the people: a paradigm

Judaism, while attentive to the universal significance of its essential teachings, has developed within a specific context of a people bound by covenant with God. In the Bible itself, the most obvious feature of this is the stress on the chosen people and the chosen land.

This has meant that Judaism, both in biblical times and subsequently, has emphasized the interrelationship of people and land, the idea that the prosperity of the land depends on the people's obedience to God's covenant. For instance:

> If you pay heed to the commandments which I give you this day, and love the Lord your God and serve him with all your heart and soul, then I will send rain for your land in season ... and you will gather your corn and new wine and oil, and I will provide pasture ... you shall eat your fill. Take good care not to be led astray in your hearts nor to turn aside and serve other gods ... or the Lord will become angry with you; he will shut up the skies and there will be no rain, your ground will not yield its harvest, and you will soon vanish from the rich land which the Lord is giving you. (Deut 11:13–17)

Two steps are necessary to apply this link between morality and prosperity to the contemporary situation:

1   The chosen land and people must be understood as the prototype of:

   (a) all actual individual geographical nations (including, of course, Israel) in their relationships with land, and
   (b) humanity as a whole in its relationship with the planet as a whole.

2   There must be satisfactory clarification of the meaning of 'obedi-

ence to God' as the human side of the covenant to ensure that 'the land will be blessed'. The Bible certainly has in mind justice and moral rectitude, but in spelling out 'the commandments of God' it includes specific prescriptions which directly regulate care of the land and celebration of its produce; some of these are discussed below.

To sum up: the Bible stresses the intimate relationship between people and land. The prosperity of land depends on:

1   the social justice and moral integrity of the people on it, and

2   a caring, even loving, attitude to land, with effective regulation of its use.

Conservation demands the extrapolation of these principles from ancient or idealized Israel to the contemporary global situation; this calls for education in social values together with scientific investigation of the effects of our activities on nature.

SABBATICAL YEAR AND JUBILEE

> When you enter the land which I give you, the land shall keep sabbaths to the Lord. For six years you may sow your fields and for six years prune your vineyards but in the seventh year the land shall keep a sabbath of sacred rest, a sabbath to the Lord. You shall not sow your field nor prune your vineyard. (Lev 25:2–4)

The analogy between the sabbath (literally, 'rest day') of the land and that of people communicates the idea that land must 'rest' to be refreshed and regain its productive vigour. In contemporary terms, land resources must be conserved through the avoidance of over-use. The Bible pointedly links this to social justice: just as land must not be exploited, so slaves must go free after six years of bondage or in the jubilee (fiftieth) year, and the sabbatical year (in Hebrew *shemittah*, 'release') cancels private debts, thus preventing exploitation of the individual.

The consequence of disobedience is destruction of the land, which God so cares for that he will heal it in the absence of its unfaithful inhabitants:

> If in spite of this you do not listen to me and still defy me ... I will make your cities desolate and destroy your sanctuaries ... your land shall be desolate and your cities heaps of rubble. Then, all the time that it lies desolate, while you are in exile in the land of your enemies, your land shall enjoy its sabbaths to the full. (Lev 26:27–35)

If in Israel today there is only a handful of agricultural collectives which observe the 'sabbath of land' in its biblical and rabbinic sense, the biblical text has undoubtedly influenced the country's scientists and agronomists to question the intensive agriculture favoured in the early years of the state and to give high priority to conservation of land resources.

CUTTING DOWN FRUIT TREES

> When you are at war, and lay siege to a city ... do not destroy its trees by taking the axe to them, for they provide you with food. (Deut 20:19)

In its biblical context this is a counsel of prudence rather than a principle of conservation; the Israelites are enjoined to use only 'non-productive', that is, non-fruit-bearing trees, for their siege works.

In rabbinic teaching, however, the verse has become the *locus classicus* for conserving all that has been created, so that the very phrase *bal tashchit* (literally, 'not to destroy') is inculcated into small children to teach them not to destroy or waste even those things they do not need. In an account of the commandments specially written for his son, Rabbi Aaron Halevi of Barcelona (*c.* 1300) sums up the purpose of this one as follows:

> This is meant to ingrain in us the love of that which is good and beneficial and to cleave to it; by this means good will imbue our souls and we will keep far from everything evil or destructive. This is the way of the devout and those of good deeds – they love peace, rejoice in that which benefits people and brings them to Torah; they never destroy even a grain of mustard, and are upset at any destruction they see. If only they can save anything from being spoilt they spare no effort to do so. (*Sefer Ha-Hinnukh Mitzvah* 529)

In view of the great esteem in which the rabbis held the Temple service, it is remarkable that they forbade the use of olive and fig wood

231

on the altar, but the destruction of such trees would frustrate settlement of the land.

LIMITATION OF GRAZING RIGHTS

The Mishnah rules: 'One may not raise small cattle [sheep, goats, etc.] in the land of Israel, but one may do so in Syria or in the uninhabited parts of the land of Israel' (M *Bava Qama* 7:7). There is evidence of similar restrictions from as early as the third century BCE.

The Mishnah itself does not provide a rationale for the law. Later rabbis suggest (a) that its primary purpose is to prevent the 'robbery' of crops by roaming animals, and (b) that its objective is to encourage settlement in the land of Israel. This latter reason is based on the premise that the raising of sheep and goats is inimical to the cultivation of crops, and reflects the ancient rivalry between nomad and farmer; at the same time it poses the question considered by modern ecologists of whether animal husbandry is an efficient way of producing food.[17]

AGRICULTURAL FESTIVALS

The concept of 'promised land' is an assertion that the consummation of social and national life depends on harmony with the land.

The biblical pilgrim festivals all celebrate the land and its crops, though they are also given historical and spiritual meanings. Through the joyful collective experience of these festivals the people learned to cherish the land and their relationship, through God's commandments, with it; the sense of joy was heightened through fulfilment of the divine commandments to share the bounty of the land with 'the Levite, the stranger, the orphan and the widow' (Deut 16:11 and elsewhere).

Specific environmental laws

Several aspects of environmental pollution are dealt with in traditional *halakhah*. Although the classical sources were composed in situations very different from those of the present, the law has been, and is, in a continuous state of development. In addition, the basic principles are in any case clearly relevant to contemporary situations.

232

WASTE DISPOSAL

Arising from Deuteronomy 23:13, 14, *halakhah* insists that refuse be removed 'outside the camp', that is, collected in a location where it will not reduce the quality of life. The Talmud and codes extend this concept to the general prohibition of the dumping of refuse or rubbish where it may interfere with the environment or with crops.

It would be anachronistic to seek in the earlier sources the concept of waste disposal as threatening the total balance of nature or the climate. However, if the rabbis forbade the growing of kitchen gardens and orchards around Jerusalem on the grounds that the manuring would degrade the local environment (BT *Bava Qama* 82b), one need have no doubt that they would have been deeply concerned at the large-scale environmental degradation caused by traditional mining operations, the burning of fossil fuels and the like. We cannot know for sure how they would have responded had they been faced by the problem of disposal of nuclear wastes, but we need not doubt that their approach would have been firm and judicious.

Smell (see also the following subsection) is regarded in *halakhah* as a particular nuisance; hence there are rules regarding the siting not only of lavatories but also of smelly commercial operations such as tanneries.[18] Certainly, rabbinic law accords priority to environmental over purely commercial considerations.

ATMOSPHERIC POLLUTION AND SMOKE

Like smell, atmospheric pollution and smoke are placed by the rabbis within the category of indirect damage, since their effects are produced at a distance. They are nevertheless unequivocally forbidden.

The Mishnah (M *Bava Batra* ch. 2) bans the siting of a threshing floor within fifty cubits of a residential area, since the flying particles set in motion by the threshing process would diminish the quality of the air.

Likewise, the second-century rabbi Nathan (T *Bava Batra* 1:7) ruled that a furnace might not be sited within fifty cubits of a residential area because of the effect of its smoke on the atmosphere; the fifty-cubit limit was subsequently extended by the Geonim to whatever the distance necessary to prevent smoke causing eye irritation or general annoyance.[19]

233

The Hazards Prevention Law, passed by the Israeli Knesset on 23 March 1961, contains the following provisions:

> #3   No person shall create a strong or unreasonable smell, of whatever origin, if it disturbs or is likely to disturb a person nearby or passerby.
> #4a   No person shall create strong or unreasonable pollution of the air, of whatever origin, if it disturbs or is likely to disturb a person nearby or passerby.

The subjectivity of 'reasonable' in this context is apparent. Meir Sichel (1985, pp. 25–43), in a study on the ecological problems that have arisen recently from the use of energy resources for power stations to manufacture electricity, and from various types of industrial and domestic consumption such as cooking, heating and lighting, has drawn on the resources of traditional Jewish law in an attempt to define more precisely what should be regarded as 'reasonable'. Citing rabbinic responsa from an 800-year period, he concludes that *halakhah* is even more insistent on individual rights than the civil law (of Israel), and that *halakhah* does not recognize 'prior rights' of a defendant who claims that he had established a right to produce the annoyance or pollutant before the plaintiff appeared on the scene.

It seems to me that in an exercise such as Sichel's, there is no difficulty in applying traditional law to the contemporary context with regard to priority of rights, and also in clarifying the relationship between public and private rights. However, it is less clear that one can achieve a satisfactory definition of 'reasonable', since ideas of what is acceptable vary not only from person to person but also in accordance with changing scientific understanding of the nature of the damage caused by smells and smoke including the 'invisible' hazards of germs and radiation unknown to earlier generations.

WATER POLLUTION

Several laws were instituted by the rabbis to safeguard the freedom from pollution (as well as the fair distribution) of water. A typical early source:

> If one is digging out caves for the public he may wash his hands, face and feet; but if his feet are dirty with mud or excrement it is forbidden. [If he is digging] a well or a ditch [for drinking water], then [whether his feet are

clean or dirty] he may not wash them. (T *Bava Metzia* 11:31, ed. Zuck-ermandel)

Pregnant with possibilities for application to contemporary life is the principle that one may claim damages or obtain an appropriate injunction to remove the nuisance where the purity of one's water supply is endangered by a neighbour's drainage or similar works. It is significant that the Geonim here also rejected the talmudic distance limit in favour of a broad interpretation of the law to cover damage irrespective of distance (cited in *Shulhan Arukh, Hoshen Mishpat* 155:21).

NOISE

Rabbinic law on noise pollution offers a fascinating instance of balance of priorities. The Mishnah lays down that in a residential area neigh-bours have the right to object to the opening of a shop or similar enterprise on the grounds that the noise would disturb their tranquillity. It is permitted, however, to open a school for Torah notwithstanding the noise of children, for education has priority. Later authorities discuss the limit of noise which has to be tolerated in the interest of education,[20] and whether other forms of religious activity might have similar priority to the opening of a school (*Shulhan Arukh, Hoshen Mishpat* 156:3).

BEAUTY

Much could be said of the rabbinic appreciation of beauty in general. Here we concern ourselves only with legislation explicitly intended to enhance the environment, and we discover that it is rooted in the biblical law of the Levitical cities:

Tell the Israelites to set aside towns in their patrimony as homes for the Levites, and give them also the common land surrounding the towns. They shall live in the towns, and keep their beasts, their herds, and all their livestock on the common land. The land of the towns which you give the Levites shall extend from the centre of the town outwards for a thousand cubits in each direction. Starting from the town the eastern boundary shall measure two thousand cubits, the southern two thousand, the western two

235

thousand, and the northern two thousand, with the town in the centre. They shall have this as the common land adjoining their towns. (Num 35:2–5)

As this passage is understood by the rabbis, there was to be a double surround to each town, first a 'green belt' of a thousand cubits, then a two-thousand-cubit-wide belt for 'fields and vineyards'. While some maintained that the thousand-cubit band was for pasture, Rashi (on BT *Sota* 22b) explains that it was not for use, but 'for the beauty of the town, to give it space' – a concept reflected in Maimonides' interpretation of the talmudic rules on the distancing of trees from residences (see *Mishneh Torah, Shekhenim*, ch. 10).

The rabbis debate whether this form of 'town planning' ought to be extended to non-Levitical towns, at least in the land of Israel, designated by Jeremiah (3:19) and Ezekiel (20:6, 15) 'the beautiful land'.

The rabbinic appreciation of beauty in nature is highlighted in the blessing they set to be recited when one sees the first blossoms in spring.

Sample ethical problems relating to conservation

ANIMAL VERSUS HUMAN LIFE

Judaism consistently values human life more than animal life. One should not risk one's life to save an animal; for instance, if one is driving a car and a dog runs into the road, it would be wrong to swerve – endangering one's own or someone else's life – to save the dog. But is it right to take a human life, e.g. that of a poacher, to save not an individual animal but an endangered species? I can find nothing in Jewish sources to support killing poachers in any circumstances other than those in which they directly threaten human life. If it be argued that the extinction of a species would threaten human life because it would upset the balance of nature, it is still unlikely that Jewish law would countenance homicide to avoid an indirect and uncertain threat of this nature.

Even if homicide were justified in such circumstances, how many human lives is a single species worth? How far down the evolutionary scale would such a principle be applied? After all, the argument about upsetting the balance of nature applies equally to microscopic species and to large cuddly-looking vertebrates like the giant panda, and to plants as much as to animals.

Judaism, true to the hierarchical principle of creation (see 'Hierarchy in creation', pp. 224–5, above), consistently values human life more than that of other living things, but at the same time stresses the special responsibility of human beings to 'work on and look after' the created order (Gen 2:15 – see 'Stewardship or domination?' above, pp. 223–4).

PROCREATION VERSUS POPULATION CONTROL

The question of birth control (including abortion) in Judaism is too complex to deal with here, but there is universal agreement that at least some forms of birth control are permissible where a potential mother's life is in danger, and that abortion is not only permissible but mandatory, up to full term, to save the mother's life.[21] Significant is the value system which insists that, even though contraception may be morally questionable, it is preferable to abstinence where danger to life would be involved through normal sexual relations within a marriage.

What happens where economic considerations rather than life danger come into play? Here we must distinguish between (a) personal economic difficulties, and (b) circumstances of 'famine in the world', where economic hardship is general. On the whole, *halakhah* places the basic duty of procreation above personal economic hardship. But what about general economic hardship, which can arise through (a) local or temporary famine, and (b) the upward pressure of population on finite world resources?

The former situation was in the mind of the third-century Palestinian sage Resh Lakish when he ruled: 'It is forbidden for a man to engage in sexual intercourse in years of famine' (BT *Taanit* 11a). Although the ruling of Resh Lakish was adopted by the codes (*Shulhan Arukh, Orach Hayyim* 240:12 and 574:4), its application was restricted to those who already had children, and the decision between abstinence and contraception is less clear here than where there is a direct hazard to life.

Upward pressure of population on world resources is a concept unknown to the classical sources of the Jewish religion, and not indeed clearly understood by anyone before Malthus. As Feldman remarks:

It must be repeated here that the 'population explosion' has nothing to do with the *Responsa*, and vice versa. The Rabbis were issuing their analyses and their replies to a specific couple with a specific query. These couples were never in a situation where they might aggravate a world problem; on the contrary, the Jewish community was very often in a position of seeking to replenish its depleted ranks after pogrom or exile.[22]

Feldman goes on to say 'It would be just as reckless to overbreed as to refrain from procreation'. Although I am not aware of any explicit traditional rabbinic source for this, I certainly know of none to the contrary. Indeed, as the duty of procreation is expressed in Genesis in the words 'be fruitful and multiply and fill the earth', it is not unreasonable to suggest that 'fill' be taken as 'reach the maximum population sustainable at an acceptable standard of living but do not exceed it'. In like manner the rabbis (BT *Yevamot* 62a) utilize Isaiah's phrase 'God made the earth . . . no empty void, but made it for a place to dwell in' (45:18) to define the minimum requirement for procreation for the individual – a requirement, namely one son and one daughter, which does not increase population.

Of course, there is room for local variation among populations. Although as a general rule governments nowadays should discourage population growth, there are instances of thinly populated areas or of small ethnic groups whose survival is threatened, where some population growth might be acceptable even from the global perspective.

NUCLEAR, FOSSIL FUEL, SOLAR ENERGY

Can religious sources offer guidance on the choice between nuclear and fossil, and other energy sources?

It seems to me that they can have very little to say and that, especially in view of the extravagant views expressed by some religious leaders, it is vitally important to understand why their potential contribution to current debate is so small.

The choice among energy sources rests on the following factors:

1   Cost-effectiveness

2   Environmental damage caused by production

3   Operational hazards

4   Clean disposal of waste products

5   Long-term environmental sustainability.

Let us consider these factors. Cost effectiveness cannot be established without weighing the other factors. There is no point, however, at which religious considerations apply in establishing whether a particular combination of nuclear reactor plus safety plus storage of waste, and so on, will cost more or less than alternative 'packages' for energy production. It is equally clear that religious considerations have no part to play in assessing environmental damage caused by production, operational hazards, whether waste products can be cleanly disposed of, or what is the long-term environmental sustainability of a method of energy production. These are all technical matters, demanding painstaking research and hard evidence, and they have nothing to do with theology.

The religions would have something to say about overall strategy. For instance, a religious viewpoint would suggest that scientists pay more attention to finding out how to use less energy to meet demands for goods than they do to finding out how to produce more energy; religions, after all, teach prudence, and should caution scientists against being carried away by the excitement of their own discoveries – one does not develop nuclear energy because it is an exciting concept, but because it is prudent to do so.

Religious leaders should take great care not to object to nuclear energy as a matter of principle. There is no spiritual value in using coal or even direct solar energy rather than nuclear energy; the costs and benefits of each, including their environmental costs and benefits, must be assessed objectively and dispassionately. Much hurt arises when the religious 'demonize' those of whom they disapprove, and in the name of love generate hatred against people who seek to bring benefit to humanity; they can be far more helpful when they ask the sort of questions suggested by their insight into our relationship with creation, and insist on adequate research being done before resources are committed to projects which may turn out to be harmful.

GLOBAL WARMING

A very similar analysis could be made of the problems relating to global warming – problems of which scientists have been aware since

239

Arrhenius in the late nineteenth century, though only recently have pressure groups developed and governments become alarmed. The fact is that, at present, no one knows the extent to which global temperatures have risen as a result of the rise in atmospheric carbon dioxide since the first reliable measurements were taken towards the end of the nineteenth century. Similarly, no one knows what would be the overall effects of the projected doubling of atmospheric carbon dioxide by the middle of next century (I leave aside the question of other greenhouse gases). Some consequences, indeed, may be beneficial, such as greater productivity of plants in an atmosphere with more carbon dioxide. Unfortunately, neither the techniques of mathematical modelling used to make the projections, nor the base of global observations at 500-kilometre intervals, can yield firm results.

So how can a government decide whether to spend hundreds of billions of dollars on reducing atmospheric carbon dioxide, and vast sums in aiding Third World countries to avoid developing along 'greenhouse' lines, when the draconian measures required greatly limit personal freedom and much of the expenditure might be better diverted to building hospitals, improving education and the like?

Essential steps, including better research, must be initiated, but it would be a lack of wisdom to rush into the most extreme measures demanded. From our point of view, however, it is clear that the decisions must be rooted in prudence, rather than in any specifically religious value (of course, all religions commend prudence).

WHO PAYS THE PIPER?

Our observations on the response to the possibility of global warming raised the question of paying for conservation. The dilemmas involved in this are exceedingly complex. Should rich nations pay to 'clean up' the technology of poorer nations (e.g. western Europe pay for eastern Europe)? Should governments distort the free market by subsidizing lead-free petrol and other 'environment-friendly' commodities? How does one assess environmental efficiency and social costs, and how should such costs be allocated between taxpayer, customer and manufacturer? Such questions are too complex, and on the whole too new, for us to find exact analogies in our sources, even though certain broad principles, such as the need for market intervention for social purposes, are well attested.

DIRECTED EVOLUTION

After writing about the progress from physical evolution through biological evolution to cultural evolution, Edward Rubinstein continues:

> Henceforth, life no longer evolves solely through chance mutation. Humankind has begun to modify evolution, to bring about nonrandom, deliberate changes in DNA that alter living assemblies and create assemblies that did not exist before.
>
> The messengers of directed evolution are human beings. Their messages, expressed in the language and methods of molecular biology, genetics and medicine and in moral precepts, express their awareness of human imperfections and reflect the values and aspirations of their species.[23]

These words indicate the area where Judaism most needs to adjust itself to contemporary reality: the area in which modern knowledge sets us most apart from those who formed our religious traditions. Religion as we know it has come into being only since the Neolithic revolution, and thus presupposes some technology,[24] some mastery of nature. Our traditional sources seem to assume that the broad situation of humanity is static, and this is now seen to be an illusion.

All at once there is the prospect, alarming to some yet challenging to others, that we can set the direction of future development for all creatures in our world. The ethics committees of our hospitals and medical schools are forced to take decisions; although the religions take part – and Judaism has a distinctive contribution to make to medical ethics – it has yet to be shown that traditional sources can be brought to bear other than in the vaguest way ('we uphold the sanctity of life') on the problems raised even by currently available genetic engineering.

Will religions, as so often in the past, obstruct the development of science? They need not. Jewish religious views have ranged from Isaac Abravanel, who opposed in principle the development of technology,[25] to Abraham bar Hiyya, who in the twelfth century played a major role in the transmission of Graeco-Arab science to the West. If Judaism (or any other religion) is to contribute towards conservation it will need to be in the spirit of bar Hiyya, through support for good science, rather than through idealization of the 'simple life' in the spirit of Abravanel.

Conclusion: religion and conservation

There is no doubt that Judaism, along with other religions, has resources which can be used to encourage people in the proper management of Planet Earth. We will now review the interaction of religion with conservation, with special reference to the sources cited.

1 We saw in 'Goodness of the physical world' (pp. 220–1) how Judaism interprets the created world, with its balanced biodiverse ecology, as a 'testimony to God', with humankind at the pinnacle holding special responsibility for its maintenance and preservation. Certainly, this attitude is more conducive to an interest in conservation than would be emphasis on the centrality of the 'next world', on the spirit versus the body, or on the 'inferior' or 'illusionary' nature of the material world.

2 One of the priorities of conservation at the present time is to control population so as not to exceed resources. Although Judaism stresses the duty of procreation, we learned that it offers the prospect of a constructive approach to population planning, including some role for both contraception and abortion (see 'Procreation versus population control', above).

3 We have noted several specific areas in which Judaism has developed laws or policies significant for conservation. Prime among them were the laws regulating the relationship between people and land, for which the 'chosen people' in the 'promised land' is the model (see 'The land and the people: a paradigm', pp. 229–32). Care of animals (see 'Concern for animals', pp. 225–9), waste disposal, atmospheric and water pollution, noise, and beauty of the environment (see 'Specific environmental laws', pp. 232–6) were also treated in the classical sources. It would be neither possible nor fully adequate to take legislation straight from these sources; but it is certainly possible to work in continuity with them, bearing in mind the radically new awareness of the need for conserving the world and its resources as a whole.

4 Religions, Judaism included, discourage the pursuit of personal wealth. While in some instances this may be beneficial to the environment – if people want fewer cars and fewer books there will be fewer harmful emissions and fewer forests will be chopped

down – there are also many ways in which poverty harms the environment: for instance, less research and development means that such technology as remains (presumably for hospitals and other welfare projects) will be less efficient and the problems of environmental pollution less effectively addressed. It is a moot point whether lower technologies generate less pollution *pro rata* than advanced ones.

5   Some religions remain strongly committed to evangelistic or conversionist aims which inhibit co-operation with people of other religions. Judaism is not currently in an actively missionary phase (some would say that it is unduly introspective, and needs to proclaim its values in a more universal context). All religions, however, must desist from ideological conflicts and espouse dialogue; conservation cannot be effective without global co-operation.

6   Mere information can motivate, as when someone who perceives a lion ready to pounce reacts swiftly. If ecological disaster were as clearly perceived as a crouching lion, ideological motivation would be unnecessary. It is better that religions support conservation than oppose it, but the world would be safer if people would act on the basis of rational collective self-preservation rather than on the basis of confused and uncontrollable ideologies.

7   Several times, particularly in discussing energy sources (see 'Nuclear, fossil fuel, solar energy', pp. 238–9) and in the global warming section, we had to stress the need to distinguish between technological and value judgements. Whether or not nuclear reactors should be built must depend on a careful, dispassionate assessment of their hazards; shrill condemnation of the 'hubris of modern technology' merely hinders judgement, though it is right and proper that religious values be considered when an informed choice is made.

   Of course, the same need for objective assessment before value judgements are made applies to all other major conservation questions, such as how to reverse deforestation, control the greenhouse effect, restore the ozone layer, and so on. This is not a recipe for moral paralysis, but a way to avoid moral arbitrariness.

8   Towards the end of the section on directed evolution (p. 241) we noted a characteristic religious ambivalence towards science. In

the interests of conservation it is essential that the 'pro-science' attitude of Abraham bar Hiyya, Maimonides and others be encouraged. The folly of 'simple life' advocates must be resisted. For a start, the present world population could not be supported if we were to revert to the simple life. Moreover, who would wish to do without sanitation, communications, electric light, books, travel, medical services and all those other benefits of 'complex' civilization? The small population which would survive the 'return to Eden' would live a very dull and insecure life.

There is indeed a question as to what level of technology – simple, intermediate, advanced – is most appropriate in a given situation. We should not be surprised if scientific evidence indicates that in some situations simple technology is preferable to advanced, whether because of availability or skills and resources, or because of side-effects such as pollution. Once again, the moral issue is straightforward (one should achieve the most satisfactory balance between people's wants and the conservation of nature), but the decision has to be based on sound technical and scientific evidence.

If science has got us into a mess (which I would dispute), the way out is not no science but better science, and science performed with a sense of moral responsibility.

Finally, let us note that Judaism, like other religions, has a vital role to play in eradicating those evils and promoting those values in society without which no conservation policies can be effective. The single greatest evil is official corruption, frequently rife in precisely those countries where conservation measures must be carried out. Next in line is drug addiction, with its associated trade. Religions must combat these evils and at the same time work intelligently for peace, not only between nations but among religions themselves.

A Model Jewish Statement on Nature

One: Creation is good; it reflects the glory of its creator 'God saw everything he had made, and indeed it was very good' (Genesis 1:31). Judaism affirms life, and with it the creation as a whole.
Two: Biodiversity, the rich variety of nature, is to be cherished. In Genesis 1, everything is said to be created 'according to its kind'. In the

story of the Flood, Noah has to conserve in the ark male and female of every species of animal, so that it may subsequently procreate.

Three: Living things range from lower to higher, with humankind at the top. Genesis 1 depicts a process of creation of order out of the primeval chaos. The web of life encompasses all, but human beings – both male and female (Genesis 1:27), 'in the image of God' – stand at the apex of this structure.

Four: Human beings are responsible for the active maintenance of all life. Setting people at the top of the hierarchy of creation places them in a special position of responsibility towards nature. Adam is placed in the garden of Eden 'to till it and to preserve it' (Genesis 2:15), and to 'name' (that implies to understand) the animals.

Five: Land and people depend on each other. The Bible is the story of the chosen people and the chosen land. The prosperity of the land depends on the people's obedience to God's covenant: 'If you pay heed to the commandments which I give you this day, and love the Lord your God and serve him with all your heart and soul, then I will send rain for your land in season ... ' (Deuteronomy 11:13–17). In the contemporary global situation, this means that conservation of the planet depends on (a) the social justice and moral integrity of its people, and (b) a caring, even loving, attitude to land, with effective regulation of its use.

Six: Respect creation – do not waste or destroy. *Bal tashchit* ('not to destroy': see Deuteronomy 20:19) is the Hebrew phrase on which the rabbis base the call to respect and conserve all that has been created. (Norman Solomon in Rose (1992), p. 21. The statement has received the endorsement of Orthodox, Conservative and Reform rabbis.)

Notes

1 Lichtenstein's paper was published (in Hebrew) in (5740/1980) *Haggut* V. Jerusalem: Religious Education Department of the Israel Ministry of Education, pp. 101–8.

2 To the third-century Palestinian Rabbi Abbahu the *Midrash Bereshit Rabbah* 3:9 attributes the statement that God 'created and destroyed worlds before he made this' – which is presumably his final, perfect design.

3 See Ehrenfeld and Bentley (1985).

4 Abraham Isaac Kook was born in Latvia and emigrated to Palestine in 1904, becoming Chief Rabbi of the Ashkenazi communities of Palestine

when the office was instituted in 1921. A man of great piety and erudition, his numerous works are imbued with mysticism, and he emphasized the role of holiness in establishing the Jewish presence in the Holy Land. A selection of his writings translated into English is published under the title (1978) *Abraham Isaac Kook* in the series 'Classics of Western Spirituality'. New York: Paulist Press.

5   This is a traditional Jewish understanding of the text. Versions such as 'For ever is mercy built' (translation of the Jewish Publication Society of America, consonant with several English versions) are more grammatically sound.

6   I have taken the quotation from the texts on protection of animals published (in Hebrew) by the Israel Ministry of Justice in February 1976, but have been unable to check the original source. This publication of the Ministry of Justice together with its volume on protection of the environment (July 1972) is an excellent resource for traditional texts on these subjects, having been compiled to assist those responsible for drafting legislation for the Knesset. The volumes were compiled by Dr Nahum Rakover, in his capacity as Adviser on Jewish Law to the Ministry of Justice.

7   In view of the ending of the verse this is a more appropriate translation of Hebrew *adam*, a generic term for humankind, than the sexist 'man'.

8   Heb. *mazzal*, literally 'constellation', but understood also as 'guardian angel'.

9   Aryeh Levine (5721/1961) *Lahai Roi*. Jerusalem, pp. 15, 16.

10   This is well explained in ch. 8 of David Novak (1983) *The Image of the Non-Jew in Judaism* (Toronto Studies in Theology no. 14). New York and Toronto: Edwin Mellen Press.

11   Moses E. Gaster (ed.) (1934) *Maaseh*, vol. 1, Philadelphia: Jewish Publication Society of America.

12   In BT *Shabbat* 128b it is suggested that this principle is of biblical status (*d'oraita*).

13   See Schwartz (1982) and Bleich (1989), pp. 237–250b for a review of the halakhic literature on vegetarianism.

14   Judah Tiktin, commentary *Baer Heitev* on *Shulhan Arukh*, *Orah Hayyim*, ch. 134, no. 3.

15   See note 6 above. Nahum Rakover gives a wide range of references to the Responsa, many of which come from Renaissance Italy, which provided most of the very few instances of Jews in pre-modern times engaging in hunting.

16   Rakover implies that participating in hunting takes one out of the company of Torah scholars and into that of those who mock at religious values.

17   Some caution is needed here. The rabbis of the Talmud did not envisage vegetarianism, and did not ban the raising of large cattle in the land. They assumed that meat would be eaten but tried to ensure that its production would not interfere with agriculture.

18   These matters are dealt with in the Talmud in the second chapter of *Bava Batra*. They are codified, with subsequent developments, in *Shulhan Arukh, Hoshen Mishpat*, ch. 145. Maimonides, in his philosophical work *Guide of the Perplexed*, Book 3, ch. 45, argues that the purpose of the incense in the Temple was to counteract the smell of the processing of the animal offerings.

19   A. Assaf (ed.) (5689/1929) *Teshuvot ha-Geonim*. Jerusalem: Darom, p. 32. The Geonim were the heads of the Babylonian academics after the completion of the Talmud; they occupy a major place in the development and transmission of rabbinic law.

20   Rashi on BT *Bava Batra* 21a. Nahmanides, in his commentary on the passage, hazards a guess that the permissible noise limit would be exceeded by a school of more than fifty pupils.

21   For a full treatment of these issues see David M. Feldman (1974) *Marital Relations, Birth Control and Abortion in Jewish Law*. New York: Schocken Books.

22   *Ibid.*, p. 304.

23   Edward Rubinstein (1989) 'Stages of evolution and their messengers', *Scientific American* (June), p. 104.

24   The ancients thought technology had come from the gods, but Genesis 4:20–22 polemically, if more accurately, credits humans with technological innovation.

25   See Abravanel's commentary on Genesis 2. He taught that in the Messiah's time, as in Eden, we would wear no clothes, build no houses, abandon technology and have no government; in this he is more indebted to Seneca's 90th *Epistle* than to Jewish sources.

References and further reading

Bleich, J. D. (1989) *Contemporary Halakhic Problems*, vol. 3. New York: Ktav.

Ehrenfeld, David and Bentley, Philip J. (1985) 'Judaism and the practice of stewardship', *Judaism* 34, pp. 310–11.

Freudenstein, Eric G. (1970) 'Ecology and the Jewish tradition', *Judaism* 19.

Gordis, Robert (1986) *Judaic Ethics for a Lawless World*. New York: Jewish Theological Seminary of America.

Kalechovsky, Roberta (1998) *Vegetarian Judaism: A Guide for Everyone*. Marblehead, MA: Micah Publications.

Kotler, David (1973) 'Jewish ecology, past and present', *Jewish Observer* (May).

Pelcovitz, Ralph (1970) 'Ecology and Jewish theology', *Jewish Life* 37(6) (New York).

Rakover, Nahum, 'Pollution of the environment in Jewish law', in the Decennial Book (1973–1982) of the *Encyclopedia Judaica*. Jerusalem: Ketev.

Rose, Aubrey (ed.) (1992) *Judaism and Ecology*. London: Cassell.

Schochet, Elijah J. (1984) *Animal Life in Jewish Tradition: Attitudes and Relationships*. New York: Schochet KTAV.

Schwartz, Richard (1982) *Judaism and Vegetarianism*. Smithtown, NY: Exposition Press.

Sichel, Meir (1985) 'Air pollution – smoke and odour damage', *Jewish Law Annual* V.

Solomon, Norman (1991) *Judaism and World Religion*. Basingstoke: Macmillan, ch. 2.

9. Worship

Dan Cohn-Sherbok

In the Jewish faith, worship is of fundamental importance. In addition to spontaneous prayer, the tradition prescribes both private and public worship. Private worship normally takes place in the home and is related to various formal occasions; public prayer is similarly fixed by time and takes place within the synagogue sanctuary where the Torah Scroll is contained within a sacred Ark. This chapter provides an introduction to these two basic patterns of prayer: the first section provides a survey of the development and nature of Jewish worship; this is followed by an outline of observances on the Sabbath, pilgrim festivals, High Holy Days, and days of joy.

For the Jewish people prayer has served as the vehicle by which they have expressed their joys, sorrows and hopes; it has played a major role in the religious life of the Jewish nation, especially in view of the successive crises and calamities in which they were involved throughout their history. In such situations Jews continually turned to God for assistance. Thus, in the Torah the patriarchs frequently addressed God through personal prayer. Abraham, for example, begged God to spare Sodom since he knew that by destroying the entire population he would destroy the righteous as well as the guilty (Gen 18:23–33). At Beth-el, Jacob vowed 'If God will be with me, and will keep me in this way that I go, and will give me bread to eat, and raiment to put on ... then shall the Lord be my God' (Gen 28:20–21).

Later Moses too prayed to God. After Israel had made a golden calf to worship, Moses begged God to forgive them for this sin (Exod 32:31–32). Joshua also turned to God for help. When the Israelites went to conquer the city of Ai, their attack was repulsed. In desperation Joshua prayed to God for help in defeating Israel's enemies (Josh 7:7). Later in the prophetic books, the prophets also offered personal prayers to God, as did the Psalmist and others. This tradition of prayer continued after the canonization of Scripture and, as a consequence, prayer has constantly animated the Jewish spirit. Through personal encounter with the Divine, Jews have been consoled, sustained and uplifted. In addition to personal prayer, throughout history Jews have turned to God through communal worship.

In ancient times Jewish communal worship centred on the Temple in Jerusalem. Twice daily, in the morning and afternoon, the priests offered prescribed sacrifices while the Levites chanted psalms. On Sabbaths and festivals additional services were added to this daily ritual. At some stage it became customary to include other prayers along with the recitation of the Ten Commandments and the *Shema* (Deut 6:4–9, 11:13–21; Num 15:37–41) in the Temple service. With the destruction of the Second Temple in 70 CE sacrificial offerings were replaced by the prayer service in the synagogue, referred to by the rabbis as *avodah she-ba-lev* ('service of the heart'). To enhance uniformity, they introduced fixed periods for daily prayer which corresponded with the times sacrifices had been offered in the Temple: the morning prayer (*shaharit*) and afternoon prayer (*minhah*) correspond with the daily and afternoon sacrifice; evening prayer (*maariv*) corresponds with the nightly burning of fats and limbs. By the completion of the Babylonian Talmud in the sixth century, the essential features of the synagogue service were established, but it was only in the eighth century that the first prayer-book was composed, by Rav Amram, Gaon of Sura.

In the order of service, the first central feature is the *Shema*. In accordance with the commandment 'You shall talk of them when you lie down and when you rise' (Deut 6:7), Jews are commanded to recite this prayer during the morning and evening service. The first section (Deut 6:4–9) begins with the phrase *Shema Yisrael* ('Hear, O Israel: The Lord our God is one Lord'). This verse teaches the unity of God, and the paragraph emphasizes the duty to love God, meditate on his commandments and impress them on one's children. In addition, it contains laws regarding the *tefillin* and the *mezuzah*. *Tefillin* consist of two black leather boxes containing scriptural passages which are bound by black leather straps on the arm and forehead in accordance with the commandment requiring that 'you shall bind them as a sign upon your hand, and they shall be as frontlets between your eyes' (Deut 6:8). They are worn during morning prayer except on the Sabbath and festivals. The *mezuzah* consists of a piece of parchment, containing two paragraphs of the *Shema*, which is placed into a case and affixed to the right-hand side of an entrance. In accordance with the same decree, male Jews wear an undergarment with fringes (the smaller *tallit*) and a larger *tallit* (prayer shawl) for morning services. The prayer shawl is made of silk or wool with black or blue stripes with fringes (*tzitzit*) at each of the four corners.

The second major feature of the synagogue service is the *Shemoneh Esreh* (Eighteen Benedictions or *Amidah*). These prayers were composed over a long period of time and received their full form in the second century. They consist of eighteen separate prayers, plus an additional benediction dealing with heretics, which was composed by the sage Samuel the Younger at the request of Rabban Gamaliel in the second century. The first and last three benedictions are recited at every service; the thirteen other prayers are recited only on weekdays. On Sabbaths and festivals they are replaced by one prayer dealing with the Holy Day. They consist of the following benedictions:

1 Praise for God who remembers the deeds of the patriarchs on behalf of the community.

2 Acknowledgement of God's power in sustaining the living and his ability to revive the dead.

3 Praise of God's holiness.

4 Request for understanding and knowledge.

5 Plea for God's assistance to return to him in perfect repentance.

6 Supplication for forgiveness for sin.

7 Request for deliverance from affliction and persecution.

8 Petition for bodily health.

9 Request for God to bless agricultural produce so as to relieve want.

10 Supplication for the ingathering of the exiles.

11 Plea for the rule of justice under righteous leaders.

12 Request for the reward of the righteous and the pious.

13 Plea for the rebuilding of Jerusalem.

14 Supplication for the restoration of the dynasty of David.

251

15 Plea for God to accept prayer in mercy and favour.

16 Supplication for the restoration of the divine service in the Temple.

17 Thanksgiving for God's mercies.

18 Request for granting the blessing of peace to Israel.

On special occasions a number of special prayers are added to these benedictions.

From earliest times the Torah was read in public gatherings; subsequently, regular readings of the Torah on Sabbaths and festivals were instituted. In Babylonia the entire Torah was read during a yearly cycle; in Palestine it was completed once every three years. The Torah itself is divided into 54 sections, each of which is known as the 'order' or 'section' (*sidrah*). Each section is sub-divided into portions (each of which is called a *parashah*). Before the reading of the Torah in the synagogue, the Ark is opened and one or more Torah Scrolls are taken out.

The number of men called up to the reading varies: on Sabbaths there are seven; on Yom Kippur, six; on Rosh Ha-Shanah and the pilgrim festivals (Pesach, Sukkot, and Shavuot), five; on Rosh Hodesh and Hol Hamoed, four; on Purim, Hanukkah and fast days, three; and on Sabbath afternoons and Monday and Thursday mornings (when the first *parashah* of the forthcoming *sidrah* is read), three. In former times those who were called up to the Torah read a section of the weekly *sidrah*; subsequently an expert in Torah reading was appointed to recite the entire *sidrah* and those called up recited blessings instead. The first three people to be called up are, in order: *Cohen* (priest), *Levi* (Levite), and *Yisrael* (member of the congregation).[1]

After the reading of the Torah, a section from the prophetic books (*Haftarah*) is recited. The person who is called up for the last *parashah* of the *sidrah* reads the *Haftarah*; he is known as the *maftir*. The section from the prophets parallels the content of the *sidrah*. Once the Torah Scroll is replaced in the Ark, a sermon is usually delivered, based on the *sidrah* of the week.

Another central feature of the synagogue service is the *Kaddish* prayer. Written in Aramaic, it takes several forms in the prayer-book and expresses the hope for universal peace under the Kingdom of God. There are five main forms:

1 Half *Kaddish*, recited by the reader between sections of the service.

2 Full *Kaddish*, recited by the reader at the end of a major section of the service.

3 Mourners' *Kaddish*, recited by mourners after the service.

4 Scholars' *Kaddish*, recited after the reading of talmudic midrashic passages in the presence of a *minyan* (quorum of ten men).

5 Expanded form of the Mourners' *Kaddish*, recited at the cemetery after a burial.

A further feature of the service is the *Hallel*, consisting of Psalms 113 to 118. In the talmudic period it was known as the 'Egyptian *Hallel*' because the second psalm (114) begins with the words 'When Israel went forth from Egypt'. (This designation was used to distinguish this group of psalms from another psalm (136) – the Great *Hallel* – which is recited on the Sabbath and festivals during the morning service.) The complete *Hallel* is recited on the first two days of Pesach, on both days of Shavuot, on the nine days of Sukkot, and the eight days of Hanukkah. Part of the *Hallel* is recited on the intermediate days (Hol Hamoed), and the last two days of Pesach.

Since the thirteenth century the three daily services have concluded with the recitation of the *Alenu* prayer which proclaims God as king over humanity. In all likelihood it was introduced by Rav in the third century as an introduction to the *Malkhuyyot*, the section recited as part of the *Musaf* service for Rosh Ha-Shanah. In the Middle Ages this prayer was the death-song of Jewish martyrs. The first part of the prayer proclaims God as king of Israel; the second anticipates the time when idolatry will disappear and all human beings will acknowledge God as King of the Universe.

The traditional liturgy remained essentially the same until the Enlightenment in the nineteenth century. At this time reformers in central Europe altered the worship service and introduced new prayers into the liturgy in conformity with current cultural and spiritual developments. Influenced by Protestant Christianity, these innovators decreed that the service should be shortened and conducted in the vernacular as well as in Hebrew. In addition, they introduced Western melodies to the accompaniment of a choir and organ, and replaced the chanting of the Torah with a recitation of the *sidrah*. Prayers viewed as anachronistic were abandoned (such as the priestly blessing given by *cohanim*, the *Kol Nidre* prayer on the Day of Atonement, and prayers for the restoration of the Temple and the reinstitution of sacrifice). Further, prayers of a particularistic character were amended so that they became more universalistic in scope.

The Conservative movement also produced prayer-books in line with its ideology. In general the Conservative liturgy followed the traditional *siddur* except for several differences, for example, prayers for the restoration of sacrifice were changed (though, unlike the Progressive Movements, mention of the sacrifices was retained) and the morning benediction thanking God that the worshipper was not made a woman was altered, and prayers for peace were altered to include all humanity.

In recent times all groups across the Jewish spectrum have produced new liturgies (such as those that commemorate Holocaust Remembrance Day, Israel Independence Day and Jerusalem Reunification Day). Moreover, a wide range of occasional liturgies exist for camps, youth groups and *havurot* (informal prayer groups). Among non-Orthodox denominations there is a growing emphasis on more egalitarian liturgies, with gender-free language and an increasingly democratic sense of responsibility. Thus prayer and worship continue to be of vital importance to the Jewish people, yet there have occurred a variety of alterations to its nature within all branches of the Jewish faith.

Sabbath

Genesis 2:1–3 declares:

> The heaven and the earth were finished, and all the host of them. And on the seventh day God finished his work which he had done, and he rested on the seventh day from all his work which he had done. So God blessed the seventh day and hallowed it, because on it God rested from all his work which he had done in creation.

This passage serves as the basis for the decree that no work should be done on the Sabbath. During their sojourn in the wilderness of Zin, the Israelites were first commanded to observe the Sabbath. They were told to work on five days of the week, when they should collect a single portion of manna; on the sixth day they were instructed to collect a double portion for the following day was to be 'a day of solemn rest, a holy Sabbath of the Lord' (Exod 16:23). On the seventh day, when several individuals made a search for manna, the Lord stated: 'How long do you refuse to keep my commandments and my laws? See! The Lord has given you the Sabbath, therefore on the sixth day he gives you bread for two days; remain every man of you in his place, let no man go out of his place on the seventh day' (Exod 16:28–29).

Several weeks later God revealed the Ten Commandments, including prescriptions concerning the Sabbath day:

> Remember the Sabbath day, to keep it holy. Six days you shall labour, and do all your work, but the seventh day is a Sabbath to the Lord your God; in it you shall not do any work, you, or your son, or your daughter, your manservant, or your maidservant, or your cattle, or the sojourner who is within your gates; for in six days the Lord made heaven and earth, the sea, and all that is in them, and rested the seventh day; therefore the Lord blessed the Sabbath day and hallowed it. (Exod 20:8–11)

The book of Deuteronomy contains a different version, emphasizing the Exodus from Egypt:

> Observe the Sabbath day, to keep it holy, as the Lord your God commanded you. Six days you shall labour, and do all your work; but the seventh day is a Sabbath to the Lord your God; in it you shall not do any work ... You shall remember that you were a servant in the land of Egypt, and the Lord your God brought you out thence with a mighty hand and an outstretched arm; therefore the Lord your God commanded you to keep the Sabbath day. (Deut 5:12–15)

According to the book of Exodus, the Sabbath is a covenant between Israel and God:

> Say to the people of Israel, 'You shall keep my Sabbaths, for this is a sign between me and you throughout your generators, that you may know that I, the Lord, sanctify you' ... Therefore the people of Israel shall keep the Sabbath, observing the Sabbath throughout their generations as a perpetual covenant. (Exod 31:12, 16)

By the time the Sanhedrin began to function in Hasmonean times the observance of the Sabbath was regulated by Jewish law. Following the injunction in Exodus 20:10, the primary aim was to refrain from

255

work. In the Five Books of Moses only a few provisions are delineated: kindling a fire (Exod 35:3); ploughing and harvesting (Exod 23:12); carrying from one place to another (Exod 16:29). Such regulations were expanded by the rabbis, who listed 39 categories of work (which were involved in the building of the Tabernacle). According to the Mishnah they are:

1. sowing; 2. ploughing; 3. reaping; 4. binding sheaves; 5. threshing; 6. winnowing; 7. sorting; 8. grinding; 9. sifting; 10. kneading; 11. baking; 12. shearing sheep; 13. washing wool; 14. beating wool; 15. dyeing wool; 16. spinning; 17. sewing; 18. making two loops; 19. weaving two threads; 20. separating two threads; 21. tying; 22. loosening; 23. sewing two stitches; 24. tearing in order to sew two stitches; 25. hunting a deer; 26. slaughtering; 27. flaying; 28. salting; 29. curing a skin; 30. scraping the hide; 31. cutting; 32. writing two letters; 33. erasing in order to write two letters; 34. building; 35. pulling down a structure; 36. extinguishing a fire; 37. lighting a fire; 38. striking with a hammer; 39. moving something.

In the Talmud these categories were discussed and expanded to include within each category a range of activities. In order to ensure that individuals did not transgress these prescriptions, the rabbis enacted further legislation which served as a fence around the law. Yet despite such ordinances, there are certain situations which take precedence over Sabbath prohibitions. Witnesses of the New Moon, for example, who were to inform the Sanhedrin or Bet Din of this occurrence, were permitted to do so on the Sabbath. Other instances include: circumcision can be performed on the Sabbath; dangerous animals may be killed; persons are permitted to fight in self-defence; anything may be done to save a life or assist a woman in childbirth.

The Sabbath itself commences on Friday at sunset. About twenty minutes before sunset, candles are traditionally lit by the woman of the house, who recites the blessing 'Blessed are You, O Lord our God, King of the universe, who has hallowed us by your commandments and commanded us to kindle the Sabbath light'. In the synagogue, the service preceding Friday *maariv* takes place at twilight. Known as *Kabbalat Shabbat*,[2] it is a late addition dating back to the sixteenth century when kabbalists (mystics) in Safed went out to the fields on Friday afternoon to greet the Sabbath queen. In kabbalistic lore the Sabbath represents the *Shekhinah* (divine presence). This ritual is rooted in the custom of Haninah (first century) who, after preparing himself for the Sabbath, stood at sunset and said 'Come let us go forth to welcome the Sabbath', and that of Yannai (third century) who said: 'Come Bride! Come Bride!' On the basis of such sentiments Solomon Alkabets composed the Sabbath hymn *Lekhah Dodi*, which has become a major feature of the liturgy. In the Sephardi[3] rite, Psalm 29 and *Lekhah Dodi* are recited, whereas the Ashkenazi rite comprises Psalms 95–99, *Lekhah Dodi* and Psalms 92–93. The Reform prayer-book offers a variety of alternative services, including abridged versions of these psalms and the entire *Lekhah Dodi*. The Reconstructionist service commences with biblical passages, continues with an invocation and meditation on the Sabbath, and proceeds to a reading of psalms and *Lekhah Dodi*.

Traditionally, when the father returns home from the synagogue, he blesses his children. With both hands placed on the head of a boy, he says 'May God make you like Ephraim and Manasseh'; for a girl, 'May God make you like Sarah, Rebekah, Rachel and Leah'. In addition, he recites the priestly blessing. Those assembled then sing *Shalom Aleikhem*, which welcomes the Sabbath angels. At the Sabbath table the father recites the *Kiddush* prayer over a cup of wine:

> Blessed are you, O Lord our God, King of the universe, who has sanctified us by your commandments and has taken pleasure in us, and in love and favour has given us your holy Sabbath as an inheritance, a memorial of the creation, that day being the first of the holy convocations, in remembrance of the Exodus from Egypt. For you have chosen us and hallowed us above all nations, and in love and favour have given us your holy Sabbath as inheritance. Blessed are you, O Lord, who sanctifies the Sabbath.

This is followed by the washing of the hands and blessing over bread (*Ha-Motzi*). The meal is followed by the singing of table hymns (*zemirot*) and concludes with the Grace after Meals. This, which Jews are obligated to recite after every meal, originally consisted of three paragraphs in which worshippers thank God for sustenance, the land and the Torah, and pray for the restoration of the Temple. Later a fourth paragraph was added, which contains the words 'Who is good and does good'. Subsequently, short prayers beginning with 'the All Merciful' were added. On the Sabbath an additional prayer is included, dealing with the Sabbath day.

On Sabbath morning the liturgy consists of a morning service, a reading of the Torah and the *Haftarah*, and the additional *Musaf* service. In the service itself, introductory prayers prior to the *Shema* differ from those of weekdays, and the *Amidah* is also different. Seven individuals are called to the Reading of the Law, and an eighth for a reading from the Prophets. In the Reform and Liberal movements the worship is abridged and has no additional service. On returning home, the morning *Kiddush* and *Ha-Motzi* are recited, followed by the Sabbath meal and then the Grace after Meals. In the afternoon service the Torah is read prior to the *Amidah*; three persons are called to the Torah, and the first portion of the reading of the law for the following week is recited. Customarily, three meals are to be eaten on the Sabbath day; the third meal is known as the *Seduah Shelishit*. It should take place just in time for the evening service. At the end of the Sabbath, the evening service takes place and is followed by the *Havdalah* service.

The *Havdalah* ceremony marks the conclusion of the Sabbath period; it is divided into four blessings. Three are recited over wine, spices and lights, and the service concludes with the *Havdalah* blessing. In the Sephardi, Ashkenazi and Yemenite rites, the blessings are similar, but the introductory sentences are different. The Ashkenazi rite contains biblical phrases with the term 'salvation'; the Sephardi requests the granting of bountifulness and success; the Yemenite prays for a successful week. The final blessing opens with the phrase 'Blessed are you, O Lord our God, King of the universe, who distinguishes' followed by a series of comparisons: between the holy and the profane, light and darkness, Israel and the nations, between the seventh day and the six days of the week. The hymn *Ha-Mavdil* follows the *Havdalah* ceremony and asks for forgiveness of sins and for the granting of a large number of children. A number of customs, including filling a cup and extinguishing the *Havdalah* candle in wine poured from it, are associated with the *Havdalah* ceremony.

Pilgrim festivals

According to the book of Deuteronomy Jews are to celebrate three pilgrim festivals each year:

> Three times each year all your males shall appear before the Lord your God at the place which he will choose, at the feast of unleavened bread, at the feast of weeks, and at the feast of booths. (Deut 16:16)

258

On the basis of this commandment large numbers of pilgrims went to Jerusalem during the First and Second Temple periods from throughout the Holy Land, Babylonia and the Mediterranean lands. There they assembled in the Temple area to offer sacrifice and pray to God.

The first of these festivals is Pesach, which is celebrated for eight days (seven in Israel) from 15 to 22 Nisan. The various names for this festival illustrate its different dimensions.

Pesach ('Passover'). This term is derived from the account of the tenth plague in Egypt when first-born Egyptians were killed whereas God 'passed over' the houses of the Israelites (whose door-posts and lintels were sprinkled with the blood of the paschal lamb). This term is also applied to the Passover sacrifice which took place on 14 Nisan; its flesh was roasted and eaten together with unleavened bread and bitter herbs.

Hag ha-Matzot ('Festival of Unleavened Bread'). This term refers to the unleavened bread baked by the Israelites on their departure from Egypt. In accordance with God's command to Moses and Aaron while the people were in Egypt, no leaven was to be eaten during future Passover celebrations, nor was it to be kept in the house. All vessels used for leavening must be put away, and their place taken by a complete set used only for Passover. Although no leaven may be eaten during this period, the obligation to eat *matzah* applies only to the first two nights during the *seder* service.

Zeman Herutenu ('Season of Our Freedom'). This term designates the deliverance from Egyptian slavery and the emergence of the Jewish people as a separate nation.

Hag ha-Aviv ('Festival of Spring'). This name is used because the month of Nisan is described in Scripture as the month of Aviv, when ears of barley begin to ripen. In accordance with the biblical command, a measure of barley (*omer*) was brought to the Temple on the second day of Passover. Only when this was done could bread be made from the new barley harvest.

In preparation for Passover, Jewish law stipulates that all leaven must be removed from the house. On 14 Nisan a formal search is made for any remains of leaven. This is then put aside and burned on the following morning. The first night of Passover is celebrated in a home ceremony referred to as the *seder*. This is done to fulfil the biblical commandment to relate the story of the Exodus to one's son: 'And you shall tell your son on the day, saying: It is because of what the Lord did for me when I came out of Egypt' (Exod 13:8). The order of the service dates back to Temple times. During the ceremony celebrants tradition-ally lean on their left sides – this was the custom of freemen in ancient times.

The symbols placed on the *seder* table serve to remind those present of Egyptian bondage, God's redemption, and the celebration in Tem-ple times. They consist of the following:

Three *matzot*. These three pieces of unleavened bread are placed on top of one another, usually in a special cover. The upper and lower *matzot* symbolize the double portion of manna provided for the Israelites in the wilderness. The middle *matzah* (which is broken in two at the beginning of the *seder*) represents the 'bread of affliction'. The smaller part is eaten to comply with the com-mandment to eat *matzah*. The larger part is set aside for the *Afikoman*, which recalls Temple times when the meal was com-pleted with the eating of the paschal lamb. These three *matzot* also symbolize the three divisions of the Jewish people: Cohen, Levi and Yisrael.

Four cups of wine. According to tradition, each Jew must drink four cups of wine at the *seder*. The first is linked to the recital of *Kiddush*, the second with the account of the Exodus and the Blessing for Redemption, the third with the Grace after Meals, and the fourth with the *Hallel* and prayers for thanksgiving. These cups also symbolize four expressions of redemption in Exodus 6:6–7.

The cup of Elijah. This cup symbolizes the hospitality awaiting the passerby and wayfarer. According to tradition, the Messiah will reveal himself at the Passover, and Malachi declared that he will be preceded by Elijah. The cup of Elijah was also introduced because of the doubt as to whether five cups of wine should be drunk rather than four.

Bitter herbs (*maror*). These symbolize the bitterness of Egyptian slavery.

Parsley (*karpas*). This is dipped in salt water and eaten after the *Kiddush*. It is associated with spring.

Haroset. This is a mixture of apples, nuts, cinnamon and wine. It is a reminder of the bricks and mortar that Jews were forced to use in Egypt.

Roasted shankbone. This symbolizes the paschal offering.

Roasted egg. This commemorates the festival sacrifice in the Temple.

Salt water. This recalls the salt that was offered with all sacrifices. It also symbolizes the salt water of the tears of the ancient Israelites.

At the *seder*, the *Haggadah* details the order of service. It is as follows:

1 The *Kiddush* is recited.

2 The celebrant washes his hands.

3 The parsley is dipped in salt water.

4 The celebrant divides the middle *matzah* and sets aside the *Afikoman*.

5 The celebrant recites the *Haggadah* narration.

6 The participants wash their hands.

7 The blessing over bread is recited.

8 The blessing over *matzah* is recited.

9 Bitter herbs are eaten.

10 The *matzah* and *maror* are combined.

11 The meal is eaten.

12 The *Afikoman* is eaten.

13 Grace after Meals is recited.

14 The *Hallel* is recited.

15 The service is concluded.

16 Hymns and songs are sung.

The second pilgrim festival, Shavuot, is celebrated for two days (or one day in Israel) on 6 and 7 Sivan. The word *Shavuot* means 'weeks'; seven weeks are counted from the bringing of the *omer* on the second day of Pesach (Lev 23:15). The festival is also referred to as Pentecost, a Greek word meaning 'fiftieth', since it was celebrated on the fiftieth day. Symbolically the day commemorates the culmination of the process of emancipation which began with the Exodus at Passover and was concluded with the proclamation of the Law at Mount Sinai. Liturgically, the festival is also called *Zeman Mattan Toratenu* ('Season of the Giving of Our Torah'). This name relates to events depicted in Exodus 19 – 20.

During the Temple period farmers set out for Jerusalem to offer a selection of first ripe fruits as a thank-offering. In post-Temple times, the emphasis shifted to the festival's identification as the anniversary of the giving of the law on Mount Sinai. In some communities it is a practice to remain awake during Shavuot night. In the sixteenth century Solomon Alkabets and other kabbalists began the custom of *tikkun*, in which an anthology of biblical and rabbinic material was recited. Today, in those communities where this custom is observed, this lectionary has been replaced by a passage of the Talmud or other rabbinic literature. Some congregations in the diaspora read a book of Psalms on the second night. Synagogues themselves are decorated with flowers or plants, and dairy food is consumed during the festival. The liturgical readings for the festival include the Ten Commandments preceded by the liturgical poems. The book of Ruth is also recited. In many communities this festival marks the graduation of young people from formal synagogue education (or Confirmation, in Reform Temples). In Israel, agricultural settlements hold a First Fruits celebration on Shavuot.

The third pilgrim festival, Sukkot, is also prescribed in the Bible: 'On the fifteenth day of this seventh month and for seven days is the feast of Tabernacles to the Lord' (Lev 23:34). Beginning on 15 Tishri, it commemorates God's protection of the Israelites during their sojourn in the desert. Leviticus commands that Jews are to construct booths during this period as a reminder that the people of Israel dwelt in booths when they fled from Egypt (Lev 23:42–3).

During this festival a *sukkah* (booth) is constructed; its roof is covered with branches of trees and plants. During the festival meals are to be eaten inside the *sukkah*. Leviticus also declares that various agricultural species should play a part in the observance of this festival: 'And you shall take on the first day the fruit of goodly trees, branches of palm trees, and boughs of leafy trees, and willows of the brook; and you shall rejoice before the Lord your God seven days' (Lev 23:40). In compliance with this prescription the four species are used in the liturgy: palm, myrtle, willow and citron. On each day of the festival the *lulav* (palm branch) is waved in every direction before and during the *Hallel*; this symbolizes God's presence throughout the world. Holding the four species, Jews make one circuit around the Torah, which is carried on the *bimah* (platform) on each of the first six days. During this circuit *Hoshana* prayers are recited. On the seventh day of Sukkot (*Hoshana Rabba*) seven circuits are made around the Torah while reciting *Hoshana* prayers. During the service the reader wears a white *kittel* (robe).

The New Year and the Day of Atonement

In ancient times the Jewish New Year (Rosh Ha-Shanah) took place on one day; it is now observed for two days, in both Israel and the diaspora, on 1 and 2 Tishri, marking the beginning of the Ten Days of Penitence which conclude on the Day of Atonement (Yom Kippur). The term *Rosh Ha-Shanah* occurs only once in Scripture (Ezek 40:1). None the less, this festival has three other biblical designations:

1   *Shabbaton* – a day of solemn rest to be observed on the first day of the seventh month.

2   *Zikhron Teruah* – a memorial proclaimed with the blast of a horn (Lev 23:24).

3   *Yom Teruah* – 'a day of blowing the horn' (Num 29:1).

Later the rabbis referred to the New Year as *Yom Ha-Din* ('the Day of Judgement') and *Yom Ha-Zikkaron* ('the Day of Remembrance').

According to the Mishnah, all human beings will pass before God on the New Year; the Talmud expands this ideal by stressing the need for self-examination. In rabbinic literature each person stands before the Throne of God, and judgement on every person is entered on the New Year and sealed on the Day of Atonement. The tractate *Rosh Ha-*

Shanah in the Talmud declares that 'there are three ledgers opened in heaven: one for the completely righteous, who are immediately inscribed and sealed in the Book of Life; another for the thoroughly wicked, who are recorded in the Book of Death; and a third for the intermediate, ordinary type of person, whose fate hangs in the balance and is suspended until the Day of Atonement'. In this light, Rosh Ha-Shanah and Yom Kippur are also called *Yamim Noraim* ('Days of Awe').

On Rosh Ha-Shanah the Ark curtain, reading desk and Torah Scroll mantles are decked in white, and the rabbi, cantor and person who blows the *shofar* (ram's horn) all wear a white *kittel*. In the synagogue service the *Amidah* of the *musaf* service contains three sections relating to God's sovereignty, providence and revelation: *Malkhuyyot* (introduced by the *Alenu* prayer) deals with God's rule; *Zikhronot* portrays God's remembrance of the ancestors of the Jewish people when he judges each generation; *Shofarot* contains verses relating to the shofar and deals with the revelation on Mount Sinai and the messianic age. Each introductory section is followed by three verses from the Torah, three from the Writings, three from the Prophets, and one from the Torah. On the first and second day of Rosh Ha-Shanah the Torah readings concern the birth of Isaac (Gen 21:1–34) and the binding of Isaac or *Akedah* (Gen 22:1–24). The *Haftarah* for the first day is 1 Sam 1:19 – 2:10, which depicts the birth of Samuel, who subsequently dedicated his life to God's service; on the second day the *Haftarah* deals with Jeremiah's prophecy (Jer 31:2–20) concerning the restoration of Israel.

On both days of Rosh Ha-Shanah (except when the first is on the Sabbath) the *shofar* is blown at three points during the service: 30 times after the reading of the Law; 30 times during *Musaf* (ten at the end of each of the three main sections); 30 times after *Musaf*; and ten before *Alenu*. In the liturgy there are three variants of the blowing of the *shofar*: *tekiah* (a long note), *shevarim* (three tremulous notes) and *teruot* (nine short notes). According to Maimonides, the *shofar* is blown to call sinners to repent. As he explains in the *Mishneh Torah*: 'Awake you sinners, and ponder your deeds; remember your creator, forsake your evil ways, and return to God'. In the Ashkenazi rite the *U-Netanneh Tokef* prayer concludes the service on a hopeful note as congregants declare that 'Repentance, Prayer and Charity can avert the evil decree'.

Traditionally it was a custom to go to the seaside or the banks of a river on the afternoon of the first day (or on the second day if the first falls on a Sabbath). The ceremony of *Tashlikh* symbolizes the casting of one's sins into a body of water. The prayers for *Tashlikh* and three verses from the book of Micah (Mic 7:18–20) express confidence in divine forgiveness. In the home after *Kiddush* a piece of bread is dipped in honey followed by a piece of apple, and a prayer is recited that the year ahead may be good and sweet. It is also a custom to eat the new season's fruit on the second night of Rosh Ha-Shanah to justify reciting the *Sheheheyanu* benediction on enjoying new things. The *hallah* loaves baked for this festival are usually round or have a plaited crust shaped like a ladder to represent hopes for a good year or the effort to direct one's life upward to God.

The Ten Days of Penitence begin with the New Year and last until the Day of Atonement. This is considered the most solemn time of the year, when all are judged and their fate determined for the coming year. During the Ten Days a number of additions are made to the liturgy, especially in the morning service. *Selihot* (penitential prayers) are recited during the morning service, and various additions are made to the *Amidah* and the reader's repetition of the *Amidah*. The reader's repetition is followed by the *Avinu Malkenu* prayer. In some synagogues it is customary to recite Psalm 130:1 in the morning service. It is also traditional to visit the graves of close relatives at this time. The Sabbath between the New Year and the Day of Atonement is called *Shabbat Shuvah*, the Sabbath of turning or repentance.

The holiest day of the Jewish calendar is Yom Kippur, which takes place on 10 Tishri. Like other major festivals, its observance is prescribed in Scripture: 'On the tenth day of this seventh month is the Day of Atonement; and you shall afflict yourselves ... It shall be to you a Sabbath of solemn rest, and you shall afflict yourselves; on the ninth day of the month beginning at evening, from evening to evening' (Lev 23:27, 32). According to the sages, afflicting one's soul involved abstaining from food and drink. Thus every male over the age of 13 and every female over 12 is obliged to fast from sunset until nightfall the next evening. Sick people, however, may take medicine and small amounts of food and drink; similarly, those who are ill may be forbidden to fast.

During the day normal Sabbath prohibitions apply, but worshippers are to abstain from food and drink, marital relations, wearing leather shoes, using cosmetics and lotions, and washing the body except for fingers and eyes. The rabbis stress that the Day of Atonement enables human beings to atone for sins against God; however, regarding transgressions committed against others, pardon cannot be obtained unless forgiveness has been sought from the persons injured; as a consequence, it is customary for Jews to seek reconciliation with anyone they might have offended during the year. Previously, lashes (*malkot*) were administered in the synagogue to impart a feeling of repentance, but this custom has largely disappeared. The *kapparot* ritual still takes place before the Day of Atonement among Sephardi and Eastern communities as well as among some Ashkenazim.[4] During this ceremony a fowl is slaughtered and either eaten before the fast or sold for money which is given to charity; its death symbolizes the transfer of guilt from the person to the bird that has been killed. In many congregations Jews substitute coins for the fowl, and charity boxes are available at the morning and afternoon services before Yom Kippur. Customarily Jews were able to absolve vows on the eve of Yom Kippur. In addition, afternoon prayers are recited earlier than normal, and the *Amidah* is extended by two formulae of confession (*Ashamnu* and *Al Het*).

Some pious Jews immerse themselves in a *mikveh* (ritual bath) in order to undergo purification before the fast. In the home, a final meal (*seudah mafseket*) is eaten and, prior to lighting the festival candles, a memorial candle is kindled to burn throughout the day. Further, leather shoes are replaced by non-leather shoes or slippers. The prayer shawl (*tallit*) is worn throughout all the services, and a white curtain (*parokhet*) adorns the synagogue Ark and the Scrolls of the Law. The reader's desk and other furnishings are also covered in white. Among Ashkenazim, rabbis, cantors and other officiants also wear a white *kittel*.

On Yom Kippur five services take place. The first, *Kol Nidre* (named after its introductory declarations), ends with the concluding service (*Neilah*). Except for the extended *Amidah*, each service has its own characteristic liturgy. In all of them, however, the confession of sins (*viddui*) is pronounced; shorter confessions as well as longer ones are in the first person plural to emphasize collective responsibility. In some liturgies there are also confessions of personal transgressions. Of special importance in the liturgy is the *Avinu Malkenu* prayer, in which individuals confess their sins and pray for forgiveness.

In most congregations the *Kol Nidre* (declaration of annulment of vows) is recited on the eve of Yom Kippur. Among the Orthodox it was a custom to spend the night in the synagogue reciting the entire book of Psalms as well as other readings. Among Sephardim and Reform Jews the memorial prayer is recited on *Kol Nidre*. In addition to *selihot* and other hymns, the morning service includes a Torah reading (Lev 16), describing the Day of Atonement ritual in the Sanctuary, and a *maftir* (additional) reading (Num 29:7–11), concerning the festival sacrifices. The *Haftarah* (Isa 57:14 – 58:14) describes the fast that is required. Ashkenazim (excluding Reform Jews) then recite memorial prayers (*yizkor*). Among Sephardi Jewry and Eastern communities, the *Hashkavah* service is repeated.

Before the *Musaf* service a special prayer (*Hineni He-Amin Mi-Maas*) is recited. A number of liturgical hymns are also included in the reader's repetition of the *Amidah*, including the *U-Netanneh Tokef* passage. Interpolated in among the *selihot* and confessions towards the end of *Musaf* is the *Elleh Ezkerah* martyrology. Based on a medieval *midrash*, this martyrology describes the plight of the Ten Martyrs who were persecuted for defying Hadrian's ban on the study of Torah. In some rites this part of the service has been expanded to include readings from Holocaust sources. In the afternoon service Leviticus 18 is read, dealing with prohibited marriages and sexual offences; the *Haftarah* is the book of Jonah. Before the concluding service (*Neilah*), the hymn *El Nora Alilah* is chanted among Sephardim. This part of the liturgy is recited as twilight approaches. During this time hymns such as *Petah Lanu Shaar* serve to remind congregants that the period for repentance is nearly over. In many congregations the Ark remains open and worshippers stand throughout the service. Worshippers ask God to inscribe each person for a good life and to seal them for a favourable fate. *Neilah* concludes with the chanting of *Avinu Malkenu*. This is followed by the *Shema*, the threefold recital of *Barukh Shem Kevod Malkhuto*, and a sevenfold acknowledgement that the Lord is God. The *shofar* is then blown, and the congregants recite *La-Shanah ha-Baah Bl-Yerushalayim* ('Next year in Jerusalem'). After the service concludes it is customary to begin the construction of the *sukkah*.

Days of joy

In the Jewish calendar there are a number of joyous festivals on which Jews are permitted to follow their daily tasks:

HANUKKAH

This festival (meaning 'dedication') is celebrated for eight days beginning on 25 Kislev: it commemorates the victory of the Maccabees over
the Seleucids in the second century BCE. At this time the Maccabees
engaged in a military struggle with the Seleucids, who had desecrated
the Temple in Jerusalem. After a three-year struggle (165–163 BCE),
the Maccabees under Judah Maccabee conquered Jerusalem and
rebuilt the altar. According to tradition, a small amount of oil for use
in the *menorah* miraculously lasted for eight days. *Hanukkah* commemorates this miracle.

The central observance of this festival is the kindling of the festive
lamp on each of the eight nights. This practice gave the holiday the
additional name of *Hag Ha-Urim* ('Festival of Lights'). In ancient
times this lamp was placed in the doorway or in the street outside to
publicize the miracle; subsequently the lamp was placed inside the
house. The lighting occurs after dark (except on Friday evenings when
it must be done before the kindling of the Sabbath lights). The
procedure for lighting the Hanukkah candles is to light one candle (or
oil lamp) on the first night, and an additional candle each night until
the last night, when all eight candles are lit. The kindling should go
from left to right. An alternative tradition prescribes that the eight
candles are lit on the first night, seven on the second night, and so
forth.[5] These candles are lit by an additional candle called the *sham-
mash* (serving light). In addition to this home ceremony, candles are lit
in the synagogue.

In the synagogue liturgy this festival is commemorated by the recitation of the *Al ha-Nissim* prayer in the *Amidah* and Grace after Meals. In
the morning service the *Hallel* is recited, and a special reading of the Law
takes place on each day of the holiday. In both the home and the
synagogue the hymn *Maoz Tsur* is sung in Ashkenazi communities;
the Sephardim read Psalm 30 instead. During Hanukkah it is customary
to hold parties which include games and singing. The best-known game
involves a *dreydel* (spinning top). The *dreydel* is inscribed with four
Hebrew letters (*nun, gimmel, he, shin*) on its side – this is an acrostic for
the phrase *nes gadol hayah sham* ('a great miracle happened here').[6]
During Hanukkah it is customary to eat *latkes* (potato pancakes) and
sufganilyyot (doughnuts).[7] In modern Israel the festival is associated with
national heroism, and a torch is carried from the traditional burial site of
the Maccabees at Modiin to various parts of the country.

PURIM

Another festival of joy is Purim, celebrated on 14 Adar to commemorate the deliverance of Persian Jewry from the plans of Haman, the chief minister of King Ahasuerus as depicted in the book of Esther. The name of this holiday is derived from the Akkadian word *pur* ('lots'), which refers to Haman's casting of lots to determine a date (13 Adar) to destroy the Jewish people (Esther 3:7–14). In remembrance of this date the Fast of Esther is observed on 13 Adar: on this day Queen Esther proclaimed a fast before she interceded with the king. On the next day, Purim is celebrated as the Feast of Lots which Mordecai, Esther's cousin, inaugurated to remember the deliverance of the Jewish people (Esther 9:20ff.). 15 Adar is *Shashan Purim*, since the conflict between the Jews and Haman's supporters in ancient Susa did not cease until 14 Adar and Ahasuerus allowed the Jews an extra day to overcome their foes. This means that the deliverance could only be celebrated a day later (Esther 9:13–18).

The laws regarding the observance of Purim are specified in the tractate *Megillah* in the Talmud. In the evening and morning services the Esther Scroll is chanted to a traditional melody. In most congregations Purim resembles a carnival: children frequently attend the reading from the Scroll in fancy dress and, whenever Haman's name is mentioned, worshippers stamp their feet and whirl noise-makers (*greggers*). In the *Amidah* and Grace after Meals, a prayer of thanksgiving is included; however, the *Hallel* psalms are excluded. During Purim it is customary to exchange gifts and donate to charity. During the afternoon a special festive meal takes place, including such traditional dishes as *Hamentashen* ('Haman's pockets') – triangular buns or pastries filled with poppyseed, prunes, dates, etc. It is usual for parents and relatives to give children money (*Purim gelt*). On Purim it is customary to stage plays, and in *yeshivot*, students imitate their teachers. In modern Israel parades take place with revellers dressed in Purim costumes.

ROSH HODESH

Rosh Hodesh is another festival of joy. It occurs with the new moon each month. Since the Jewish calendar is lunar, each month lasts a little more than 29 days. Because it was not possible to arrange the calendar with months of alternative length, the Sanhedrin declared whether a month had 29 or 30 days. If the outgoing month had 29 days, the next day was Rosh Hodesh. When a month had 30 days, the last day of the outgoing month and the first day of the new month constituted Rosh Hodesh. In early rabbinic times, the Sanhedrin was responsible for determining the day of the new moon on the basis of eye-witnesses who had claimed to see the new moon. Only in the fourth century was a permanent calendar fixed by Hillel II.

During the period of the First Temple, Rosh Hodesh was observed with the offering of special sacrifices, the blowing of *shofars*, feasting and a rest from work. By the end of the sixth century BCE, Rosh Hodesh became a semi-holiday. Eventually even this status disappeared, and Rosh Hodesh became a normal working day except for various liturgical changes. The liturgy for Rosh Hodesh includes the *Yaaleh Ve-Yavo* prayer, read in the *Amidah* and in Grace after Meals, which asks God to remember his people for good, for blessing and for life. In the morning service the *Hallel* psalms of praise are recited. The Bible reading is from Numbers 28, which describes the Temple service for the new moon. An additional service is also included, corresponding to the additional sacrifice which was offered on the new moon.

TU BI-SHEVAT

A further joyous festival is the New Year for Trees (Tu Bi-Shevat) which takes place on 15 Shevat. Although this festival is not referred to in the Bible, it appeared in the Second Temple period as a fixed cut-off date for determining the tithe levied on the produce of fruit trees. Once the Temple was destroyed, the laws of tithing were no longer applicable; as a result, this festival took on a new character. Wherever Jews resided, it reminded them of their connection with the Holy Land. During the fifteenth century a number of new ceremonies and rituals were instituted by the mystics of Safed. Through the influence of Isaac Luria, it became customary to celebrate the festival with gatherings where special fruits were eaten and hymns were sung and readings from Scripture were recited. Among the fruits eaten on Tu Bi-Shevat were those of the Holy Land. In modem Israel new trees are planted during this festival.

15 AV

Another further joyous occasion is 15 Av, which was a folk festival in the Second Temple period. At this time bachelors selected their wives from unmarried maidens. According to the Mishnah, on both this day and the Day of Atonement young girls in Jerusalem dressed in white garments and danced in the vineyards where young men selected their brides. In modern times this festival is marked only by a ban on eulogies or fasting. In the liturgy the *Tahanun* prayer is not recited after the *Amidah*.

INDEPENDENCE DAY

The final festival is Independence Day: this is Israel's national day which commemorates the proclamation of its independence on 5 Iyyar 1948. The Chief Rabbinate of Israel declared it a religious holiday and established a special order of service for the evening and morning worship. This service includes the *Hallel*, and a reading from Isaiah (Isa 10:32 – 11:12). The rabbinate also suspended any fast which occurs on the day, the recital of the *Tahanun* prayer, and mourning restrictions of the *omer* period. In Israel the preceding day is set aside as a day of remembrance for soldiers who died in battle. *Yizkor* prayers (including the *Kaddish*) are recited then and next-of-kin visit the military cemeteries. At home, memorial candles are fit and Psalm 9 is recited in many synagogues.

For the Jew, God is the creator and sustainer of the universe who has chosen the Jewish people from all nations. Out of covenantal loyalty the Jewish people have turned to their God in times of both joy and sorrow; through prayer and worship the nation has expressed its deepest spiritual longings and hope for the dawn of a new age when God will rule over all creatures. Both private and public prayer have thus played a central role in the Jewish tradition.

Notes

This chapter is based on Dan Cohn-Sherbok, *The Jewish Faith*. London: Society for Promoting Christian Knowledge. The notes have bee added for this publication.

1 This practice of calling up a *Cohen* and a *Levi* is usually not followed in Reform or Liberal synagogues. There is also variation in the number of people called to the Torah by the different movements. [Ed.]
2 Literally 'Receiving (or welcoming) the Sabbath'. [Ed.]
3 The Jewish community is broadly divided into two main divisions, Sephardim and Ashkinazim. Sephardic Jews are said to be descended from Jews living in Spain (but also include Jewish communities from other parts of the Arab world); Askenazic Jews are descended from those living in central, northern and eastern Europe. (For more information see Chapter 4, p. 115–16.). [Ed.]
4 This ritual is not practised by any of the non-Orthodox movements and is also not common even among Orthodox Jews. [Ed.]
5 Although this second practice is mentioned in the Talmud, it is not followed by any modern Jewish communities. [Ed.]
6 In Israel the letter Shin is replaced by the letter pe as the last word of the phrase is changed from 'there' (*sham*) to 'here' (*po*). [Ed.]
7 These foods are eaten because they are cooked in oil in commemoration of the oil which burned for eight days. [Ed.]

Further reading

De Lange, N. (1986) *Judaism*. Oxford: Oxford University Press.
Jacobs, L. (1987) *The Book of Jewish Practice*. New York: Behrman House.
Neusner, J. (1974) *The Way of Torah: An Introduction to Judaism*. Florence, KY: Dickenson.
Pilkington, C. M. (1991) *Judaism*. London: Hodder and Stoughton.
Siegel, R., Strassfeld, M. and Strassfeld, S. (eds) (1973) *The Jewish Catalog*. Philadelphia: Jewish Publication Society.
Steinberg, M. (1947) *Basic Judaism*. London: Harcourt Brace Jovanovich.
Strassfeld, S. and Strassfeld, M. (eds) (1966) *Encyclopedia of the Jewish Religion*. London: Holt, Rinehart & Winston.
Strassfeld, S. and Strassfeld, M. (eds) (1976) *The Second Jewish Catalog*. Philadelphia: Jewish Publication Society.
Werblowsky, R. J. and Wigoder, G. (eds) (1966) *Encyclopedia of the Jewish Religion*. London: Holt, Rinehart & Winston.
Wouk, H. (1968) *This Is My God*. New York: Doubleday.

10. Making moral decisions

Norman Solomon

Introduction: law and morality

A moral decision is one that the man or woman making it makes in the light of what he or she believes is right or wrong. It is not a decision made simply to gain material advantage or pleasure, or merely to conform with habit, rule or law.

Of course, a moral decision might result in material advantage or pleasure to whoever makes it; being moral does not mean being miserable. Though happiness in this world is not, in Jewish teaching, the criterion of right and wrong, it is virtuous to make others happy and, under normal circumstances, sinful to be miserable oneself.

A moral decision might also be made in conformity with a rule or law; after all, the rule or law itself might express moral values. Can moral decisions, then, be distinguished from legal decisions? The relationship between law and morality is complex, and this complex relationship of law and morality is a major factor in decision-making within traditional Judaism. A decision doesn't stop being moral just because it is made in the light of 'divinely revealed law'. On the contrary, since it is a self-evident moral duty to do what God wants, and since he would only want us to do what is good, then if there really is a known 'divine law', obviously we ought to follow it. Traditional Jewish belief is that the Torah (that is, in particular, the first five books of the Bible) is the authentic record of God's self-revelation. The Hebrew word *torah* is by no means co-extensive with 'law', though it is often convenient to translate it as 'law'. When Jews speak of the Torah as 'God's law', what they mean is that it expresses what God wants us to do; it is how God himself formulated the 'moral law' – 'the Torah of the Lord is perfect' (Psalm 19:8). It is not law *as opposed to* morality, but law which *is* morality.

The problem here, for all except the 'true believer', is how to be sure that God commanded this, that or the other. How do we know that the Bible is 'true', or that the rabbis of the Talmud[1] interpreted it correctly? We shall see later that doubts of this kind underlie the sectarian divisions among Jews today. For the time being, however, we will assume the traditional orthodox point of view.

Ought the law to be followed only because God commanded it? Certainly it should not be obeyed with the objective of gain: 'Be not like servants who serve their master in order to receive a reward', counselled Antigonos of Socho[2] (first century BCE). Torah should be observed *lishmah* (for its own sake), ultimately for the love of God. Psalm 119 beautifully expresses the love and joy in the commandments of God as taught by the Pharisees and their successors, the rabbis.

Are moral decisions distinguished from legal decisions by their subject matter? Sometimes people use 'moral' to refer to a decision made on a matter not covered by law, or not enforceable. This, as we shall see, is not a distinction that Judaism can make. Or again, to take another question, does the term 'moral' refer to decisions which exceed the standards demanded by law? The traditional Jewish concept corresponding to this form of morality is *lifnim mishurat ha-din* ('beyond the line of the law'). For instance, although a court cannot demand more than correctness or justice, the individual is called upon to exceed this by restraint from making the full legal demand on the other party, from demanding the 'pound of flesh'.[3] This restraint plays a major role in Jewish ethics. The third-century Palestinian Rabbi Yohanan said 'Jerusalem was destroyed only because people did not act beyond the strict requirement of law'.[4] That the law of Torah did not completely encompass its moral demands was recognized in the traditional *mi shepara'*:

> If (the purchaser) had handed over the money but had not yet taken possession of the goods (the vendor) has the right to withdraw from the sale; but he who punished (*mi shepara'*) the generation of the flood and the generation of the tower (of Babel) will punish him who does not stand by his word. (M *Bava Metzia* 4:2)

Does the concept of *lifnim mishurat ha-din* indicate that the law is not always just, or is *lifnim mishurat ha-din* itself part of one's legal responsibility – that there is, so to speak, a 'law' which tells you to go beyond the law?[5]

Another area of rabbinic Judaism in which the distinction between law and morality becomes fuzzy is that of alms-giving and benevolence. Alms-giving features prominently in Jewish teaching and practice, and the rabbis constantly impressed on their followers the need for compassion and charity. One of the Hebrew words for 'alms-giving' is *tzedakah*, derived from a root meaning 'to be right, fair or correct'. Alms-giving is not so much an act of piety as one of fairness, ensuring correct distribution of the wealth God has entrusted to us. The overall concept within which alms-giving is contained is *hesed*, a biblical Hebrew word which can be translated by 'love' or 'compassion' and has frequently been translated 'loving-kindness'. Yet the rabbis were not content to preach a moral value, but felt the need to formulate the duty of alms-giving in legal fashion, setting down limits as to how much, how often, to whom, and in what manner and form help ought to be given. But even this law-like formulation allows ample space for individual choice.

Isadore Twersky[6] has skilfully used a talmudic story to illustrate the polarity, in rabbinic Judaism, of law (*halakhah*) and ethics, or morality:

> It has been taught: R. Meir used to say: The critic [of Judaism] may bring against you the argument, 'If your God loves the poor, why does he not support them?' If so, answer him, 'So that through them we may be saved from the punishment of Gehinnom.' This question was actually put by Turnus Rufus to R. Akiba: 'If your God loves the poor, why does He not support them?' He replied: 'So that through them we may be saved from the punishment of Gehinnom.' 'On the contrary,' said the other, 'it is this which condemns you to Gehinnom. I will illustrate by a parable. Suppose an earthly king was angry with his servant and put him in prison and ordered that he should be given no food or drink, and a man went and gave him food and drink. If the king heard, would he not be angry with him? And you are called "servants", as it is written, For unto me the children of Israel are servants.' R. Akiba answered him: 'I will illustrate by another parable. Suppose an earthly king was angry with his son, and put him in prison and ordered that no food or drink should be given to him, and someone went and gave him food and drink. If the king heard of it, would he not send him a present? And we are called "sons", as it is written, Sons are ye to the Lord your God.' He said to him: 'You are called both sons and servants. When you carry out the desires of the Omnipresent, you are called "servants". At the present time you are not carrying out the desires of the Omnipresent.' R. Akiba replied: 'The Scripture says, Is it not to deal thy bread to the hungry and bring the poor that are cast out to thy house?

275

> When "dost thou bring the poor who are cast out to thy house?" Now; and
> it says [at the same time], is it not to deal thy bread to the hungry?[7]

The first inference Twersky derives from this passage is that God
has, so to speak, abdicated to people part of a function of his own in
order to enable them to transcend mere biological existence, to escape
damnation. In the practice of *hesed* one does not merely 'imitate' God,
one shares directly in his work. The second is that we are all equal, all
'children' of God; even our sin and temporary disgrace do not abro-
gate this relationship.

Twersky's third point is that the fact that God's judgement has
condemned an individual to poverty does not allow us to sit in
judgement on that person and to desist from giving help; on the
contrary, we are challenged to vigorous ethical response to his or her
situation. Fourth, we cannot 'dismiss a destitute person with a coun-
terfeit expression of faith: "Rely on God . . . ! He will help you" '. Faith
or trust (*bitahon*), to the poor, means trusting in God's mercy; to the
rich, on the other hand, 'it suggests the obligation of sustained and
gracious liberality'.

Twersky finally draws our attention to the 'dialectic' nature of the
halakhic approach to charity. While the essential achievement of
halakhah is the system of rules by which a principle of faith is
anchored into a detailed ethical code, it sought 'to combine the thesis
of free, spontaneous giving with the antithesis of soulless, obligatory
contribution and produce a composite act which is subjective though
quantified, inspired yet regular, intimate yet formal'. This dialectic is
indicated in the polarities between the attitude and manner of giving,
and the determination of the amount of giving, as well as between
individual and community responsibility; both of these polarities are
delicately handled within *halakhah*.

The tradition-conscious Jew is thus faced by the need to make a
characteristically 'moral' decision whenever he engages in a charitable
act; even as *halakhah* sets bounds to the act, he (or, in those commands
which affect her, she) is challenged as to its moral dimension.

The Hebrew scriptures

There is some truth in the description of Judaism and Christianity as
'two religions divided by a common scripture'. Both regard the

Hebrew scriptures as sacred, yet neither is simply 'the religion of the Old Testament', for both have evolved distinctive traditions of reading scripture.

Rabbinic Judaism reads the first five books of the Bible (Genesis, Exodus, Leviticus, Numbers, Deuteronomy) collectively as 'Torah', often translated 'law', though 'law' must here be understood in a very broad fashion; 'teaching', 'guidance', or 'the way' are possible translations of 'Torah', less misleading than 'law'. The *mitzvot* ('commandments', 'laws') contained in these books cover all aspects of life, from the most personal to the constitution of the state, and ranging from 'you shall love your neighbour as yourself' and 'you shall love the Lord your God' to the minutiae of Temple sacrifice or judicial procedure.

The rest of scripture is secondary to Torah, consisting of history, prophecy and wisdom, which confirm, but neither add to nor detract from, the substance of Torah.

HETERONOMOUS LAW?

The most obvious feature of scripture, when read from this perspective, is that it proclaims a set of laws, or system of behaviour, apparently independent of the observer. The source of law is transcendent; Torah proceeds from the eternal God, who is infinitely greater than the individual human.

Many theologians refer to this as 'heteronomous' law, opposing it to 'autonomous', that which comes from the individual, arising out of his or her own 'nature'. But this is a confused opposition. The distinction between 'outside' and 'inside' just does not apply to the transcendent; in some experiences we may know God as the 'other', but in other experiences we know him through our innermost self. Indeed, it is only when we are divided from our selves that we sense God as imposing, as demanding, from 'outside'. When we are reconciled with our selves, God's demands flow, as it were, from our own being. This is what is meant when humans, both male and female, are said to be made 'in the image of God' (Genesis 1:27). Thus even the stringent law code of Deuteronomy is presented, not as a 'scandal' (to use Paul's term) or profound 'mystery', but as totally accessible and in conformity with human understanding:

277

The commandment that I lay on you this day is not too difficult for you, it is not too remote. It is not in heaven, that you should say, 'Who will go up to heaven for us to fetch it and to tell it to us, so that we can keep it?' Nor is it beyond the sea, that you should say, 'Who will cross the sea for us to fetch it and to tell it to us, so that we can keep it?' It is a thing very near to you, *upon your lips and in your hearts ready to be kept.* (Deuteronomy 30:11–14, New English Bible (NEB); my emphasis)

People, individually or collectively, do not always obey the law, whether it be the 'inner law' of conscience, or some imposed system. Conflicts arise, and that is when authority intervenes, and the individual is deprived of freedom of action and perhaps severely punished. Much as scripture might assume that the individual conscience, freely exercised, would coincide with the 'law of God', it thoroughly disapproves of individuals who 'follow the promptings of [their] stubborn heart' (Deuteronomy 29:19) to run after false gods. Here we see the essential conflict of religion – rather, of any religious establishment – with the individual. The establishment will always characterize as 'stubborn' those who disagree with it. But, assuming integrity on both sides, who is to say the establishment is right and the individual wrong? The establishment may well affirm the freedom of conscience, even primacy of conscience, but so long as it also assumes 'If you truly followed your conscience you would do as we say', there is no real freedom, no recognition of the autonomy of the individual conscience.

RESOLVING DOUBT

What does one do in circumstances where the Torah offers no clear-cut solution to a problem? In biblical times, one would 'seek guidance of the Lord' (Genesis 25:22). But what did this mean in practical terms?

In appropriate cases, one would work through the available judicial process, including courts of appeal:

When the issue in any lawsuit is beyond your competence, whether it be a case of blood against blood, plea against plea, or blow against blow, that is disputed within your courts, then go up without delay to the place which the Lord your God will choose. There you must go to the levitical priests or to the judge then in office; seek their guidance, and they will pronounce the sentence. You shall act on the pronouncement which they make from the place which the Lord will choose. (Deuteronomy 17:8–10, NEB)

An individual, or even the king on behalf of the nation, might turn to some authority figure, for instance a judge, a prophet or a priest, perhaps using an oracle such as the Urim and Thummim (Numbers 27:21).

There are many instances in the Bible of the 'question and answer'. For instance, Zelophehad had no sons, but five daughters; their problem became the pretext for clarifying the laws of inheritance:

The heads of the fathers' families of Gilead son of Machir, son of Manasseh, one of the families of the sons of Joseph, approached Moses and the chiefs, heads of families in Israel, and addressed them. 'Sir,' they said, 'the Lord commanded you to distribute the land by lot to the Israelites, and you were also commanded to give the patrimony of our brother Zelophehad to his daughters. Now if any of them shall be married to a husband from another Israelite tribe, her patrimony will be lost to the patrimony of our fathers and be added to that of the tribe into which she is married, and so part of our allotted patrimony will be lost. Then when the jubilee year comes round in Israel, her patrimony would be added to the patrimony of the tribe into which she is married, and it would be permanently lost to the patrimony of our fathers' tribe.'
So Moses, instructed by the Lord, gave the Israelites this ruling: 'The tribe of the sons of Joseph is right. This is the Lord's command for the daughters of Zelophehad: They may marry whom they please, but only within a family of their father's tribe ... '. (Numbers 36:1–9, NEB)

Centuries later, the same procedure of enquiry from the Lord through a prophet is followed by the Babylonian exiles. Should they continue to observe the fasts by which they had commemorated the destruction of the Temple, now about to be rebuilt? Zechariah, however, hijacks the question as an opportunity to inculcate a moral lesson:

Bethel-Sharezer sent Regem-Melech with his men to seek the favour of the Lord. They were to say to the priests in the house of the Lord of Hosts and to the prophets, 'Am I to lament and abstain in the fifth month as I have done for so many years?' The word of the Lord of Hosts came to me: Say to all the people of the land and to the priests, When you fasted and lamented in the fifth and seventh months these seventy years, was it indeed in my honour that you fasted? And when you ate and drank, was it not to please yourselves? ... These are the words of the Lord of Hosts: Administer true justice, show loyalty and compassion to one another, do not oppress the orphan and the widow, the alien and the poor, do not contrive any evil against one another ... (Zechariah 7:2–10, NEB)

FREE WILL

The rabbinic reading of scripture fairly consistently endorses Ezekiel's statement that it is 'the soul that sins, and no other, that shall die; a son shall not share a father's guilt, nor a father his son's' (Ezekiel 18:20). The well-known phrase in the Ten Commandments, 'visiting the sins of the fathers upon the third and fourth generations of those who hate me', is glossed by the Targum: 'if they continue in the way of their fathers'.

There are few places where traditional Jewish and Christian exegesis diverges so radically as the story of Adam and Eve. Jewish exegetes understand the sin of Adam as a prototype, not as a burden of guilt to be inherited by his descendants. Though the power of the *yetser ha-ra* ('evil inclination') is acknowledged, humans are created with the strength to resist. They should, indeed, turn to God for mercy and help, for true penitence is not easy; but there is no burden of inherited guilt which can only be expiated by vicarious sacrifice. Adam and Eve were themselves penitents.

In this light, it is easy to appreciate Deuteronomy's stress on human ability to choose, and to choose aright:

I summon heaven and earth to witness against you this day: I offer you the choice of life or death, blessing or curse. Choose life, and then you and your descendants will live. (Deuteronomy 30:19, NEB)

What then, O Israel, does the Lord your God ask of you? Only to fear the Lord your God, to conform to all his ways, to love him and to serve him with all your heart and soul. This you will do by keeping the commandments of the Lord. (Deuteronomy 10:12–13, NEB)

There is no suggestion here that humanity labours beneath an inescapable burden of sin, or is destined to suffer.

Equally absent from scripture, on the rabbinic reading, is the notion of fatalism, that certain individuals are fated, or 'predestined', to sin, or that for each individual there is mapped out some inescapable path in life. Some rare individuals – Jeremiah, for instance – might indeed be 'called' to a particular vocation, but this is not the same as being 'fated'; Jeremiah might well have rejected the call, or failed, for there was no compulsion, however much Jeremiah felt it to be so, as a 'fire burning in his bones'.

Against this background it is noteworthy that post-rabbinic Judaism, including Jewish folk custom, sometimes veered away from the rabbinic stress on the freedom of the will. Kabbalah, for instance, developed the concept of the sin of Adam as a cosmic fault. Popular Judaism toys with astrological determinism, reflected in the *mazal tov* (literally 'a good constellation') greeting, and with fatalism, reflected in the common response to events as *beschärt* (cut out, preordained by God).

One of the strongest contrasts between the Hebrew scriptures and the New Testament is the prominence of demonic spirits – 'powers', 'dominions' – and possession (devils being driven out) in the latter. Though demons (*shedim*) figure in many talmudic anecdotes, and are thought to tempt people to sin and to cause damage, their power is very circumscribed. Much the same could be said of Satan who, as in Job, is not a great power challenging God, but rather a 'licensed tempter', whom it is always possible to resist.

Rabbinic decision-making

Towards the end of the Second Temple period a 'hidden revolution'[8] took place within Judaism. The 'power of decision', previously in the hands of the priests, passed to the scribes, or interpreters of the law, and eventually to their successors, the rabbis. An extraordinary tale referring to events at the beginning of the second century makes plain how the mantle of Torah had passed from men claiming direct inspiration (prophets) and from the priesthood to creative teachers:

> It was taught: On that day Rabbi Eliezer responded to every question (that was raised against his opinion that a certain type of oven was not subject to impurity), but (the other sages) would not accept (his view). He said to them 'If the law is in accordance with my opinion, let this carob tree prove it!' The carob moved a hundred, some say four hundred, cubits from its

place. They said to him 'One does not prove the law from a carob tree'. Then he said to them 'If the law is in accordance with my opinion, let this stream of water prove it!' The stream thereupon flowed backwards. They said to him 'One does not prove the law from a stream of water'. Then he said to them 'If the law is in accordance with my opinion, let the walls of this House of Study prove it!' The walls of the House of Study began to cave in. Rabbi Joshua rebuked them, saying 'If the learned sages debate with one another, what has it to do with you?' Out of respect to Rabbi Joshua they fell no further; out of respect to Rabbi Eliezer they did not rise ... (Rabbi Eliezer) then said 'If the law is in accordance with my opinion, let the heavens prove it'. A heavenly voice then proclaimed 'What do you want with Rabbi Eliezer! The law is according to him in all matters!' Rabbi Joshua rose to his feet and proclaimed 'It is not in heaven (Deuteronomy 30:12)!' (BT *Bava Metzia* 59b)

Of course, this is not a denial of the need for divine guidance. On the contrary, it is allied with a deep conviction that the correct deliberations of the rabbis are guided by *ruah hakodesh* (the holy spirit). 'Whoever judges one law aright', runs another rabbinic adage, 'is a partner of the Holy One, Blessed be He, in creation.' The correct understanding and application of Torah is a divine task, in which we are humble, if privileged, participants. The part of this process which we can accomplish is the work of study and reflection on that which has already been revealed, a painstaking collaborative work in which decisions are reached by a majority of those competent, not by claims of special divine intervention.

The sources and levels of authority are many. There are laws carrying direct scriptural authority (*d'oraita*), there are rabbinic enactments (*d'rabbanan*), whether for the protection of the biblical laws or whether directly for the improvement of society, there is customary law (*minhag*) and there are local enactments (*taqqanah*). God's law has been revealed, and is to be pursued in an orderly and peaceful manner, with faith and love. It is not 'in heaven'; rather, heaven, through the Torah, has come down upon earth.

Freedom of the will

Some indication was given above of how the rabbis read scripture with a hermeneutic of free will. We must now see how the doctrine developed.

'All is foreseen, yet freedom is granted; the world is judged to the good side, and all is according to the effort expended' (*Mishnah Avot* 3:19). This statement is attributed to Rabbi Akiva (early second century).

The most powerful expression of the doctrine of free will is that of Moses Maimonides (1135–1204), in the seventh chapter of the 'Laws of Penitence' in his great Code, the *Mishneh Torah*. Here is part of it (note that the Hebrew term *reshut* is variously translated as 'power', 'ability', 'freedom' as well as 'free will'):

> Free will is granted to every human being. Should he so wish, he has the power to incline himself to the good way and to be just; should he so wish, he has the power to incline himself to the evil way and to be wicked ...
> Let that not enter your head, which is claimed by stupid gentiles and by numerous Jewish fools, that the Holy One, blessed be He, decrees on anyone at the time of his birth that he should be just or wicked. It is not so, but everyone possesses the ability to be as just as Moses our teacher or as evil as Jeroboam, or wise or foolish, or compassionate or cruel, or generous or mean, and likewise with other aspects of character. No one forces him, decrees upon him, or constrains him to either path, but he himself determines of his own free will which path he will follow ...
> This is a major principle and pillar of Torah and of the commandments, as it is said 'Behold I set life before you this day' (Deuteronomy 30:15) ... that is to say, you have the power, and whatsoever you wish to do of human deeds, whether good or evil, you can do ...
> If God decreed that any individual should be righteous or evil, or if anything in the formation of a person led him to any (predetermined) path, character or understanding, as senseless astrologers fabricate, how could He command us through prophets 'Do this and don't do that' ... what would be the point of the whole Torah and what justice would there be either in the punishment of the wicked or the reward of the just ... ?

Notwithstanding Maimonides' example, philosophers such as Crescas greatly narrowed the scope of free will, and where Maimonides had totally ridiculed astrology and reviled those who believed that the stars determined human action, ibn Ezra and most medievals continued to believe that our fate, if not our actions, is determined for us. German Hasidism of the twelfth century, and much liturgical poetry, manifest an overwhelming sense of sin. Yet the fundamental principle of freedom of the will was never abandoned entirely, nor the faith that the sinner, through penitence, could be reconciled with God.

Natural law

The idea of natural law (*nomos phuseos*) goes back to Aristotle, to whom ethics was essentially the science of how to fulfil the true nature of humanity. It is reflected in the Roman law concept of *obligationes naturales*. This is 'teleological' ethics, for it presupposes that humans have a 'purpose' – in Aristotle's terminology, a final cause. Jewish theology in the past consistently maintained that God created human beings for a purpose, even if that purpose transcended human reason. Since the Torah was given to help humans achieve the purpose for which they were created, its laws are a teleological ethic; they correspond to the aim of human nature as created by God 'in his own image'.

However, when one actually looks at the detailed provisions of Torah and attempts to explain them, problems arise. Is Torah indeed a rational system which can be related to human nature? Do the dietary laws, for instance, or the precise sexual regulations, correspond to the 'human purpose', or are they, to use the rabbinic term, *huqim* (statutes), which must be observed as 'decrees of the king', but have no intrinsic rationale? One might regard such regulations as 'positive law'. Such questions were discussed at great length by the medieval Jewish philosophers; some argued that these regulations have 'inner meanings', others that, though arbitrary in form, they constituted tests of our obedience, and in this way contributed to the fulfilment of human nature.

Clearly, some concept of ideal human nature underlies the system of Torah. But one may still ask how Torah actually operates as a legal system. Does one, as with 'natural law' systems, make decisions on the basis of broad principles of human nature and purpose? Or do Torah judges adopt a more positivist approach, treating the actual formulation of law as the 'given', and deciding cases by reference to it rather than by reference to human purpose?

Torah as natural law

Possibly the first Jew consciously to express Torah as a sort of 'natural law' was Philo, who may well have used the term *agraphos nomos* ('unwritten law') to refer to that law which did not have to be written down, because it was already in people's hearts.[9] It has been argued by many scholars that the talmudic 'Noahide laws', which constitute the Torah's provisions for gentile behaviour, are a rabbinic attempt at formulating natural law; this question turns on whether the Noahide is expected to follow these laws for their intrinsic merit, or because they are a 'positive law' revealed by God.[10]

Recently, serious consideration has been given to the extent to which Jewish law as a whole is a natural law system. Emanuel Rackman, recognizing the artificiality of imposing such a philosophical framework on a legal system which developed in another tradition, observes:

> In *halakhic* literature one can find support for virtually every theory of legal philosophy known to secular jurisprudence.[11]

Commenting on this, in the following year, the late Julius Stone wrote:

> Dr Rackman is concerned to point out that this hospitality of the *halakhic* tradition to a diversity of legal theories is not inconsistent with the view of Jewish law as commanded by God.[12]

Certainly, many traditional authorities have expounded Jewish law in a manner consistent with a natural law approach. However, they refer not to the law as a whole, but to parts of it, as rational, hence Saadiah Gaon's (882–942) distinction between *mitzvot sikhliyot* and *mitzvot shim'iyot* (rational and revealed commandments), or Albo's (fifteenth century) explicit reference to natural law as the basis for the prohibitions of murder, theft and robbery which are essential to the stability of society (Joseph Albo, *Sefer Ha-Iqqarim*, 1:5). Among attempts to present Judaism as a whole as a rational, natural law system is David Novak's extension of the biblical notion of 'covenant' to incorporate even the 'positive law' of revelation into the rationality of covenantal obligation.

ARE THERE 'SECOND ORDER' PRINCIPLES BY WHICH DECISIONS ARE GUIDED?

Another approach to assessing the natural law aspect of Judaism is to examine the way in which 'second order' moral principles are invoked to decide cases.

In his commentary on the verse 'And you shall do what is upright and good in the eyes of the Lord your God' (Deuteronomy 6:18), Nahmanides (1194–1270) commented:

Our rabbis interpreted this with reference to compromise and to exceeding the bare requirement of law. What they mean by this is that (scripture) first says that you should observe the statutes and testimonies He commanded you, and then it says that even in those matters He did not (explicitly) command you should take care to do that which is good and upright in His eyes, for He loves what is good and upright. This is a very important matter, for it would be impossible for the Torah to mention every detail of man's relationship with his neighbour and fellow, or all his transactions, or every detail of social and political arrangements. But as it gives several examples, for instance 'Do not go spreading tales amongst your people' (Leviticus 19:16), 'Do not take vengeance or bear a grudge' (Leviticus 19:18), 'Do not stand on your brother's blood' (Leviticus 19:16), 'Do not curse the deaf' (Leviticus 19:14), 'Rise before the hoary head' (Leviticus 19:32) and similar things, it repeats in a general manner that you should do what is good and upright in everything, to the extent that you should be ready to accept a compromise and to act beyond the requirement of law . . .

This illustrates that within the Torah itself – for the verse cited is one of the commandments – there is the assumption of a rational ethic, and provision for invoking it in the interpretation and application of other laws. This will be discussed below.

Of principles and cases

GENERAL AND PARTICULAR

One of the most obvious features of the source texts cited by exponents of Jewish ethics is that they tend to consist of anecdotes, rules, examples, rather than generalizations. Even the general exhortations to virtue more often than not take the form of encouragement to observe the commandments, that is, they relate to specific instances of, or rules of low generality about, desirable behaviour. This approach stands in marked contrast to that of the Greek philosophers, or of mainline Christian theologians, who have tended, at least in their theoretical writing, to base ethics on much more general concepts, such as human nature or justice or love. Thomas Aquinas, for instance, utilizing the concept of 'natural law', derives the detail of his moral philosophy and the criteria for acceptable legislation from his understanding of human nature.

This dissimilarity is evident in the way in which Jews and Christians today, addressing the identical ethical problem, tend to approach it from opposite directions. In discussions on the environment, for instance, one will find Christians primarily concerned with what they call 'creation theology'; from this they infer the desired attitude towards creation, and they then address themselves, adopting this attitude, to the specific problems of pollution, depletion of resources, threat to species or whatever else they are concerned with.

Traditional Jews tend to reason in the opposite direction, from particular to general. Addressing the problem of depletion of natural resources, they will immediately call to mind the rule of *bal tashchit* ('do not destroy', Deuteronomy 20:19), rooted in the very specific context of the conduct of war; they will then move from the particular to the general, arguing that the rule against destroying fruit trees in time of war implies a general principle of care for the environment, even in time of war; from that, they will make inferences to the specific problems of pollution, depletion of resources, threat to species or whatever else they are concerned with.

I do not wish to imply that Jews and Christians necessarily or always argue along these lines. This would be a form of stereotyping that does justice to neither tradition. Indeed, it is fascinating to observe, among the traditional sources, how the two approaches interrelate. How, for instance, does Aquinas relate his 'moral law' concept to the specifics of Roman law, canon law, the scriptures and the Church's traditions, which effectively tie down the way he argues from general to particular? How does Maimonides accommodate the halakhic system and rabbinic *obiter dicta* on ethics to his adoption of Aristotle's 'doctrine of the mean'?[13]

Moreover, the 'mainline Christian' tendency I have spoken of is Catholic rather than Protestant, and perhaps more strongly characteristic of high medieval and early modern times than of other epochs in church history; at the opposite end of the Christian spectrum, the British-based Jubilee Trust furnishes an intriguing recent instance of 'bottom up' argumentation in basing many of its social policy recommendations on the biblical law of the jubilee and sabbatical year, and in so doing draws on a strong Protestant tradition of turning direct to the Bible for detailed guidance.

287

Why are both approaches, the 'top down' and the 'bottom up', needed? For pragmatic reasons: to use either approach on its own would generate great uncertainty. The 'top down' approach used alone means that one has to argue from general to particular without any guidance as to how to proceed. Liberation theologians, for instance, are fond of arguing from the general moral principle 'identify with the poor' (itself derived from the even more general principle of love) to calling for specific forms of regulation of economic activity. The trouble is that there is no way, at least within the realm of moral discourse, to determine which economic regulations will work to the benefit of the poor, so you cannot argue 'because one should identify with the poor, one should tax the rich heavily' – taxing the rich heavily may well result in the destruction of means of production and the general loss of wealth to the detriment of the poor.

The 'bottom up' approach offers greater certainty at the practical level, but only in the given cases. 'Do not remove your neighbour's landmark' (Deuteronomy 19:14) is a clear enough rule in its biblical context, but to apply it (as rabbis do) to the copyright of books demands, first, that a fairly general moral principle be supplied as the rationale ('do not act in such a way as to deprive any other person of a proprietary right'), and from that one works 'top down' to the particular case of intellectual property. The 'bottom up' approach, if used alone, leaves one searching for the rationale of the given case, that is, for the general principle underlying it; but without this rationale, it is impossible to proceed to the case under discussion and to know whether it can validly be compared with the original one. Indeed, the rabbinic discussions of the hermeneutic rules of *ribbui umiut* and *klal ufrat* reflect this problem, albeit at a lower level of generalization than that of abstract moral principles.[14]

THE DATA OF MORAL PERCEPTION

But in fact there is a more profound issue at stake in this question of the direction of moral argument. Presumably, one argues from that which is subjectively more certain to that which is less certain. But at what level is there moral certainty? (I am not committing myself here to 'intuitionist' ethics.) What are the basic known 'data' of ethics? Indeed, at what level do we know or experience anything?

The neurologist Oliver Sacks, reflecting on his experience with people with learning difficulties, is led to assess the relationship between the abstract and the concrete in human psychology. Regarding one (brain-damaged) patient, he writes 'He remains a man, quintessentially a man, with all the moral weight and rich imagination of a man, despite the devastation of his abstract and propositional powers ... '. Sacks adds:

> I believe all this to be true of the simple also – the more so as, having been simple from the start, they have never known, been seduced by, the abstract, but have always experienced reality direct and unmediated, with an elemental and, at times, overwhelming intensity.[15]

Sacks should be more careful in claiming 'direct and unmediated' experience, but his remarks serve to remind us of the possibility that all abstract generalizations – and this would include moral principles – are intellectual constructions at a further remove from reality than our already heavily mediated perceptions of particular situations.

Lawrence Kohlberg, from a rather different perspective, has attempted to describe what he refers to as levels of moral development, and he sees these as a progression from the recognition of 'is' to that of 'ought'.[16] The main levels are preconventional, conventional and postconventional, and they are subdivided into six stages. At stage six, decisions are guided by 'logical comprehensiveness, universality and consistency'. Kohlberg sees this as possessing greater 'moral adequacy' than stage five, at which there is 'an emphasis upon the possibility of changing law in terms of rational considerations of social utility'. However, it is unclear just why greater logicality should lead to objective moral superiority (Kohlberg prudently does not claim this), even though it might produce greater consistency. If the 'raw material' of morals – the cases where our moral conviction is strongest that x, y and z ought to be done – is available only at a low level of generality, let alone if it is tied to specific situations, there is a danger that in constructing general rules we will fail to sum the 'data' correctly, and then will make wrong inferences to other cases. Therefore, the maximum of 'known' cases must be recorded and preserved as a check on inference from the general rules.

Stephen R. L. Clarke has aptly written, with reference to philosophical attempts to reduce ethics to a small number of highly general principles:

> The idea that parental obligation, for example, is a minor corollary of some

abstract duty, binding on all moral beings, to maximize happiness, or to allow all other moral or potentially moralizing beings an equal liberty, is a quite hopeless fantasy.[17]

It is often said, as Clarke does (citing MacIntyre among others), that the detailed interpretations that philosophers put on their general principles are not necessitated by those principles but shaped by their general world outlook. True, but it should also be recognized that the broad outlook itself has meaning only through the very specific commitments that those philosophers, often as members of their class or society, have.

MORAL AND SCIENTIFIC REASONING

An important point arises here in reasoning. In science, one reasons from general to particular by a process of deduction. The well-known laws of Boyle and Charles relate the volume, temperature and pressure of gases, within a certain range of conditions. If the temperature of a gas increases and the volume is held constant, the pressure rises according to a known formula; therefore, if I increase the temperature of this gas, its pressure will increase, according to the formula. This is a deductive inference, and if measurements do not accord with prediction I will call into question either the theory or the measurements.

Moral reasoning is different, especially when mixed up with theology. Consider the controversy about what is popularly referred to as 'virgin birth', but is actually artificial insemination of single women. Dr John Habgood, when Archbishop of York, is alleged to have rejected this practice in the words: 'Single parents who are single by choice play truant from the school of charity, and that is bad for them and bad for their children.'[18] Now this is simply an argument from general to particular. Everyone ought always to practise charity (meaning here, to love their neighbour); ergo, if this woman wants a child she ought to be married or in a stable relationship. Put thus baldly, the argument is manifest nonsense; but Habgood's real argument is far more complex, and assumes the desirability of certain forms of social structure and certain forms of child care. Those people who believe that there are ways in which a single mother can provide an adequate environment for her child would not argue from the general principle of love to the particular conclusion that single women ought not to conceive children; indeed, bearing in mind some of the awful things that happen to children in two-parent families, they might be led to argue in favour of single mothers, at least in some cases. Moreover, the argument has no bearing on the method by which the child is conceived. Clearly, there is no deductive inference from the principle of charity to the specific decision about a single woman who cannot find a satisfactory husband and wishes to conceive by artificial insemination. A wide range of decisions is logically compatible with the principle of charity, in sharp contrast with the 'gas laws' above, where the general law is compatible with only one consequence in the particular instance. Whereas physical laws are generalized summaries of clearly definable classes of observations, moral 'laws' are broad statements of value relating to ill-defined classes of action.

The artificial insemination debate highlights the difference of approach between 'top down' and 'bottom up' moral arguments. Jewish discussions of artificial insemination hinge not on any broad principle of charity (though all Jews subscribe to such principles), but on the permissibility or not of certain acts. One would need to establish whether the introduction of semen into a vagina by means of a syringe constitutes an act of sexual intercourse (it does not), whether the ejaculation of sperm for this purpose is permissible, and whether a child conceived in this way is related to the sperm donor in respect of various consequences, such as inheritance, degree of consanguinity for marriage, and so on.[19] Whatever the overall relationship of *halakhah* to moral principles, it is the *halakhah* and not the principles which would be evoked at this stage of the argument. Only after clarifying these basic *halakhot* would one proceed to consider the more 'social' aspects of the case, and these might well be decided in terms of higher-level principles. There is an analogy here with some theories of legal reasoning, according to which hard cases are decided by reference to 'second-order rules' which are more general than the actual law, and may well be broad moral assumptions.

Daniel H. Gordis[20] has argued that the classic halakhic approach to problems in medical ethics, which he dubs 'precedent-based or formalist', should be replaced by deducing from the halakhic material 'a defensible, positive Jewish conception of human life', and on the basis of this conception the specific problems should be addressed. As an example of the wrong inferences being made by attempting to work directly from the precedent of an existing traditional source, he cites authorities who forbid artificial insemination absolutely on what are obviously spurious grounds. He suspects that their real motive is one of moral repugnance, and rightly observes that if this is the case the correct approach would be to spell out that moral repugnance as a clear moral doctrine and to admit that that is the basis of their judgements. Gordis himself tries to set up a concept of 'humanness', perhaps based on 'God's image', as a basis for judgement of bio-ethical questions. However, apart from the misgivings I have already expressed about teleological ethics, I do not understand how such a vague and ill-defined notion can give any better determination of specific issues than the admittedly strained logic of the halakhists (see Meier, 1986).

IMITATIO DEI

The concept of *imitatio dei* provides an example from within Judaism both of the use of a broad general moral principle and of the difficulty in drawing inferences from it. The Talmud records the following interpretation of the verse 'After the Lord your God shall you walk . . .' (Deuteronomy 13:5):

> Said Rabbi Hama bar Hanina: How can a person walk after God? Is it not written 'For the Lord your God is a consuming fire' (Deuteronomy 4:24)? But follow God's attributes. As He clothes the naked . . . as He visits the sick . . . comforts the bereaved . . . buries the dead . . . so should you.[21]

What Rabbi Hama bar Hanina neglects to tell us is how he knows that precisely these attributes of God are to be imitated and no others, for instance God's vengeance (Psalm 94:1). The answer, of course, lies in scripture, which proclaims 'Do not be vengeful, do not bear a grudge' (Leviticus 19:18). That is, no deduction can be made direct from the general moral principle that it is good to 'imitate' God; one still needs the check on inference which is provided by the specific laws of Torah.

GENERAL MORAL PRINCIPLES IN LEGISLATION ON NON-JEWS

Further study is needed of the efforts of the rabbis of the Talmud to regulate behaviour towards non-Jews. On the one hand, they tended (not always consistently) to interpret biblical legislation with narrow

292

reference to Israelites. On the other hand, there is a counterbalancing tendency to invoke broad general principles to guide behaviour towards non-Jews, among them *tiqqun olam* ('putting the world right'), *darkhei shalom* ('the ways of peace'), *kiddush Hashem* (sanctification of God's name – in the sense of acting in such a way as to bring honour to God's name).

ON MORAL ABSOLUTISM

Are there absolute moral principles or only *prima facie* ones? If it is absolutely wrong to kill people or to tell lies, what happens when some moral duty, for instance to protect the innocent or to avoid deep personal distress, demands that one kill the aggressor or speak an untruth?

Traditional *halakhah*, since it presents itself as a law system rather than as a table of vices and virtues, resists the tendency to moral absolutism. The law of *kiddush Hashem* (martyrdom) does indeed assume three absolutes, for even at the risk of one's life it is forbidden to worship idols, to commit adultery (as defined in the codes) or to shed innocent blood. However, a major part of rabbinic literature is concerned with ranking priorities of obligation, a simple example being that the saving of human life takes precedence over observance of the Sabbath laws.

In terms of moral philosophy we would have to say that Jewish ethics, as expressed in the system of halakhic priorities, is consequentialist; it is never the case, apart from the three exceptions cited, that a virtue is to be pursued or a vice avoided irrespective of the consequences.

Additional contemporary examples

Here are two further examples of the way in which decisions are reached on the basis of traditional Jewish sources.

TERRITORY FOR PEACE

In 1967, defending itself from Arab attack, Israel occupied surrounding territory, including the West Bank and Gaza, both of which lie within the biblical boundaries of the Land of Israel. These territories remained under Israeli control after the 1973 'Yom Kippur' war, and after the accommodation with Egypt under Begin and Sadat in 1978.

In 1973 a major religious debate erupted over the question of whether the West Bank and Gaza might be voluntarily handed over to Arab control in return for peace. In 1980 a religious peace movement, Oz Veshalom, published some papers on this topic, and on the treatment of minorities according to *halakhah*, by Shilo Refael, a *dayan* (judge) of the rabbinical court in Jerusalem. At the front of the booklet stands a summary of the halakhic rulings as agreed by Refael and the then Sephardic Chief Rabbi of Israel, Ovadiah Yosef. The summary reads as follows:

> According to the majority of early authorities[22] *they shall not dwell in your land* [Exodus 23:33] does not refer to Muslims, since they are not idolaters.
>
> All authorities agree that nowadays, when Israel does not have power to drive out nations from the land, that the prohibition *they shall not dwell in your land* has no application.
>
> According to many of the greatest authorities, both early and late, the prohibition *lo tehanem*[23] applies only to idolaters.
>
> Even if it were prohibited to sell land (in Israel) to non-Israelites, the possibility would remain of exchanging it.
>
> According to all authorities it is permitted to return territories of (biblical) Israel in order to remove the possibility of war, for nothing stands in the way of *pikuah nefesh* (the saving of life).
>
> Even if there were disputes as to (whether this was a case of) *pikuah nefesh*, wherever there is a doubt in a matter of life and death we take the more lenient view (and avoid risk).
>
> In a generation where all are righteous, and immersed in (a life of) Torah, one might trust in God even where there is risk to life, but in our generation we cannot rely on miracles, and therefore we should return the territories to remove enemies from ourselves.
>
> Even according to Nahmanides, who maintains that it is a religious duty to wage war for the conquest of the Land of Israel, there is no religious duty on us today to risk our lives to hold on to the territories we have conquered against the will of the nations of the world.
>
> With the agreement of the leaders of the community not only converts but non-Jews may be appointed to any public office.

What is of interest in the above is the manner in which Ovadiah Yosef and Shilo Refael relate to the classical sources of Judaism.

First, they do not go directly to biblical texts, but to rabbinic interpretation of those texts. Second, they cite a principle formulated by the rabbis, that the safeguarding of life has priority over all of the commandments (except murder, idolatry, and adultery/incest) and use it in a context for which there is no clear talmudic precedent, namely the circumstance where part of the historical territory of Israel is occupied by non-idolators. How is this extrapolation justified? In fact, it would seem that they engaged in a characteristic process by which theologians effect change: they selected one value from a number of available, but conflicting, values in the tradition, and accorded it priority. The selection of the value of *pikuah nefesh* over that of settlement of the land is not dissimilar, for instance, to the selection of the value of human dignity over that of the ownership of slaves. Both represent a creative decision, determining the direction in which the faith and law are to proceed.

Finally, though the value priority has been established, nothing very definite follows in practice. Surely they are not suggesting that if Arabs threatened to kill just one person they would relinquish the land rather than run such a risk? Clearly, other priorities come into operation in the actual situation, for we know that Yosef and Refael both support defensive wars and even pre-emptive strikes in certain circumstances. In the end, the decision has to be made in the light of a critical assessment of all circumstances, military and political options, and the like, so although there may be a value input from theology (based on *halakhah*), *halakhah* alone does not determine the decision. We see here another line of demarcation between theology and practical decision-making.

MATERNITY IN FOETAL IMPLANTS

The following example demonstrates the method of rabbinic argument from case law. Note that all areas of law are considered relevant, and are regarded as belonging to a single comprehensive and coherent system.

It is possible to remove an embryo from one woman and implant it in another, who gives birth to the baby. Does conception or birth determine maternity? Dependent on this are questions of inheritance, of personal status, of relationship with other children of the first and second women.[24]

A *prima facie* proof that maternity depends on conception is derived from a responsum of Rabbi Akiva Eger (1761-1837) on the subject of whether the prohibition of cooking milk and meat together applies to the milk of a *treifa* (an animal suffering a defect rendering it forbidden for eating). The relevant part of Eger's responsum runs as follows:

> It is questionable whether the milk of a *treifa* is contained in the prohibition, according to the principle that a *treifa* cannot give birth, and hence is unable to be a mother. See Sanhedrin 69a (where the Talmud excludes from the laws of the rebellious son one who has reached majority three months earlier, as he is considered to be a (potential) father and not a 'son'. He is capable of impregnating a woman from when he obtains majority and after three months the pregnancy is evident, at which time he is called a 'father'). This implies that the father of an embryo is considered to be a father. Similarly, in our case, the *treifa* is capable of being a mother, since she can conceive, although she cannot deliver ... The mother of an embryo is also considered a mother. However, it is possible that the parent of an embryo is considered a parent only if the embryo will be delivered in the future. A *treifa*, however, who cannot deliver, is not considered to be a mother while pregnant. Subsequently, I discovered that the *Issur Veheter* (31, 14) ruled that the milk of a *treifa* is included in the Torah prohibition of milk–meat because if she was impregnated before she became a *treifa*, she is capable of delivering even when a *treifa*. Accordingly, the milk of an animal born *treifa* will not be included in the prohibition.

From this, it would appear that maternity depends on conception; hence the foetal implant would be regarded in law as the child of the first, not the second, woman. Against Eger, Rabbi Yosef Engel (1859–1920) argued that a distinction should be made between maternity and paternity. Paternity is indeed established at conception. Maternity, however, depends on birth. Engel derives this distinction from a comment of Rashi (1040–1105) on an apparently redundant statement in the book of Esther.

Engel proceeds to demonstrate that birth rather than conception determines maternity from the following talmudic passage:

> Twin brothers who are converts or emancipated slaves do not perform *yibum* or *chalitza* (for each other), nor is one prohibited (from marrying) the other's widow. (Rashi – Even if the [first] marriage was contracted after the conversion, as a convert he is like a new-born child and therefore he does not have the relationship of brotherhood, even [with a child] from the same mother.) If their conception was before conversion and their birth

after conversion, they do not perform *yibum* or *chalitza* ... but are prohibited from marrying each other's widow. (BT *Yevamot* 97b)

Since, in the second case, conception took place before conversion, it cannot serve as a determinant of maternity, for the brothers are like new-born children from the time of conversion. As they are evidently considered brothers from the point of view of incest, it seems that birth, not conception, is the determinant of maternity.

Several similar arguments are considered before reaching the conclusion that the child relates exclusively to the mother who gives birth. It is a matter of speculation as to what extent the argumentation is controlled by unstated assumptions as to moral principles. Certainly, it would not be difficult to show that the arguments are not strictly deductive.

Jewish sectarian differences

In all the preceding we have assumed a position within traditional Orthodoxy. Contemporary Jewish Orthodoxy is itself diverse,[25] but in its hardest form it treats the words of scripture, from Genesis to Deuteronomy, as verbally inspired, and the words of the talmudic rabbis as guided by *ruah ha-kodesh* (the holy spirit); high authority is accorded to the literature within this tradition, including law codes and responsa still being produced today. Rabbis within this 'hard' tradition are by no means insensitive to the conflicts of conscience faced by Jews today when called upon to follow traditional rulings meticulously. Perhaps their greatest sensitivity is shown in *agunah* cases, where (perhaps for some technical reason) a woman is prevented from remarriage; undoubtedly they strive hard, within what they perceive as the limits of *halakhah*, to find grounds on which to make permissive rulings. Ultimately, however, in this as in other conflicts between correct Torah rulings (as they see them) and personal compassion, the former has priority. The autonomous individual conscience can never overrule the 'superior wisdom of God' as handed down by the sages.

Conservative[26] Judaism differs from 'hard' Orthodoxy in allowing greater rein to historical factors. Historical criticism of the Bible is accepted, and the rabbinic sages and their interpretations placed within historical context. This enables some degree of relativism so

297

that, for instance, Conservatives have permitted mixed seating in the synagogue, and since 1985 they have ordained women rabbis, in the belief that the segregation of women and their diminished role in public life are not of the 'essence' of Judaism, but were related to social circumstances which have changed in modern times. Conservatives nevertheless attach great weight to *halakhah*, and claim that they, rather than the Orthodox, stand in the Hillelite tradition of interpretation in accordance with the needs of the times.

Reform Judaism, originating in Germany in the early nineteenth century and quickly achieving dominance in the United States, takes a more radical approach than Conservativism to the modification of religious observances and to the revision of theological doctrines. Both the 1885 'Pittsburgh Platform' and the 1937 'Columbus Platform' strongly emphasize ethical and moral values at the expense of ritual and tradition. In so doing, Reform has ensured a prominent role for the 'voice of conscience', even where that conflicts with tradition. Recent issues where the autonomy of the individual conscience has claimed recognition include the claim that homosexuals be given equal rights within the community. The range of responses to questions of this type reflects the broad spectrum of opinion within the World Union for Progressive Judaism (founded 1926), of which Reform is the major component.

The greatest freedom of the individual conscience is granted within the Reconstructionist movement, which owes its inspiration to Mordecai M. Kaplan (1881–1982). Though the movement was founded in 1922, it was originally conceived as an 'umbrella' for all Jews, whatever their sectarian attachment. However, in 1967 it set up its own Rabbinical College, in Philadelphia, and since 1970 has had its own congregations. In these, decisions are made collectively by members, who form a democratic *havurah* (society) in which the rabbi is no more than a 'resource person'. Autonomy of individual conscience is paramount, however, and it is the individual who is the final arbiter of which rituals or folkways to practise.

Thus the Jewish sects provide between them a full spectrum of approaches to moral decision-making, ranging from the insistence of 'hard Orthodoxy' on a non-historical acceptance of sources, with only limited opportunity for compassionate interpretation, to Reconstructionism, where individual conscience reigns supreme.

Notes

1   The Palestinian (completed *c.* 450) and Babylonian (completed *c.* 550) Talmudim are expansions of the Mishnah (completed *c.* 215), and together form the classical exposition of rabbinic Judaism. See Chapter 4, pp. 119–22.

2   Mishnah, *Avot* 1:3.

3   The early versions of the 'pound of flesh' story (best-known from Shakespeare's *Merchant of Venice*), such as that in the tale of the fourth wise master of the 'Seven Wise Masters of Rome' in the Sinbad series, have no Jewish reference.

4   Babylonian Talmud (BT), *Bava Metzia* 30b. There is an excellent chapter on *lifnim mishurat ha-din* in S. Federbush (5708/1947) *Ha-Musar v'ha-Mishpat b'Israel* (in Hebrew) Jerusalem: Mosad Harav Kook, ch. 11.

5   See the discussion in Louis E. Newman (1989) 'Law, virtue and supererogation in the Halakha', *Journal of Jewish Studies* XL, pp. 61–88. Newman, following Menachem Elon's Hebrew work *Ha-Mishpat Ha-Ivri* (Jerusalem: Magnes Press), cites several instances where later authorities have made legally enforceable something which the Talmud referred to as *lifnim mishurat ha-din*.

6   'Some aspects of the Jewish attitude toward the welfare state' in Twersky (1982), pp. 137ff.

7   BT *Bava Batra* 10a: Twersky's translation.

8   This is the title of a book by Ellis Rivkin.

9   There are two other interpretations of the term used by Philo in, for instance, *de Specialibus Legibus* IV, 148–9. Many scholars have incorrectly surmised that he was referring to the 'oral Torah', but this is an anachronism. Others, probably correctly, have interpreted it as 'unwritten law as custom'. See John W. Martens (1992) 'Unwritten law in Philo', *Journal of Jewish Studies* 43/1 (Spring), pp. 38–45.

10 J. David Bleich (1988) 'Judaism and natural law', *Jewish Law Annual* VII, pp. 5–42; Bleich's article should be consulted for a fuller treatment of the topic of this section. See also David Novak (1988) 'Natural law, Halakhah and the Covenant', *Jewish Law Annual* VII, pp. 43–67.

11 E. Rackman (1987) 'Secular jurisprudence and the Halakha', *Jewish Law Annual* VI, pp. 45–63.

12 Julius Stone (1988) 'Leeways of choice, natural law and justice in Jewish legal ordering', *Jewish Law Annual* VII, pp. 210–51, at p. 211.

13 The *locus classicus* for this difficulty is *Mishneh Torah, De'ot* 2:3.

14 See Norman Solomon, 'Extensive and restrictive interpretation of terms in rabbinic literature' in Rakover (1984), pp. 37–54, and (1985) in *Jewish Law Association Studies* I (Scholars Press), pp. 125–39.

15   Oliver Sacks (1986) *The Man Who Mistook His Wife for a Hat*. Orig. London: Gerald Duckworth & Co. (1983); Picador edn, London; Pan Books, p. 165.

16   Lawrence Kohlberg, 'From is to ought' in Theodore Mischel (ed.) (1971) *Cognitive Development and Epistemology*. New York: Academic Press, pp. 151–235.

17   Stephen R. L. Clarke, 'Abstract morality, concrete cases' in J. D. G. Evans (ed.) (1987) *Moral Philosophy and Contemporary Problems*. Cambridge: Cambridge University Press (for the Royal Institute of Philosophy), p. 42.

18   *The Times*, 12 March 1991, p. 2. Undoubtedly this is an inadequate account of Dr Habgood's views.

19   There is a substantial and growing literature on the subject. See for instance Moshe Drori's article 'Artificial insemination: is it adultery?' in Rakover (1984), pp. 203–16. See also the article by Daniel H. Gordis referred to in note 20.

20   Daniel H. Gordis (1989), 'Wanted – the ethical in Jewish bio-ethics', *Judaism* 3811 (Winter), pp. 28–40.

21   BT *Sota* 14a. See Maimonides, *Mishneh Torah, Hilkhot De'ot* 1:6 for a reconstruction of this passage.

22   In this context, 'early authorities' means the post-talmudic rabbis preceding Joseph Caro (1488–1575); 'late authorities' are any from that time onwards.

23   Deuteronomy 7:2. Literally, 'do not show them kindness'. By a play on words, this was taken to mean 'do not give them dwelling (*haniyyah*) in the land'.

24   See Goldberg (1987), in *Crossroads*, pp. 71–7.

25   On the range of contemporary Orthodoxy, see Jonathan Sacks (1989) *Traditional Alternatives: Orthodoxy and the Future of the Jewish People*. London: Jews' College Publications.

26   Conservative Judaism is strongest in the United States, where it originated towards the end of the nineteenth century in reaction to Reform. The much more recent British offshoot is referred to as 'Masorti' Judaism, the Hebrew name adopted by its Israeli counterpart.

References and further reading

Bleich, J. David (several vols from 1981) *Contemporary Halakhic Problems*. New York: Ktav.

Cohn, Haim (1984) *Human Rights in Jewish Law*. London: Institute of Jewish Affairs.

Crossroads: Halakha and the Modern World (1987) Jerusalem: Zomet Institute (no editor given).

Feldman, David M. (1974) *Marital Relations, Birth Control and Abortion in Jewish Law*. New York: Schocken.

Greenberg, Blu (1981) *On Women and Judaism: A View from Tradition*. Philadelphia: Jewish Publication Society of America.

Jakobovits, L. (1976) *Jewish Medical Ethics*. New York: Bloch.

Meier, Levi (1986) *Jewish Values in Bioethics*. New York: Human Sciences Press.

Neusner, Jacob (1988) *The Mishnah: A New Translation*. New Haven and London: Yale University Press.

Novak, David (1998) *Natural Law in Judaism*. Cambridge: Cambridge University Press.

Rakover, N. (ed.) (1984) *Jewish Law and Current Legal Problems*. Jerusalem: Jewish Legal Heritage Society.

Rose, Aubrey (ed.) (1992) *Judaism and Ecology*. London: Cassell.

Steinsaltz, Adin (1977) *The Essential Talmud*. New York: Bantam Books.

Tamari, Meir (1987) *'With All Your Possessions': Jewish Ethics and Economic Life*. London: Collier Macmillan.

Twersky, Isadore (1982) *Studies in Jewish Law and Philosophy*. New York: Ktav.

Index